THE GREAT DIVIDE

THE GREAT DIVIDE
A Lutheran Evaluation of Reformed Theology

JORDAN COOPER

WIPF & STOCK · Eugene, Oregon

THE GREAT DIVIDE
A Lutheran Evaluation of Reformed Theology

Copyright © 2015 Jordan Cooper. All rights reserved. Except for brief quotations in critical publications or reviews, no part of this book may be reproduced in any manner without prior written permission from the publisher. Write: Permissions, Wipf and Stock Publishers, 199 W. 8th Ave., Suite 3, Eugene, OR 97401.

Wipf & Stock
An Imprint of Wipf and Stock Publishers
199 W. 8th Ave., Suite 3
Eugene, OR 97401

www.wipfandstock.com

ISBN 13: 978-1-4982-2423-9

Manufactured in the U.S.A.   07/15/2015

To R.C. Sproul, whose writings inspired me to study theology.

Contents

Introduction | ix

Part I: Predestination and Free Will

1 Chosen in Christ: The Doctrine of Predestination | 3
2 Once for All: The Extent of the Atonement | 34
3 Shipwrecked Faith: A Lutheran Approach to Perseverance and Apostasy | 62

Part II: Worship and the Sacraments

4 Praising the Triune God: The Nature and Essence of Worship | 89
5 The Washing of Regeneration: The Sacrament of Baptism | 109
6 The Medicine of Immortality: The Lutheran Doctrine of Holy Communion | 136

Part III: Salvation

7 Justification by Faith: The Doctrine upon Which the Church Stands or Falls | 161
8 New Life in Christ: Sanctification and Vocation | 180

Bibliography | 211

Introduction

IN A 2009 ISSUE of *Time* magazine, the "New Calvinism" was named among the "Ten Ideas Changing the World Right Now."[1] Within the past five years, several Calvinistic preachers have gained immense popularity.[2] Reformed websites, blogs, and podcasts are prominent on the Internet. Reformed publishing houses have had more sales than they have seen in years. Whether one agrees with Calvinism or not, it is apparent that interacting with these ideas is necessary for anyone who is trying to impact the modern church.

Now, perhaps more than any time in American Lutheran history, is a time when interacting with the Calvinistic Reformation is crucial. It is an unfortunate truth of history that it is Calvinism rather than Lutheranism which has defined and shaped much of American Evangelical Christianity. Thus in contemporary theological conversations, it is often supposed that there are only two theological options: Calvinism, or revivalist Arminianism. Lutheranism has often remained its own entity, avoiding interaction with the broader Evangelical church in America. This has had both positive and negative effects. It has been helpful in that Lutherans have avoided (though certainly not always) the various trends which come and go in the Evangelical world, whether that be regarding the "purpose-driven life," a new way to get God to speak to you, or some kind of magical prayer which brings all sorts of supposed blessings to your life. Though this avoidance has been positive, and Lutherans have been somewhat shielded from such theologically vapid material, it is unfortunate that the Lutheran tradition

---

1. Van Biema, "The New Calvinism," 50.

2. The relationship between the terms "Calvinistic" and "Reformed" is somewhat fluid. By "Calvinistic" in this context, I am referring to a belief in the five points of Calvinism. "Reformed" is a more specific term, referring to those churches which hold to one of the historic Reformed confessions of faith, including the Westminster Standards, the Three Forms of Unity, or the 1689 London Baptist Confession of Faith.

has not been able to proclaim its unique approach to law and gospel to Christians throughout America.

This is especially true regarding the Reformed and Presbyterian tradition. Since Luther refused to shake Zwingli's hand at the Marburg Colloquy, these two sides of the Reformation have been ever divided. This is a necessary situation, as attempts at union have proven unfruitful and ignore rather than confront serious theological differences between the two movements. In the seventeenth century, with the rise of scholasticism, there was extensive interaction between the Lutheran and Reformed churches. At some point, this serious interaction became caricature and avoidance. As a convert from Presbyterianism to Lutheranism, I find myself constantly correcting misrepresentations from both sides. This includes misrepresentations from professors, pastors, and lay people.

What is needed is not unionism, nor hostility to those with opposing views, but fruitful dialogue and polemical defenses of why these differences are significant and important. This work is an attempt to begin dialogue with the other side, and to defend the Lutheran branch of the Reformation. The intended audience of this work is twofold:

First, I intend this book to be read by curious Reformed Christians. This work will hopefully demonstrate a respectful and correct understanding of the Calvinistic Reformation, while giving important (and hopefully convincing!) exegetical and theological defenses of the Lutheran distinctives. This work will not convert every Reformed Christian immediately to Lutheranism, but will hopefully serve to bring greater understanding about what Lutherans teach, and why we believe the way we do.

Second, I hope that this book will be read by Lutheran theologians, pastors, and concerned laity. It will help to clarify what the Reformed actually teach on specific subjects, so that misrepresentations and caricatures can be avoided. I also hope to strengthen Lutherans in their own faith, demonstrating that the Confessions of the Lutheran church truly do contain teachings that are consistent with God's word.

One of the difficulties I have found when writing this work is the variety of views within the realm of Reformed Christianity. While many in the contemporary Calvinist movement have formulated their theology primarily through the so-called five points, others have argued for a more covenantally grounded Confessional approach to the Reformed tradition. I consulted both popular and scholarly resources on these topics, from the Presbyterians, the Dutch Reformed tradition, and Calvinistic Baptist

Introduction

traditions. The first three chapters give an overview of the "five points" and utilize material from various perspectives. I cite popular resources along with scholarly resources due to their prominence in contemporary Calvinism. My goal is to make this work accessible to both the learned lay reader as well as the scholar, so I urge scholars not to be put off by the utilization of popular writers. In the later chapters, which deal with the nature of worship and the sacraments, I narrow in on the Confessionally Reformed tradition as defined in the Westminster Confession and the Three Forms of Unity. I intend to deal with historic Reformed sacramental theology and ecclesiology rather than the broadly evangelical approach to these issues, which would go beyond the scope of this work. I have consulted with pastors, scholars, and lay people in the Reformed tradition so as to ensure an accurate representation of their position, and to capture the many perspectives which are represented by various branches of the Reformed church. Though no short treatment of this subject can capture all of the nuances of either the Reformed or Lutheran traditions, this work will hopefully begin to explain and clarify many of the issues which continue to divide the two branches of the magisterial Reformation. May the following pages stir your mind, enrich your understanding of God's grace, and be a reminder of our great Reformation heritage. *Soli Deo Gloria!*

PART I

Predestination and Free Will

1

Chosen in Christ
The Doctrine of Predestination

PREDESTINATION IN THE REFORMED TRADITION

FOR SOME, THE NAME John Calvin is associated with the teaching that God predestines everything that occurs in the universe, especially as regards salvation and damnation. Calvin is seen as a supporter of fatalism, a man with misplaced theocratic hopes, and even as a murderer.[1] Despite these charges, which do little other than frighten the audience away from Reformed theology, the Calvinistic system is much broader and more nuanced than it is often given credit for. The Reformed theological system is all encompassing; it has its own unique approaches to the sacraments, church, eschatology, and redemptive history.[2] That being said, the Reformed church does focus much attention to the subject of predestination and the sovereignty of God. This flows from the Reformed tendency to view God's glory as a

---

1. For an example of a popular vitriolic critique of both the Calvinistic system and John Calvin himself, see Bryson, *Dark Side of Calvinism*.

2. R. Scott Clark has written a helpful work titled *Recovering the Reformed Confession*, which explains the historic Reformed confessional tradition in contrast to what is often mischaracterized as Reformed.

Part I: Predestination and Free Will

central tenant of theology.[3] In contrast to this, soteriology is central for the Lutheran tradition.[4]

John Calvin was highly influenced by the predestinarian theology of Augustine and Luther's treatise *On the Bondage of the Will*.[5] In contrast to certain strands of medieval Roman Catholic theology, Calvin held to a high view of original sin, arguing that salvation is impossible apart from irresistible grace. This irresistible grace is given to the elect alone. Calvin went beyond much of the earlier Augustinian tradition[6] in his affirmation of double predestination, purporting that God predestines the reprobate as well as the saved to their eternal destiny. There is some debate regarding Calvin's view of the atonement. Some have proposed that the doctrine of limited atonement was an innovation of Calvin's student Theodore Beza (1519–1605) and does not reflect Calvin's own teaching.[7]

---

3. There is, of course, some debate as to the validity of a *Centraldogmen* in Christianity. Muller argues against the idea of a central dogma in *Christ and the Decree*. Whether or not one will label predestination or the glory of God as *the* central tenant of Reformed theology, it is apparent that these ideas are far more prominent in the Reformed than the Lutheran tradition.

4. Herman Bavinck says as much when he defines the difference between the two traditions in the following words: "The difference seems to be conveyed best by saying that the Reformed Christian thinks theologically, the Lutheran anthropologically. The Reformed person is not content with an exclusively historical stance but raises his sights to the idea, the eternal decree of God. By contrast the Lutheran takes his position in the midst of the history of redemption and feels no need to enter more deeply into the counsel of God. For the Reformed, therefore, election is at the heart of the church; for Lutherans, justification is the article by which the church stands or falls. Among the former the primary question is: How is the glory of God advanced? Among the latter it is: How does a human get saved? The struggle of the former is above all else paganism—idolatry; the latter against Judaism—works-righteousness. The Reformed person does not rest until he has traced all things retrospectively to the divine decree, tracing down the 'wherefore' of all things, and has prospectively made all things subservient to the glory of God; the Lutheran is content with the 'that' and enjoys the salvation in which he is, by faith, a participant" (Bavinck, *Reformed Dogmatics* 1:177).

5. The best translation of this work is that of J. I. Packer, though it is to be noted that the forward has a clear Calvinistic bias. The influence of Augustine on Calvin is shown most clearly in Calvin, *Bondage and Liberation of the Will*.

6. Such as in the Canons of the Council of Orange in 529. These canons can be found in Stucco, *Not without Us*, 117–23. The post-Augustinian tradition, as taught by the late Prosper of Aquitaine and Caesarius of Arles, denies any sense of double predestination while affirming universal grace.

7. The major work which argues that a distinction exists between Calvin and the later Reformed tradition is R. T. Kendall, *Calvin and English Calvinism*. In contradistinction to this view, see Raymond A. Blacketer's article "Blaming Beza: The Development

The Arminian conflict in many ways defined the Calvinist movement. The "five points of Calvinism" were formulated in response to Arminian protests and have become a popular means of confessing the teachings of the Calvinist Reformation.[8] The Arminian, or "Remonstrant," movement followed the teachings of Jacob Arminius (1560–1609). Though he admired Calvin and was a student of Beza, Arminius disagreed with certain tenants of Reformed theology. According to Arminius's reading of Paul's struggle with sin in Romans 7, Paul described himself as struggling between good and evil prior to conversion.[9] This negates a Calvinistic understanding of total depravity, wherein it is only after irresistible grace confronts the sinner that a struggle between good and evil begins. Arminius also feared that Calvin's views led to determinism and made God the cause of evil. Thus, Arminius argued that this doctrine should be amended. In his view, predestination is not unconditional but is based upon foreseen faith. In contrast to Calvin's insistence, Arminius defended the position that grace is resistible. Arminius quickly drew much support behind his cause.[10]

The young Remonstrant movement ran into several difficulties with the necessity of agreeing with the Heidelberg Catechism and the Dutch Confession as a prerequisite for ordination. These documents contained unambiguous statements about Calvinistic predestination. In response to this, a petition was drawn which contained five points that defined Arminian theology: limited depravity, election based on foreseen faith, universal atonement, the resistible nature of grace, and the reality of apostasy.[11]

In response to the five statements of the Remonstrants, the Dutch church convened a council in 1618 known as the Synod of Dort.[12] At this synod, the Heidelberg Catechism was reaffirmed and the Arminian position

---

of Definite Atonement in the Reformed Tradition," in Gibson and Gibson, *From Heaven He Came,* 121–42.

8. Historically, Calvinism has been defined as a much broader theological movement than the five points. However, due to the popularity of the New Calvinist movement, and following such Calvinist writers as Lorraine Boettner, it has become the primary way in which Calvinism is popularly known.

9. This is discussed in his essay, "A Dissertation of the True and Genuine Sense," in Arminius, *Works* 2.

10. Arminius's most important works relating to predestination have been compiled in the volume *Arminius Speaks.*

11. However, it is to be noted that there was a variety of opinion on the topic of apostasy within the Arminian movement.

12. The Canons of Dort as well as a brief history may be found in Scott, *Articles of the Synod of Dort.* This is where much of the above history is cited from.

was condemned as heretical. At first both ecclesiastical and governmental punishments were enacted against the Arminians; they were released from ordination and were banished from the country. There were even certain cases of more severe punishment. Eventually, toleration was promoted and the Arminians and Calvinists continued in their own diverging streams of theology.

PREDESTINATION IN THE LUTHERAN TRADITION

Lutherans are more often than not left out of the discussion regarding predestination. It is common to hear Calvinism and Arminianism expressed as two alternative theological systems, to the neglect of a third option.[13] The Lutheran approach to predestination serves as a mediating view between both Calvinistic particularism and Arminian free will theology. A biblical approach adopts both the Arminian insistence of the universal nature of God's saving will, along with the Calvinist contention that salvation occurs *sola gratia*.

The history of the doctrine of election within the Lutheran church is a complex one. Martin Luther famously defended a monergistic understanding of predestination against the humanist Erasmus in his *Bondage of the Will*. Like Augustine before him, Luther argued that man's will is captive to sin. Of his own power, man is not able to come to faith.[14] Luther expresses this idea clearly in his Small Catechism: "I believe that I cannot by my own reason or strength believe in Jesus Christ, my Lord, or come to Him; but the Holy Spirit has called me by the Gospel, enlightened me with His gifts, sanctified and kept me in the true faith."[15] Luther argued that God's election is the cause of man's conversion and preservation in the faith. In an explanation of the election of Jacob in Romans 9, Luther writes that "God called Jacob before he was born, because He loved him, and that He was not loved by Jacob first, nor influenced by any desert on Jacob's part."[16] This election is a free gift without any foreseen merit or faith on the part of man.

---

13. See, for example, Horton, *For Calvinism*, and Olson, *Against Calvinism*. This series attempts to give both the Arminian and Calvinistic views of election, and Lutheranism is glaringly absent from the discussion.

14. Gerhard Forde and Robert Kolb have both written on the importance of Luther's *Bondage of the Will*. See Forde, *Captivation of the Will*, and Kolb, *Bound Choice*.

15. Luther, *Small Catechism*, 17.

16. Luther, *Bondage of the Will*, 226.

After the death of Luther, the Lutheran party split into two primary factions. One was the Phillipist school, under the leadership of Melanchthon, and the other the Gnesio Lutheran party, under the leadership of Matthius Flacius.[17] The Phillipist school rejected Luther's Augustinianism and viewed man's free will as an instrument of conversion. The chief proponents of this view were Johann Pfeffinger and Viktorin Strigel. For support, these theologians used a statement made by Melanchthon in his 1535 edition of the *Loci Communes*, in which he attributed to conversion three causes, including the Holy Spirit, the word of God, and man's will. The Gnesio Lutherans responded by arguing that the effect of Adam's fall was so great that apart from grace, man would never assent to the gospel. God must first enlighten man's mind and free his will that he may repent and believe; man's will is purely passive in conversion. This discussion was settled by the Formula of Concord in favor of the Gnesio Lutheran party. Article II of the Solid Declaration states, "people who are spiritually dead in sins cannot on the basis of their own strength dispose themselves or turn themselves toward appropriate spiritual, heavenly righteousness and life, if the Son of God has not made them alive and freed them from the death of sin" (FC SD II.11).[18] The Formula of Concord says of election that "it is false and incorrect to teach that not only the mercy of God and the most holy merit of Christ but also something in us is a cause of God's election, and for this reason God chose us for eternal life. For he had chosen us in Christ not only before we were born [Rom 9:11], indeed 'before the foundation of the world'" (FC SD XI.88). Thus, Luther's doctrine of both free will and predestination is defended. It is confessed that man is so affected by sin that faith is impossible apart from grace, and that election is unconditional.

The first great dogmatic text of the Lutheran scholastic period, Martin Chemnitz's *Loci Theologici*, defended the position outlined in the Confessions.[19] However, into the seventeenth century, Lutheran dogmaticians began to soften the doctrine of predestination. It was said that God chose man *intuitu fidei* (in view of faith), rather than the unconditional predestination taught by both Luther and the Lutheran Confessional documents.[20] While

17. On this debate see Klug, "Free Will, or Human Powers," in Preus et al., *A Contemporary Look*, and also Kolb, *Bound Choice*.

18. All references to the Book of Concord are from Kolb and Wengert, *The Book of Concord*, unless otherwise noted.

19. Chemnitz, *Loci Theologici*, 393–474.

20. Robert Preus identifies this shift, writing, "In only one article is there clearly a departure from the theology of the Formula of Concord on the part of seventeenth century

the scholastics affirmed that man is converted and saved apart from his own works, and they still held to the deadness of man in sin, they argued against the Calvinists that God's election is conditional.[21] Because grace is universal, they argued, and man's unbelief is a result of his own resistance rather than God's predetermination, those whom God elected were those who did not resist grace. Thus non-resistance became a cause of election.[22]

In the nineteenth century, predestination again became a subject of controversy within Lutheranism. American theologian and pastor C. F. W. Walther unintentionally found himself in a controversy over the issue of predestination.[23] During a Missouri Synod convention in 1868, Walther made a statement about God's election being unconditional. This statement was soon attacked by Gottfried Fritschel. A heated controversy began over the relationship between faith and predestination. For the Waltherian party, election is unconditional. It is a free act of God wherein God elects certain individuals unto salvation. He argued that proposing anything else negated the principle of *sola gratia*, giving humans credit in some manner for personal salvation.[24] Walther was accused of being a closet Calvinist, and Walther defended himself by demonstrating his rejection of double predestination and limited atonement, and by showing the continuity of his own view with that of Luther and the Confessions.[25] This led some churches

---

Lutheranism: the doctrine of predestination and election" (Robert Preus, "The Formula of Concord," in Klemet I. Preus, *Doctrine Is Life*, 249). This essay is helpful in explaining the nature of this divergence.

21. B. B. Warfield argues that Lutheranism is essentially on the same side as Arminianism due to its confession of conditional election in his book *Plan of Salvation*. Unfortunately, Warfield ignores the Synodical Conference's position on the issue.

22. The earlier writers who used this phrase, such as Hunnius and Gerhard, still defended a monergistic approach to election. According to Gerhard, God chooses man based on foreseen faith. However, the faith that is foreseen is in no way the work of man, but is the work of God through Word and Sacrament. See Gerhard's discussion on election in *On Creation and Predestination*, 122–250. Later writers were not so careful, and argued that the human will is in some sense a cause of conversion. Hollaz writes, for example, "The election to eternal life of men corrupted by sin was made by the most merciful God, in consideration of faith in Christ remaining steadfast to the end of life" (quoted in Schmid, *Doctrinal Theology*, 288).

23. This controversy is documented rather well in August R. Suelflow's biography of Walther, *Servant of the Word*.

24. This debate has been summarized well Thuesen, *Predestination*, 136–71.

25. Walther's essays on the topic have been compiled in Walther, *Predestination in Lutheran Perspective*.

to split away from the Synodical Conference[26] under Walther's leadership, while other major figures within the Synodical Conference, such as Adolf Hoenecke and Francis Pieper, defended Walther's critique of *intuitu fidei*.[27] Ultimately, the Waltherian position would become that of the Missouri Synod, Wisconsin Synod, and various other American Lutheran church bodies.[28]

EXAMINING THE FIVE POINTS OF CALVINISM

Though it may be somewhat simplistic to explain a Lutheran approach to election by examining the five points of Calvinism, it is a helpful means to organize the discussion around certain topics confessed in the Reformed tradition.[29] The issues of both the extent of the atonement and the nature of perseverance have their own chapters in this present work; thus limited atonement and perseverance of the saints will not be discussed here.

Total Depravity

The first of the five points of Calvinism is total depravity. The Westminster Confession describes this doctrine as the concept that "Man, by his fall into a state of sin, hath wholly lost all ability of will to any spiritual good accompanying salvation; so as a natural man, being altogether averse from that good, and dead in sin, is not able, by his own strength, to convert himself, or to prepare himself thereunto" (WCF IX.3). The phrase "total depravity" may lend itself to confusion; it seems to imply that the children of Adam are as depraved as is possible. However, as the Westminster Confession demonstrates, the proposal is not utter depravity (the view that people are as evil as they possibly could be), but that human depravity is so deep that

---

26. The Synodical Conference was one of four major groups of Lutheran church bodies in early American Lutheranism. The Synodical Conference was generally the most conservative.

27. Pieper catalogues the controversy and gives a defense of the Missourian position in *Conversion and Election*.

28. The Waltherian approach to predestination was adopted by the Synodical Conference, but both the General Synod and the General Council generally rejected this view. For a defense of the opposing doctrine of predestination, see Keyser, *Election and Conversion*.

29. This is essential to do in light of the contemporary utilization of the "five points" as a summary of Reformed predestinarian theology.

Part I: Predestination and Free Will

it hinders one from approaching God apart from grace.[30] Apart from grace, no human being would have faith; faith is a divine gift.

On this point, the Lutheran Reformation agrees. Luther confessed similar concerns to that professed in the first point of Calvinism. Article II of the Formula of Concord contains a lengthy discussion and defense of a Lutheran perspective on free will. The Confessions state,

> That in spiritual and divine matters, the mind, heart, and will of the unreborn human being can in absolutely no way, on the basis of its own natural powers, understand, believe, accept, consider, will, begin, accomplish, do, effect, or cooperate. Instead, it is completely dead to the good—completely corrupted. This means that in this human nature, after the fall and before rebirth, there is not a spark of spiritual power left or present with which human beings can prepare themselves for the grace of God or accept grace as it is offered. (FC SD II.7)

Along with the Reformed, the Lutheran Reformation confessed that apart from grace, all are in a state of spiritual death. It takes the divine work of God to cause one to repent and believe. Both repentance and faith are gifts from God, given by grace.

Though in agreement with the Reformed confessions of faith, there are some common Reformed explanations of depravity which go beyond that of the Lutheran Confessions. In the mid-eighteenth century, Jonathan Edwards published a much discussed work titled *Freedom of the Will*.[31] In this volume, Edwards sought not to contradict Luther's concept of the bondage of the will, but to defend it through philosophical argumentation. However, in doing so, Edwards purports a pure determinism regarding every action of will rather than simply defending man's inability to approach God due to sin.[32] Edwards does this through defining the will as "that

---

30. R. C. Sproul explains this distinction: "Total depravity means radical corruption. We must be careful to note the difference between total depravity and 'utter' depravity. To be utterly depraved is to be as wicked as one could possibly be. Hitler was extremely depraved, but he could have been worse than he was. I am sinner. Yet I could sin more often and more severely than I actually do. I am not utterly depraved, but I am totally depraved. For total depravity means that I and everyone else are depraved or corrupt in the totality of our being. There is no part of us that is left untouched by sin. Our minds, our wills, and our bodies are affected by evil. We speak sinful words, do sinful deeds, have impure thoughts. Our very bodies suffer from the ravages of sin" (*Essential Truths*, 147–48).

31. Edwards, *Works* 1

32. Reformed scholar Richard Muller points this out in his lecture "Jonathan Edwards

power, or principle of mind, by which it is capable of choosing: an act of the Will is the same as an act of choosing or choice."[33] Thus one's choices and actions are initiated in the mind. The way that the mind chooses, according to Edwards, is not by a process of contemplation and consequently making a libertarian free-will decision, but according to one's greatest desire. One always chooses what is desired most. Edwards purports that the "very act of choosing one thing rather than another, is preferring that thing, and that is setting a higher value on that thing . . . Choice or preference cannot be before itself in the same instance . . . it cannot be the foundation of itself, or the consequence of itself."[34] Within this framework, Edwards promotes an argument for total depravity. A sinner is born to desire sin rather than goodness and truth. Therefore, since desire determines choice, one must choose sin and cannot choose good. The problem with Edwards's argument is that it promotes a view of free will that goes beyond the intention of biblical statements on the topic. Scripture emphasizes human lack of free will regarding conversion, but not as a general principle. In Edwards's view, no action of human beings is free because every action is determined by one's greatest desire, which one has an inability to change. In contrast to Edwards's approach, the Augsburg Confession states, "Concerning free will they [the Lutheran churches] teach that the human will has some freedom in producing civil righteousness, and choosing things subject to reason. However, it does not have the power to produce the righteousness of God or spiritual righteousness without the Holy Spirit" (AC XVIII.1–3). The lack of free will that man has is not in reference to ordinary actions such as which parking space one should take, what one should eat for breakfast, etc., but it references a lack of spiritual freedom.[35]

The Lutheran and Reformed traditions are in agreement regarding the nature of depravity and one's sinful state before God. For both, the extent of sin negates the possibility of faith and repentance apart from an act of grace. However, the popular explanation of Edwards of the nature of bondage and freedom adopted by many Reformed writers goes beyond the

---

and the Absence of Free Choice." Muller argues that Edwards's position has more in common with eighteenth-century British philosophy than classical Calvinism.

33. Edwards, *Freedom of the Will*, 4–5.

34. Ibid., 19.

35. Gustaf Wingren speaks of this in terms of freedom in things "below us," but not in things "above us." See Wingren, *Luther on Vocation*, 15–23.

Part I: Predestination and Free Will

Lutheran approach by adopting pure determinism and addresses an issue not intended by Lutheran discussions of bondage and free choice.[36]

Unconditional Election

The second point in the Calvinistic system is unconditional election. This is the teaching that predestination is an unconditional act. God's act of choosing people for salvation, therefore, is not in view of future faith or merit but is the cause of future faith and good works. In eternity past, God chose specific individuals unto salvation. The Canons of Dort express the idea with the following words:

> Election is the unchangeable purpose of God, whereby, before the foundation of the world, he hath out of mere grace, according to the sovereign good pleasure of his own will, chosen, from the whole human race, which had fallen through their own fault, from their primitive state of rectitude, into sin and destruction, a certain number of persons to redemption in Christ, whom he from eternity appointed the Mediator and Head of the elect, and the foundation of Salvation. (CD I.7)

In this statement it is demonstrated that the cause of God's act of predestination is God's "sovereign good pleasure" and an act of "his own will." There is no human condition behind God's choice, but only an act of grace.

There is some agreement in the Lutheran Confessions regarding the unconditional nature of one's election. The Formula of Concord states,

> God's eternal election not only foresees and foreknows the salvation of the elect but is also a cause of our salvation and whatever pertains to it, on the basis of the gracious will and good pleasure of God in Christ Jesus. As this cause, it creates, effects, aids, and promotes our salvation. Our salvation is founded upon it so that "the gates of hell" [Matt. 16:18] may not have any power against this salvation, as is written, "No one will snatch the sheep out of my hand" [John 10:28]. And again, "As many as had been destined for eternal life became believers" [Acts 13:48]. (FC SD XI.8)

In contrast to the *intuitu fidei* approach of later scholastic Lutheranism and the Arminian position, the Lutheran reformers argued that election is not a decision of God based merely on foreseen faith, but is itself a cause of

---

36. Edwards's explanation has been popularized especially by the work of John Gerstner. See, for example, Gerstner, *Jonathan Edwards*.

faith. Election is an unconditional act, wherein God freely gives salvation through faith, apart from any work on the part of man. Regarding the positive aspect of predestination, there is thus agreement on its unconditional nature.

However, the Calvinist and Lutheran Reformations proceeded with divergent views regarding the nature of damnation. In the Lutheran tradition, it is confessed that

> The eternal election of God, however, or *praedestinatio* (that is, God's preordination to salvation), does not apply to both the godly and the evil, but instead only to the children of God, who are chosen and predestined to eternal life, "before the foundation of the world" was laid, as Paul says (Eph. 1[:4, 5]): He chose us in Christ Jesus and "preordained us to adoption as his children." (FC SD XI.5)

Thus it is confessed that predestination is single. Election extends only to the children of God and not to the reprobate. Lutheran theology has been purposefully careful about the attribution of evil to God's will. Though God's providence extends over all things both good and evil, and nothing happens apart from God's allowance, God is not active in the predestinating decree of evil actions. The purpose of the doctrine of election is to give assurance to God's people and to serve as a reminder that salvation comes *sola gratia* and is not an abstract discussion regarding God's sovereignty.[37]

Reformed Lapsarian Views

In the Reformed tradition, there are various approaches to the decree of reprobation. Some theologians have argued for an active decree of reprobation by God, whereas others have argued that the act is merely passive. These have been divided into the infralapsarian and supralapsarian traditions, along with the less prominent tradition of Amyrauldianism.[38]

---

37. I recognize that many Reformed writers will object to this characterization, but it is stated by Bavinck that "The Reformed person does not rest until he has traced all things retrospectively to the divine decree, tracing down the 'wherefore' of all things, and has prospectively made all things subservient to the glory of God; the Lutheran is content with the 'that' and enjoys the salvation in which he is, by faith, a participant" (Bavinck, *Reformed Dogmatics* 1:177).

38. However, some theologians, such as Bavinck, have rejected any attempt to formulate a lapsarian view. See Bavinck, *Reformed Dogmatics*. These theologians argue (I think rightly) that such discussion is speculative and unhelpful.

Part I: Predestination and Free Will

The divide in the Reformed camp regarding double predestination centers on a discussion of God's eternal decrees and their logical order. It is argued that the "golden chain of salvation" in Romans 8 gives precedence for such a distinction.[39] In Romans 8, Paul distinguishes between God's decrees of foreknowledge, predestination, justification, and glorification. This allows for further distinctions in the divine will. These distinctions do not refer to a temporal order of decrees because all are simultaneous, but they are related to the logical order of God's decree.

The most prominent Reformed view is infralapsarianism.[40] Infralapsarianism means "after the fall" (coming from the Latin prefix *infra*, meaning "after" or "below," and the term *lapsus*, meaning "fall"). In the infralapsarian system, the order of God's decrees is as follows: First, God decreed to create the human race; secondly, God decreed the fall, causing everyone to fall into sin; third, God decreed to save some fallen people and leave those remaining in sin; and finally, God decreed the atonement for the elect alone. While still remaining double predestinarian, this perspective takes a less active approach to the act of reprobation. God reprobates only in view of the fall and sin. God is active in that he decides specifically not to grant redemption or atonement for these reprobate individuals, but not in creating sin in them or causing their specific rebellion. This perspective is reflected in the Westminster Confession of Faith, as well as the Canons of Dort. The majority of those in attendance at the formation of each of these confessional documents were infralapsarian, though not exclusively. It is held by several of the most popular Calvinistic theologians, including Charles Hodge, Lorraine Boettner, and Francis Turretin.[41]

For a defense of Amyraut's theology, see Armstong, *Calvinism and the Amyraut Heresy*. In this work, Armstrong argues that Amyraut represents Calvin's theology better than does the scholastic tradition. I am not ultimately persuaded by Armstrong's thesis, as the writing is often more hagiographic than convincing as scholarship.

39. "For those whom he foreknew he also predestined to be conformed to the image of his Son, in order that he might be the firstborn among many brothers. And those whom he predestined he also called, and those whom he called he also justified, and those whom he justified he also glorified" (Rom 8:29–30). John Murray utilizes the text in this manner in *Redemption Accomplished and Applied*.

40. See Hodge's discussion of the infralapsarian position in *Systematic Theology* 2:319–21.

41. Dr. Curt Daniel gives a list of those committed to this position, including those mentioned, and to the supralapsarian position, in *History and Theology of Calvinism*.

The other lapsarian perspective is that of supralapsarianism.[42] This term means "before the fall" (the Latin prefix *supra* meaning either "before" or "above"). In this system, the logical order of decrees is first to reprobate some and elect others; secondly to create human beings to bring about such election and reprobation; thirdly to cause the fall; and finally to send Christ so that atonement might be made for the elect only. In this system, predestination to both death and life is active. Creation is a means to bring about the giving of life through election and death through reprobation. God does not elect and reprobate in view of sin, but allows for sin as a means to elect and condemn. God's glory in damnation and salvation is thus the purpose of creation itself.[43] Due to its implications regarding the relationship between sin and God's decree, this approach has failed to gain much support. There were, however, several supralapsarians present at both the Synod of Dort and the Westminster Assembly, though the other perspective is reflected in the confessional documents of both synods. Popular supralapsarian theologians include Theodore Beza, Abraham Kuyper, and Herman Hoeksema.[44] The supralapsarian position is also that of the nineteenth-century hyper-Calvinist movement in Europe. However, most supralapsarians reject hyper-Calvinism.[45]

Finally, there is a third school in the discussion which seeks to limit God's role in damnation, known as Amyraldianism.[46] The seventeenth-century French Reformed theologian Moses Amyraut argued that both a Calvinistic doctrine of election and universal atonement could be main-

42. Hodge's discussion of this perspective in *Systematic Theology* 2:316–19 is also quite helpful.

43. This is explicated throughout Herman Hoeksema's *Reformed Dogmatics*. More recently, Robert Reymond is a proponent of what he labels a "modified supralapsarianism." See Reymond, *New Systematic Theology*.

44. I would point again to Dr. Curt Daniel's book *History and Theology of Calvinism*.

45. Though some claim that all extreme Calvinists are hyper-Calvinists, there is a historical belief system and movement with defining characteristics differing from that of most Calvinists. Hyper-Calvinists believe that unbelievers do not have a duty to believe since God does not want them to. Thus, unbelief is not a sin for the reprobate. They also oppose the free offer of the gospel confessed by traditional Calvinism. Other views prominent within hyper-Calvinism are eternal justification, the denial of common grace, the neglect of evangelism, denial that non-Calvinists (or even non-hyper-Calvinists) can be saved, and the belief that God actively creates sin in the hearts of the reprobate. A prominent contemporary example of hyper-Calvinism (albeit in a more moderate form) can be found in Engelsma, *Hyper Calvinism*.

46. Hodge also writes about this view with the term "hypothetical universalism" in *Systematic Theology* 2:321–24.

Part I: Predestination and Free Will

tained. Amyraut argued that God's decree of atonement precedes the decree of election and reprobation. God first decrees that Christ will die as the universal substitute for humankind. Because none would believe due to sin, then apart from election none would benefit from the atonement. Because of this, God chose to elect some and leave others in sin. Thus, Amyraut argued, it can be confessed both that election is particular and atonement is universal. In this sense, Amyraut's perspective is similar to that of the Lutheran Confessions, though Amyraut still maintained the doctrine of double predestination. Prominent Amyraldians include Richard Baxter, John Bunyan, and contemporary Baptist theologian Bruce Ware.[47]

Lutheran theologians have historically rejected all three of these positions, especially because of their adamant denial of double predestination. In the Lutheran perspective, election refers to the children of God alone and has no reference to the rejection of grace on behalf of the reprobate.[48] While one's salvation is attributed solely to grace, one's damnation is attributed solely to a rejection of grace rather than God's decree. A distinction has often been made between God's antecedent and consequent will. God's antecedent will is universal, for the salvation of all; his consequent will, which is in view of the rejection that is offered toward the gospel, is for the salvation of the elect and the damnation of those who reject the gospel. Revere Franklin Weidner writes:

> The will of God is said to be antecedent and consequent, a) not with regard to time, as though the former preceded the latter in time; b) nor with regard to the divine will itself, as though two actually distinct wills in God were affirmed, for the divine will is the essence itself of God, with a connoted object, conceived under the mode of an act of volition; c) but from the order of our reason, according to a diverse consideration of the objects, because, according to our mode of conception, God's willing eternal salvation to men, and His providing the means of grace, are anterior to His will to confer in act eternal salvation upon those who would to the

---

47. See Amar Djaballah, "Controversy on Universal Grace: A Historical Survey of Moise Amyraut's," in Gibson and Gibson, *From Heaven He Came*.

48. Pieper, for example, writes, "Clearly and emphatically Scripture teaches that Christians owe their whole Christian state in time, specifically also their faith, to their eternal election; but with the same clarity and emphasis Scripture also excludes the thought that the unbelief of the lost can be traced to predestination to damnation" (Pieper, *Christian Dogmatics* 3:495).

end believe in Christ, or to assign eternal condemnation to the impenitent.[49]

In contrast to the Reformed theology, God's antecedent will, in view of the fallen human race in its entirety, is for the salvation of all. It is only in view of the active rejection of God's call that anyone is damned. There are several reasons for accepting the Lutheran approach to predestination in contrast to the various lapsarian views.

First, this discussion delves into areas of God's eternal will and nature which are both theologically unnecessary and irrelevant to the central scriptural themes. Scripture does not extensively discuss abstract truths about God or the nature of eternal decree, but speaks rather to that which affects the hearer. Though the developments of systematic theology can be a valid extrapolation of biblical material, Scripture is not primarily a philosophical text; it does not give any precedent for abstract speculation about that which is not directly addressed. Paul's argument in Romans 8 regarding foreknowledge, election, justification, and glorification is not grounds for distinguishing eternal decrees. Paul does not contextually propound a logical order of God's decrees, but gives assurance to his readers that they are elect and justified and will receive eternal life.[50] Even if Paul was attempting to propose an order to God's decrees, this would still not be justification for further speculation regarding the order of God's other decrees which have not been explicitly stated.[51] The Lutheran Reformation openly denied such speculation in the following section of the Formula of Concord:

49. Weidner, *Theologia*, 71. Weidner's statement is a summary of Hollaz and Quenstedt.

50. I do not deny that this text does give some grounds for treating an *ordo salutis*, though this must not remain abstract. The *ordo salutis* is a historic Lutheran teaching, as in Schmid, *Doctrinal Theology*.

51. It is to be noted that Calvin himself cautioned against such speculation: "Not to take too long, let us remember here, as in all religious doctrine, that we ought to hold to one rule of modesty and sobriety: not to speak, or guess, or even to seek to know, concerning obscure matters anything except what has been imparted to us by God's Word. Furthermore, in the reading of Scripture we ought ceaselessly to endeavor to seek out and meditate upon those things which make for our edification. Let us not indulge in curiosity or the investigation of unprofitable things. And because the Lord willed to instruct us, not in fruitless questions, but in sound godliness, in the fear of his name, in true trust, and in the duties of holiness, let us be satisfied with this knowledge. For this reason, if we would be duly wise, we must leave those empty speculations which idle men have taught apart from God's Word concerning the nature, orders, and number of angels" (*Institutes* I.XIV.4). The Reformed tradition has often cautioned against speculation, but on this point they have not heeded their own warnings.

Part I: Predestination and Free Will

> Nor is this eternal election or ordination of God to eternal life to be considered in God's secret, inscrutable counsel in such a bare manner as though it comprised nothing further, or as though nothing more belonged to it, and nothing more were to be considered in it, than that God foresaw who and how many were to be saved, who and how many were to be damned, or that He only held a [sort of military] muster, thus: "This one shall be saved, that one shall be damned; this one shall remain steadfast [in faith to the end], that one shall not remain steadfast." (FC SD XI.9)[52]

That which pertains to God's decree is part of the "hidden God," of the aspects of God not to be peered into by humans. Rather than giving an explanation of the hidden God, the doctrine of election is meant to give assurance, and to promote the gracious and eternal nature of God's promise.[53]

Another significant difficulty with the first two lapsarian approaches is that election necessarily becomes the central and primary soteriological category. In both approaches, the eternal decree of election and reprobation precedes that of the atonement. Thus, the cross and resurrection become a means to bring about election. First God elects and only secondly God decrees the cross as an instrument of saving the elect. This is necessitated with the confession of limited atonement. This displaces the cross as the primary soteriological event in redemptive history. In a Lutheran and biblical approach, election is God's means to bring people to the cross, as opposed to the Calvinistic approach, which argues the opposite.[54] This is demonstrated especially in the first chapter of Ephesians:

> Blessed be the God and Father of our Lord Jesus Christ, who has blessed us in Christ with every spiritual blessing in the heavenly

---

52. From the Triglotta.

53. The hidden/revealed God distinction is explicated by Luther in *Bondage of the Will*. Richard Muller defines this doctrine, writing, "The paradox of God's unknowability and self-manifestations as stated by Luther. The issue is not that God has been hidden and has now revealed himself, but rather that the revelation that has been given to man defies the wisdom of the world because it is the revelation of the hidden God. God is revealed in hiddenness and hidden in his revelation. He reveals himself paradoxically to thwart the proud, under the opposite, omnipotence manifest on the cross" (*Dictionary*, 90).

54. Lutherans have continually emphasized the Christological nature of God's election. Weidner writes, "The true judgment concerning predestination must not be learned 1) from reason, 2) nor from the Law of God, 3) but alone from the Holy Gospel concerning Christ, in which it is clearly testified that 'God hath shut up all unto disobedience that he might have mercy upon all' (Rom. 11:32), 'not wishing that any should perish, but that all should come to repentance' (2 Pet. 3:9)" (*Theologia*, 69).

places, even as he chose us in him before the foundation of the world, that we should be holy and blameless before him. In love he predestined us for adoption as sons through Jesus Christ, according to the purpose of his will, to the praise of his glorious grace, with which he has blessed us in the Beloved. In him we have redemption through his blood, the forgiveness of our trespasses, according to the riches of his grace, which he lavished upon us, in all wisdom and insight making known to us the mystery of his will, according to his purpose, which he set forth in Christ as a plan for the fullness of time, to unite all things in him, things in heaven and things on earth. (Eph 1:3–10)

Notice the centrality of Christ in the discussion of election. One is chosen "in Christ," not abstractly. In the Reformed view, one could not be chosen "in Christ" because the decree of the incarnation is a response to election. However, in Paul's view, election is already in view of Christ, the incarnate God. The incarnation is a universal solution for sin which God brings to individuals through election. If Paul had believed in either a supralapsarian or infralapsarian view of predestination, he could have stated that one was chosen by God through the second person of the Trinity or in the Spirit, but not *in Christ*—the title of the incarnate Messiah. Paul also assumes that election is unto the blessings he enumerates, including the forgiveness of sins through the cross. This is the opposite of what the Reformed purport.[55] It is clear that Paul placed the incarnation, death, and resurrection of Christ at the center of his theology. All other soteriological categories are merely means to bring this salvation to God's people.

Finally, all three of these approaches err in the context in which election is placed.[56] Sovereignty becomes a—or *the*—central category in all

---

55. The Reformed tradition has not always placed election in a more central place than the cross. Calvin urges, for example, "We cannot find the certainty of our election in ourselves; and not even in God the Father, if we look at him apart from the Son. Christ, then, is the mirror in which we ought, and in which, without deception, we may contemplate our election . . . if we are in communion with Christ, we have proof sufficiently clear and strong that we are written in the Book of Life" (*Institutes* III.XXIV.5). The problem is in the consistency of holding to the cross as central when one argues that the cross is a secondary consideration in God's eternal decree. If the cross is a means to bring about election, this necessarily makes election a more fundamental soteriological category.

56. Many Reformed dogmaticians include the doctrine of election under Theology Proper, thus placing it in the midst of a discussion of God's decrees in general. Some examples of this tendency are Frame, *Systematic Theology*, 216–17; and Bavinck, *Reformed Dogmatics* 2:337–405. This is a departure from Calvin himself, who places the doctrine of predestination in a soteriological context (Calvin, *Institutes* Book III, XXI).

Part I: Predestination and Free Will

theological discussions. Election often centers on God's decree and self-glorification, rather than God's gracious response to his creation, which fell through sin.[57] One text which is often utilized in such discussions is also from Ephesians 1. It is observed that God "works all things according to the counsel of his will" (Eph 1:11).[58] However, the broader discussion is not about God's sovereignty and self-glorification through damnation and salvation, but is in reference to the cross and all of the blessings that Christians obtain through Christ. The above statement of Paul is not a ground for arguing that lapsarian approaches to sovereignty are valid; rather, it demonstrates that the biblical context of the doctrine of sovereignty is to give assurance to the anxious Christian that God's providential care is powerful and unending. To argue otherwise removes election from its Pauline context.

Refuting Double Predestination

There are several theological and exegetical arguments proposed in support of double predestinarianism. Perhaps the most common is that of the logic of its relation to positive predestination unto life. If God has elected some for salvation, as Scripture teaches, then logically predestination unto death follows. If God elects some, he chooses specifically not to elect others.[59] Though logically coherent, this approach negates the scriptural confession of God's universal saving will. This will be demonstrated in the following chapter regarding the extent of the atonement. Though there is no logical solution to the dilemma of God's active role in election and his non-involvement in reprobation, this paradox reflects New Testament teaching. God's will is mysterious, and one must not go beyond the biblical testimony regarding the subject in an attempt to harmonize two truths which are seemingly in tension with one another.[60]

    57. This, again, is demonstrated by Bavinck, who notes that idolatry is the primary enemy for Reformed theology, due to its emphasis on the glory of God, and legalism for the Lutheran, because of the Lutheran soteriological emphasis (*Reformed Dogmatics* 1:177). There are, however, likely some Reformed theologians who would disagree with this statement.

    58. For example, see Frame, *Systematic Theology*, 169.

    59. Lorraine Boettner argues this way in *Reformed Doctrine of Predestination*, 113–17.

    60. Steven P. Mueller notes that "Double predestination is logical, and it takes part of the Scriptures very seriously, but it also adds to the Scriptures by means of logic. It may seem logical to assume that God has predestined some to hell, but it is not Biblical"

The truth of single predestination can be demonstrated by looking at various texts which discuss the difference between God's active role in election unto life, and his inactive role in damnation. Scripture often speaks of hell as that which was prepared specifically for the devil. Matthew writes, "Then he will say to those on his left, 'Depart from me, you cursed, into the eternal fire prepared for the devil and his angels'" (Matt 25:41). In God's act of sending people to judgment, it is not claimed that this punishment was foreordained for these individuals; rather this judgment was foreordained for fallen angels. Contrast this with God's active role in preparing heaven for the elect: "In my Father's house are many rooms. If it were not so, would I have told you that I go to prepare a place for you? And if I go and prepare a place for you, I will come again and will take you to myself, that where I am you may be also" (John 14:2–3). In contrast to the fate of the wicked, the reward of the righteous had been predestined and prepared beforehand. One is consciously prepared, while the other is an unfortunate result of unbelief.[61] This does not reflect either the supralapsarian or infralapsarian approach to double predestination, which both argue for an active role of God in reprobation to some extent.

Sovereignty, election, and predestination are terms used in the context of salvation, giving encouragement to Christians and reminding them of their continual dependence on grace.[62] They are not used to describe the actions or fate of those who are damned. Rather, damnation is always a result of personal sin and rejection of Christ. Paul attributes damnation to those "who do not obey the gospel" (2 Thess 1:8), thus placing the cause of damnation solely on unbelief. Peter writes that heretics bring "upon themselves swift destruction" (2 Pet 2:1). In this epistle, Peter later speaks of a condemnation of these particular heretics from "long ago" (2 Pet 2:3). However,

---

(Mueller, *Called to Believe*, 291–92).

61. "Even though God desires the salvation of all humans (1 Timothy 2:4), Scripture warns us that not all will receive his free gift of salvation. There will be people who reject God's grace and choose to follow their own will and ways (Romans 2:8). The means of grace, including the Gospel, may be resisted (Matthew 23:37, Acts 13:46). While God does not want anyone to reject his gift of salvation, he will not force salvation on them. He will allow them to choose eternity without him" (Mueller, *Called to Believe*, 287).

62. John Molstad writes, "Our election gives us assurance because it drives us to the Word, where we are told that, through Christ's saving work, places in heaven are reserved for us believers" (Molstad, *Predestination*, 57).

Part I: Predestination and Free Will

this does not necessitate double predestination, but merely that in view of their heresies, these men would be punished and suffer damnation.[63]

The most common text used to defend the concept of double predestination is Romans 9.[64] This chapter is an extended discussion on the election of grace, the nature of true Israel, and God's sovereignty. The Pauline argument begins:

> But it is not as though the word of God has failed. For not all who are descended from Israel belong to Israel, and not all are children of Abraham because they are his offspring, but "Through Isaac shall your offspring be named." This means that it is not the children of the flesh who are the children of God, but the children of the promise are counted as offspring. For this is what the promise said: "About this time next year I will return, and Sarah shall have a son." And not only so, but also when Rebekah had conceived children by one man, our forefather Isaac, though they were not yet born and had done nothing either good or bad—in order that God's purpose of election might continue, not because of works but because of him who calls—she was told, "The older will serve the younger." As it is written, "Jacob I loved, but Esau I hated." (Rom 9:6–13)

Paul has a specific purpose in this argument other than delving into God's sovereign decrees regarding election and reprobation. In chapters 9–11 of Romans, Paul deals with the question of the nature of true Israel. He puts forth a lengthy argument that those who constitute Israel, inheritors of the Abrahamic promise, are those who have faith in Christ rather than simply those born into Jewish ethnicity. It might seem to some that since ethnic Jews did not accept the messianic claims of Jesus, this implies that God's promises regarding Israel's redemption have not been fulfilled. Thus,

---

63. When speaking of double-predestination Calvinists fail to distinguish between God's foreknowledge and predestination. The Formula of Concord argues that predestination refers only to salvation, whereas damnation and evil actions are not eternally decreed by God, but simply foreknown. Weidner writes, "The foreknowledge of God is nothing else than that God knows all things before they happen (Dan. 2:28). This foreknowledge is occupied alike with the godly and the wicked; but it is not the cause of evil or of sin, nor the cause that men perish, for which they themselves are responsible" (Weidner, *Theologia*, 69).

64. The most in-depth discussion of this issue from a Calvinistic perspective is John Piper's doctoral dissertation, published as *Justification of God*. This work merits a much more in-depth rebuttal than can be offered in a work such as this. Perhaps this will be a future doctoral student's work rather than my own.

it seems that the word has failed to do what was promised. Paul argues that the word of God has not failed, because these promises refer not to the nation as a whole, but to specific individuals who have faith. In light of this, Paul promotes the idea of election. The Old Testament witnessed to the corporate election of Israel, wherein God chose one specific nation among others to give his promises. Paul argues that behind corporate election there is a more profound reality that God has elected individuals as the true Israel. Thus, by grace, people are elected, given faith, and made part of the true Israel.

Note that the quotation Paul utilizes regarding Jacob and Esau originally had reference to the nations which descended from each of them (Mal 1:1–3). The statement does not mean that God predestined Jacob unto life and Esau unto death.[65] That being said, Paul does expand the national principle used in its original context to make a point about individuals. The point has nothing to do with damnation, but has reference to the election of grace. Paul does not utilize this quotation to emphasize that God hated Esau, but that God loved Jacob. He writes that the twins had "done nothing good or bad." This is a demonstration of election, of God's gracious choice to bless Jacob regardless of his merits or demerits. The point Paul is making is this: the story of Jacob and Esau is about a firstborn son who loses his birthright to his younger brother, who, according to normal human law, would not be given the birthright. God decided before their birth that Jacob would be chosen as the one who would carry the line of Israel to his descendants, rather than Esau. God did not make this choice based on anything that Jacob would do, but solely by an act of grace. This example of God's unconditional and unmerited favor corresponds with the nature of true Israel. Just as Jacob was made a great nation and given the promise by grace alone, God creates the true Israel by grace alone, choosing people apart from their works.[66]

The Pauline argument then continues,

---

65. Johann Gerhard writes, "[Calvinists] corrupt the genuine meaning of the words, for 'hating' here should not be taken positively for an absolute hatred, but negatively, so that it is the same thing as esteeming less, namely, in the conferral of external privileges and benefits" (Gerhard, *Theological Commonplaces VIII–XI*, 154).

66. Gerhard adopts this interpretation, writing, "The true spiritual seed of Abraham is reckoned not on the basis of carnal birth nor on the basis of the merits of works, but on the basis of God who calls and by virtue of faith which embraces the divine promise" (ibid.).

Part I: Predestination and Free Will

> What shall we say then? Is there injustice on God's part? By no means! For he says to Moses, "I will have mercy on whom I have mercy, and I will have compassion on whom I have compassion." So then it depends not on human will or exertion, but on God, who has mercy. For the Scripture says to Pharaoh, "For this very purpose I have raised you up, that I might show my power in you, and that my name might be proclaimed in all the earth." So then he has mercy on whomever he wills, and he hardens whomever he wills. (Rom 9:14–18)

Paul continues his argument by promoting the concept that mercy and compassion are unmerited. Grace does not depend "on human will or exertion, but on God, who had mercy." This supports Paul's insistence that the true Israel includes those who are saved by grace. Paul then expands this concept to a discussion regarding God's sovereignty more broadly. He does this through the example of Pharaoh, whom God is said to harden. Some claim that this is a reference to reprobation. Notice, however, the original context in which Pharaoh was said to be hardened by God. Throughout the book of Exodus, a process is described wherein Pharaoh becomes more hardened toward the people of Israel. It does not speak exclusively of God's act of hardening, but also of Pharaoh hardening his own heart. Exodus 8 states for example that "when Pharaoh saw that there was a respite, he hardened his heart and would not listen to them, as the Lord had said" (Exod 8:15). Hardening Pharaoh's heart is not evidence of God's active predestination of Pharaoh unto death, but is a result and punishment for Pharaoh's own sin. Pharaoh's continual resistance to God's grace and his harsh attitude toward the Israelites resulted in a punishment wherein God gave Pharaoh over to his sin. This is consistent with what Paul writes in the beginning of Romans, wherein he speaks of God's giving one over to sin as a punishment for previous unbelief and sinful indulgence. "Therefore God gave them up in the lusts of their hearts to impurity, to the dishonoring of their bodies among themselves, because they exchanged the truth about God for a lie and worshiped and served the creature rather than the Creator, who is blessed forever! Amen" (Rom 1:24–25). The example supports Paul's insistence on God's sovereignty, but it does not necessitate the concept of double predestination. Pharaoh's hardening is a result of his own sin rather than being predestined unto death.

The rest of Paul's argument is along similar lines. Paul defends God's right to harden hearts and to choose people apart from works. God is said to "endure with much patience vessels of wrath prepared for destruction" (Rom 9:22). Johann Gerhard explains this text, writing,

> The application is as follows. As the potter has the power to fashion out of one and the same lump some vessels for honor and some for dishonor, so God is not unjust if He prepares vessels of mercy for glory and very tenderly tolerates vessels of wrath suited for destruction to make known his power. The Apostle states this with precisely these words, which move from the lesser to the greater. If one cannot accuse the potter for making a vessel for dishonor out of material that does not fight back, all the less can one accuse God of injustice for taking away His grace from people (such as Pharaoh) who insolently resist Him, and for surrendering to Satan for hardening that workmanship which fought back against its Maker, and for discarding it unto destruction.[67]

After discussing the patience God has toward vessels of wrath, Paul gets back to his original theme that not all of national Israel is of true Israel by telling his readers that God calls people from both the Jews and the Gentiles. He then gives the reason that not all of national Israel is saved. It is not because they had been predestined to death; rather, "Because they did not pursue it by faith, but as if it were based on works" (Rom 9:32). The Jews did not accept the doctrine of salvation by grace—that which Paul is attempting to prove in this chapter—but sought justification through the law. Thus, the cause of reprobation is unbelief.

This discussion continues for two more chapters. In chapter 10, Paul emphasizes salvation by grace, the unity of Jews and Gentiles, and the necessity of evangelism. After a lengthy discussion of the relationship between Jews and Gentiles in the covenant in chapter 11, he expresses his desire for the salvation of all, both Jews and Gentiles:

> For just as you were at one time disobedient to God but now have received mercy because of their disobedience, so they too have now been disobedient in order that by the mercy shown to you they also may now receive mercy. For God has consigned all to disobedience, that he may have mercy on all. (Rom 9:30–32)

The nature of the parallel between those who have been "consigned to disobedience" and those on whom God desires to have mercy necessitates that "all" is universal. As all have sinned, all are given grace. The conclusion to Paul's discussion which extends from chapters 9 through 11 is that God

---

67. Ibid., 159.

convicts all so that he might have mercy on all. Because in Paul's perspective this is a conclusion which can be drawn from his writing, double predestination is clearly not intended in chapter 9 because this would contradict Paul's insistence that God's desire for salvation is universal.

Double predestination is not a biblical concept. It is a logical extrapolation from the teaching of positive predestination, but it does not have exegetical support. Scripture blames damnation entirely on one's own sin and not in any sense on God's foreordination. While Romans 9 is an admittedly difficult text, it does not necessitate a double-predestinarian reading. This is confirmed by examining the cited verses in their original context, following the logic of Paul's argument regarding true Israel, and through the application Paul himself makes at the conclusion of his argument that God desires to have mercy on all.

Irresistible Grace

The doctrine of irresistible grace is the belief that saving grace always results in conversion. The Westminster Confession describes the doctrine as follows:

> All those whom God hath predestinated unto life, and those only, he is pleased, in his appointed and accepted time, effectually to call, by his Word and Spirit, out of that state of sin and death, in which they are by nature, to grace and salvation, by Jesus Christ; enlightening their minds spiritually and savingly to understand the things of God, taking away their heart of stone, and giving unto them a heart of flesh; renewing their wills, and, by his almighty power, determining them to that which is good, and effectually drawing them to Jesus Christ: yet so, as they come most freely, being made willing by his grace. (WCF X.1)

This statement confesses two primary convictions. The first is that all who are predestined unto life will receive salvation; God's grace will not fail to convert those whom he has elected in eternity past. The second is that it is the elect alone who receive saving grace; thus, saving grace is always irresistible and results in eschatological blessing.

The first of the two statements is confessed by the Lutheran Confessions. The elect will be finally saved. The Formula of Concord states, for example, that "Thus he wills, finally, to save and glorify forever in eternal life those whom he has elected, called, and justified" (FC SD XI.22). Pieper writes similarly that "The elect are only those actually saved, for Scripture teaches that without fail all elect enter eternal life."[68] In this sense the Lutheran tradition confesses irresistible grace, in that those who are elect will be effectually saved. Election always results in salvation; however, grace is not limited to the elect. Regeneration, justification, adoption, sanctification, and other soteriological blessings are given through the means of grace indiscriminately. They are not the property of the elect alone.

The Reformed can speak of the universal nature of grace in a different sense than regenerating or justifying grace. It is proposed that there is a "common grace"[69] which is given to all people.[70] This refers to various external benefits which God can bestow upon people. The Westminster Confession purports that "Others, not elected, although they may be called by the ministry of the Word, and may have some common operations of the Spirit, yet they never truly come unto Christ, and therefore cannot be saved" (WCF X.4). Restraining grace is that by which God restrains the evil desires and intentions of people, allowing them to live externally honorable lives. Common grace is also demonstrated in that God gives talents to the non-regenerate. Unbelievers are allowed to benefit the world with great art, literature, architecture, etc.[71] They also are given the undeserved benefits of life and happiness.

Common grace is not soteriological, and refers primarily to external blessings rather than genuine spiritual good.[72] Because of the limited nature of common grace, the Reformed also promote the concept of a universal gospel offer.[73] The gospel is truly offered to all people, elect and reprobate alike. Thus, people can reject and resist grace in the sense of a refusal to accept the universal offer. There is, however, no true grace given to the non-elect in the sense of that which regenerates and saves.

---

68. Pieper, *Christian Dogmatics* 3:479.

69. See Keller, *What Is Common Grace?*

70. There are some Calvinists, notably those associated with the Presbyterian Reformed Church, who reject the teaching of common grace. Herman Hoeksema rejected the teaching of common grace which was associated with Abraham Kuyper. See Engelsma, *Common Grace Revisited*.

71. This is discussed in some detail by Abraham Kuyper in *Lectures on Calvinism*.

72. However, it is to be noted that sometimes this terminology can be used to discuss the temporal delay of judgment prior to death. See Kline, *Kingdom Prologue*, 153–60.

73. This has been emphasized in discussions with hyper-Calvinism. See Murray, *Spurgeon v. Hyper-Calvinism*.

Part I: Predestination and Free Will

The Means of Grace

Lutherans confess that grace is universal in nature. This does not refer simply to external benefits that God grants all men, or to an external call. In the Lutheran view, God connects his grace to concrete means. In Reformed theology, a distinction is often made between an outward call and an internal call. As Sproul writes, "[T]he outward call refers to preaching of the gospel."[74] It is the proclamation of the word which extends to all. This is distinct from the inward call with which the Spirit calls individuals through regeneration.[75] While the outward and inward call often accompany one another, there is no organic connection between the two. For the Lutheran tradition, these calls are one and the same. The physical is not divorced from the spiritual. Calling is given through words heard by the ear, and by water poured on a person's head. There is no such thing as an outward call that does not simultaneously call inwardly.

In discussions of the *ordo salutis*, Lutheran writers have contended that the call (or *vocatio*) is, in contrast to Calvinism, both universal and resistible. Weidner explains:

> The vocation is serious. God is in earnest, He means it. The words of vocation do not mean less than their sound, but in consequence of the very imperfection of language, the meaning, when they convey a divine call, is more than their sound. If the earnest call of a father to a wandering child to come, means come, then does the call of God, equally serious, yet more urgently, means come. It is not as Calvin teaches, merely the manifestation by sign and command, but it arises out of the deepest purpose and good pleasure of God who seriously desires the saving illumination and conversion of all men.[76]

The call is a real and intended call. Every time that the gospel is preached and baptism administered, God's Spirit is at work in the call. The differentiating

---

74. R. C. Sproul, *Chosen by God*, 108.

75. Michael Horton writes, "Regeneration (or effectual calling) is the Spirit's sovereign work of raising those who are spiritually dead to life in Christ through the announcement of the gospel" (Horton, *Christian Faith*, 572). There is some disagreement among Reformed theologians over whether or not regeneration and the effectual call are distinct acts. Horton argues that they are synonymous, whereas, in *Redemption Accomplished and Applied*, John Murray differentiates them.

76. Weidner, *Pneumatology*, 34.

factor is not whether God intends the call or not, but the resistance of man. Quenstedt further explains:

> No call of God, whether of itself and its intrinsic quality or the intention of God, is inefficacious, so that it cannot and should not produce a salutary effect; but every call is efficacious (for the preached Word of God has a divine and sufficient power and efficacy to effect regeneration, conversion, etc., by the ordination and appointment of God Himself), although it may be prevented from obtaining its effect by *men presenting an obstacle, and thus becomes inefficacious by the fault of the wicked and perverse will of men.*[77]

The call is efficacious, in that it does indeed work faith in the sinner apart from any free movement of the will. However, it is not irresistible, but can be rejected. In this way, those who are converted by the call can give credit only to God's work within his word, but those who are not have only themselves to blame for resisting God's earnestly intended call.

Grace is connected to both word and sacrament. In the Lutheran view, the word of God is not merely descriptive but it is also active. The word acts as both law and gospel, convicting of sin and granting grace.[78] This is true and valid regardless of the response of the hearer. If the hearer despises the gospel and rejects it, that does not negate the fact that the Spirit is present in its proclamation and acts to save the hearer. Rejection of the gospel does not negate the power of the gospel. The Apostle Peter speaks of the power of God's word, for example, when he says to his readers, "You have been born again, not of perishable seed but of imperishable, through the living and abiding word of God" (1 Pet 1:23). The word itself is an instrument of grace, through which the Spirit acts to regenerate. If the Spirit does not regenerate through the word, it is not through a lack of his presence, but through the rejection of the listener.

In the same manner as the word, the Spirit accompanies the sacraments by granting grace and forgiveness. Baptism puts the sinful self to death and brings the new man to life. The later chapter on baptism will expound upon all of the benefits attributed to it throughout Scripture. These benefits are never limited to the elect, but are tied to the baptismal act. Thus baptismal grace is universal, and consequently, resistible.[79] Some will reject

---

77. Schmid, *Doctrinal Theology*, 445–46 (italics original).

78. Oswald Bayer emphasizes this as an important aspect of Luther's theology. See Bayer, *Martin Luther's Theology*.

79. Some writers have argued, within the Reformed tradition, that baptism effects

what the Spirit does through the water, and again this is due to the unbelief of the recipient rather than an absence of grace. This is true in the same manner regarding the Eucharist. In the Supper, Christ offers himself to all who partake of the bread and wine. His presence is not negated by unbelief, but the benefit is negated by unbelief, making the sacrament an instrument of judgment rather than blessing.[80]

Because of the nature of God's presence within both word and sacrament, it must be confessed that grace is universal. While election is particular, regarding only those who gain eternal life, grace is sacramental, and is thus given to all who receive word and sacrament.

The Doctrine of Predestination in Ancient Christianity

Much of the discussion of predestination has reference to the Pelagian controversy of the early fourth century, in which St. Augustine defended the doctrines of original sin and predestination.[81] The Calvinistic system has often been labeled "Augustinian" in its approach to these topics.[82] The Lutheran tradition has claimed Augustine to some extent, but has been vocal in opposing errors which are similar to the views of Calvin.[83] However, the agreement between Calvinism and Augustinianism has been greatly overstated. Both the Reformed and Lutheran traditions are Augustinian in reference to their confession of depravity and divine monergism, but Augustine's own theology is much more nuanced than that of Calvin.

The doctrine of baptismal regeneration was essential for Augustine's soteriology.[84] It may be said with confidence even that the doctrine of baptism is the foundation for Augustine's theology of grace. In arguing with the

---

an external and covenantal union with Christ for all who receive the sacrament. See Leithart, *Baptized Body*.

80. This important differentiation between Lutheran and Reformed Eucharistic theologies is expounded in Herman Sasse's book *This Is My Body*.

81. A good selection of Augustine's anti-Pelagian works can be found in *Fathers of the Church: St. Augustine*.

82. Loraine Boettner writes, "The Reformation was essentially a revival of Augustinianism and through it evangelical Christianity again came into its own" (Boettner, *Reformed Doctrine of Predestination*, 367).

83. Francis Pieper, for example, is outspoken in his rejection of certain Augustinian teachings.

84. Especially see his work "On Forgiveness of Sins, and Baptism," in *St. Augustine: Anti-Pelagian Writings*, 15–78.

Pelagians, who denied original sin, Augustine often referred to the practice of infant baptism and its connection with regeneration. At this time in the early fourth century, all of Christendom had seemingly practiced infant baptism. This includes the Pelagians as well as the Augustinian party. Augustine argued against Pelagius that baptismal regeneration would be pointless if infants were not sinful. Thus, acceptance of infant baptismal regeneration necessitates that infants have sin. The grace given in baptism is consistently referred to. Augustine is even willing to call baptism necessary for one's salvation. He writes, "as so many and such divine witnesses agree, neither salvation nor eternal life can be hoped for by any man without baptism and the Lord's body and blood."[85] Augustine's is a theology in which grace is connected to the means of word and sacrament, rather than the purely spontaneous approach of many Calvinists.[86]

Augustine did not teach the doctrine of limited atonement, at least not in its fullest Calvinistic sense. While Augustine did at times speak of irresistible grace and the limiting of grace to the elect,[87] he also adopted the perspective that grace is universal. Augustine accepted the common belief that baptism saves each infant who receives it. Christ "engrafts into His body even baptized infants."[88] Augustine was not willing to claim that all infants are indiscriminately elect. Thus because of the connection between grace and the sacraments, grace is broader than election. Not merely common grace but grace which regenerates and justifies applies to more than the elect.

---

85. "On Forgiveness of Sins, and Baptism," Ch. 33, in *ANPNF* I.5.

86. The efficacy of the means of grace within Calvinism is a complex topic. Though many of the Confessionally Reformed have confessed that God's grace is *in some sense* connected to the sacramental acts of the church, much of the "New Calvinism" has rejected the means of grace as efficacious. This division among Reformed theologians in America can be traced to the nineteenth-century debate between William James Nevin and Charles Hodge. Hodge argues that the sacraments were primarily symbolic, and his approach has generally been definitional for American Reformed Christianity.

87. Certain quotations seem to teach limited atonement, such as, "Hence things that are lawful are not all good, but everything unlawful is not good. Just as everyone redeemed by Christ's blood is a human being, but human beings are not all redeemed by Christ's blood, so too everything that is unlawful is not good, but things that are not good are not all unlawful. As we learn from the testimony of the apostle, there are some things that are lawful but are not good" (Kearney, *Adulterous Marriages*, 15–16).

88. "On the Forgiveness of Sins, and Baptism," Ch. 10, in *ANPNF* I.5.

Part I: Predestination and Free Will

This demonstrates Augustine's rejection of the fifth point of Calvinism as well.[89] All who are baptized are regenerated. However, not all who are regenerated will remain in the Christian faith. Some will depart from Christian profession through licentious living or through heresy. Though regenerated and justified, some fall away from the faith and are ultimately damned. Augustine writes, for example, that

> if anyone falls before he dies he is, of course, said not to have persevered; and most truly it is said . . . For if anyone have continence, and fall away from that virtue and become incontinent,—or, in like manner, if he have righteousness, if patience, if even faith, and fall away, he is rightly said to have had these virtues and to have them no longer; for he was continent, or he was righteous, or he was patient, or he was believing, as long as he was so; but when he ceased to be so, he no longer is what he was.[90]

Commensurate with his perspective on divine election, Augustine proposes that perseverance is a gift of God, not given to all alike, but only to the elect. Thus, as in the Lutheran doctrine of predestination, perseverance is a divine monergistic work,[91] but it is not universal with regard to everyone who has been regenerated.

Finally, the Augustinian definition of double predestination, at least as explained by later writers, is not Calvinistic. Augustine expressed himself in double-predestinarian terms but never identified the nature of reprobation. However, the later Augustinian tradition as developed by Prosper of Aquitaine, Fulgentius of Ruspe, and ultimately the Council of Orange—when defining double predestination—consistently made it apparent that when some are predestined unto death, they are only predestined based upon foreseen future demerits.[92] This is in contradistinction to both the supralapsarian and infralapsarian approaches. While infralapsarianism defends double predestination, it does so only in reference to Adamic sin rather than the individual sins and unrepentance of the reprobate. As in the later Lutheran formulation of the concept, predestination unto life is

---

89. See his work "A Treatise on Perseverance," in *ANPNF* I.5.

90. "On the Gift of Perseverance," Ch.1, in *NPNF* I, 5.

91. "I assert, therefore, that the perseverance by which we persevere in Christ even to the end is the gift of God" (ibid.).

92. See Stucco, *Not without Us*. Stucco has an excellent treatment of the various predestinarian views in the post-Augustinian patristic tradition.

unconditional, while one's damnation is purely conditional, based upon one's own sin.

Lutheran theologian and reformer Martin Chemnitz recognizes this difference and is even willing to adopt the concept of double predestination in its historic meaning. In his *Loci Theologici*, Chemnitz cites Augustine's affirmation of double predestination and approves of Fulgentius of Ruspe's formulation of the concept.[93] Fulgentius argues that predestination is twofold. First God predestines the elect unconditionally unto salvation. Second God predestines, not individuals unto death, but to punish the sins of those who reject the gospel. As Chemnitz writes, "God foreknows the evil intentions and actions of the godless, but he does not predestine them. But he has predestined that the punishment for these sins shall take place with righteous judgment."[94] In other words, what God predestines for the damned is merely that those in unbelief and who reject the gospel should be punished. This is based only on the fact that grace is continually rejected and one remains unrepentant unto death. The punishment rather than the individual is predestined.

CONCLUSION

While there are significant agreements on the doctrine of predestination between the two Reformation traditions, especially with regard to the confession of divine monergism, ultimately the two approaches are incompatible. It is the Lutheran approach which holds the paradox of God's unconditional election and the sinner's sole responsibility for damnation in its full biblical sense. Grace is universal, and God desires the salvation of all. In Lutheranism, grace is sacramental, and is present wherever the word is proclaimed and the sacraments are administered. At the same time, election is particular and refers only to those who are finally saved. There is agreement on the point of the bondage of the will; a sinner cannot approach God apart from grace. There is also agreement on the gracious nature of God's election unto salvation; the elect are chosen, apart from merit or faith, unto salvation. Faith and repentance are an effect of election, rather than its cause. The paradox of both the universality of grace and the efficacious nature of grace is consistent with both the biblical testimony and the early Christian teaching on the subject.

93. See his work "To Monimus," in Fulgentius, *Selected Works*.
94. *Loci Theologici*, 328.

2

Once for All
The Extent of the Atonement

INTRODUCTION

Of all of the points of disagreement regarding the five points of Calvinism, the most problematic for Lutheran theologians has been limited atonement. In Calvinist orthodoxy, it is taught that Christ died only for the elect. The Canons of Dort state,

> For it was the entirely free plan and very gracious will and intention of God the Father that the enlivening and saving effectiveness of his Son's costly death should work itself out in all his chosen ones, in order that he might grant justifying faith to them only and thereby lead them without fail to salvation. In other words, it was God's will that Christ through the blood of the cross (by which he confirmed the new covenant) should effectively redeem from every people, tribe, nation, and language all those and only those who were chosen from eternity to salvation and given to him by the Father; that he should grant them faith (which, like the Holy Spirit's other saving gifts, he acquired for them by his death); that he should cleanse them by his blood from all their sins, both original and actual, whether committed before or after their coming to faith; that he should faithfully preserve them to the very end; and

> that he should finally present them to himself, a glorious people, without spot or wrinkle. (CD II.8)

In this approach, on the cross, Christ propitiated God's wrath for a specific group of individuals, namely, the elect. It is only the elect who are regenerate, called, justified, sanctified, and glorified. None of these benefits of the atonement can or will be applied to those who are lost. While some Calvinists confess that common grace was bought for all people on the cross, it is the common Reformed confession that saving grace is limited to the elect and Christ's act of propitiation occurs specifically for elect individuals. The confession of universal grace on behalf of the Lutheran Reformation necessitates a universal atonement. Christ died for all indiscriminately, even though all do not ultimately benefit from his saving activity because of unbelief.

IMPORTANT TEXTS TEACHING UNIVERSAL ATONEMENT

Those who write against Calvinistic particularism often do so with flippant references to universalistic verses void of context and neglect interaction with Calvinistic responses.[1] A quick reference to John 3:16 claiming that the term "world" negates limited atonement is hardly enough to convince the studied Calvinist. Here are presented three of the most clearly universalistic verses referring to the atonement, which have garnered much attention from Reformed writers because of their seemingly perspicuous statements of universal atonement. When context and syntax are considered, the Calvinistic responses, while creative, are negated. The plain meaning of the text stands.

1 Timothy 2:4

> This is good, and pleases God our Savior, who wants all men (πάντας ἀνθρώπους) to be saved (σωθῆναι) and to come to a knowledge of the truth. For there is one God and one mediator between God and men, the man Christ Jesus, who gave himself as a ransom for all (πάντων) men—the testimony given in its proper time. (1 Tim 2:3–6)

---

1. An example of this type of argumentation is found in Hunt, *What Love Is This?*

Part I: Predestination and Free Will

Proponents of universal atonement approach this verse as a statement that God desires every person, without distinction, to be saved, and that Christ was given as a ransom indiscriminately. Many Calvinistic interpreters, however, have interpreted this statement as "all kinds of men." Reformed Baptist theologian James White promotes this approach, writing, "Who are kings and all those in authority? They are kinds of men, classes of men."[2] White supports this by citing the earlier text, which states, "I urge, then, first of all, that requests, prayers, intercession and thanksgiving be made for everyone—for kings and all those in authority, that we may live peaceful and quiet lives in all godliness and holiness." Commensurate with this preceding verse, in the Calvinist approach, Paul is making a statement that all kinds of men can be saved. This includes people from different social groups. Paul is referring to types of people, including regular citizens as well as those in authority. White argues that a command to pray for kinds of men would be necessary due to the state of persecution in the church. Those in authority were often those who were active in persecuting the church. As White purports, "It is easy to understand why there would have to be apostolic commandments given to pray for the very ones who were using their power and authority to *persecute* these Christians."[3] He then continues to support this possibility by pointing to other instances in the Pauline literature in which the phrase "all men" can refer to kinds of men, rather than all men indiscriminately. The example he utilizes is from Titus 2:11, "For the grace of God has appeared, bringing salvation for all people." According to White, in this text Paul "clearly means all *kinds* of men."[4]

While this interpretation of 1 Timothy 2:4 is understandable, there are several problems with White's argument. First, the text from Timothy does not bear the supposed "clear" meaning that Paul is referencing only some men. In Lutheran theology, grace and salvation *have* appeared for all people; the problem is that people bound to sin reject this grace and salvation, not that it isn't present.[5] Thus, this doesn't prove that the phrase refers to kinds of men. Second, even if it could be proven that Paul sometimes used the concept of "kinds of men" when referring to all men, that wouldn't

---

2. White, *Potter's Freedom*, 139.
3. Ibid.
4. Ibid.

5. As Pieper writes, "God's gracious disposition in Christ is not limited to a part of mankind, but extends over all men without exception. Saving grace is universal grace" (Pieper, *Christian Dogmatics* 2:21).

necessitate such an interpretation in this specific verse. Thus, the use of the phrase in this specific text must be examined. One problem with the particularist interpretation of this text is that it would seem to necessitate that prayers should be made only for the elect. The "everyone" whom we should pray for is linked to the "all men" whom God desires to be saved. White attempts to refute this argument by saying, "Paul is not instructing Timothy to initiate never-ending prayer meetings where the Ephesian phone book would be opened and every single person listed therein would become the object of prayer."[6] This misses the point of what Paul is saying. Just because Paul does not indicate that literally every individual on the planet must be prayed for, this does not necessitate that he is simply asking that the elect among types of men are to be prayed for. Rather, Paul's point is that prayers should be universal and indiscriminate. This corresponds to Christ's atonement, which is also universal and indiscriminate. The meaning of this passage seems to be that because Christ died for every man, including those in authority, we should pray for every man, including those in authority. This is the plain meaning of the text.

There is evidence to support this view when one examines the rest of the epistle to Timothy. Look how Timothy uses the term "all" ($πᾶς$) throughout his epistle. There is a passage parallel to 2:4 later in the book which should be taken into careful consideration.

> This is a trustworthy saying that deserves full acceptance (and for this we labor and strive), that we have put our hope in the living God, who is the Savior of all men, and especially of those who believe. (1 Tim 4:9–10)

Paul once again uses the concept of salvation (the word used is $σωτήρ$) with the concept of "all men" ($πάντων ἀνθρώπων$). Clearly in 4:10, the "all men" are distinct from those who are believers. Paul specifically differentiates between "all men" and "those who believe." Believers are merely one section of the group "all men." This has sometimes troubled interpreters because of its universalistic tone. Does this verse imply that every individual will be saved? The explanation of what Paul means by calling Christ the "savior of all men" can be found in the earlier verse, where the same topic is being discussed. This occurs in 2:4–6. These two verses, containing similar concepts and terms, interpret one another. Most likely, Paul utilizes the phrase "all men" earlier in the epistle in a universalistic sense, as it is

---

6. White, *Potter's Freedom*, 139.

in 4:10. This is necessitated by the consistency of Paul's language. In these verses it is apparent that Christ is the savior of "all men" in that:

1. He desires them to be saved.

2. He gives himself as a ransom for them.

To be a consistent exegete, it must be admitted that "all men" in 1 Timothy 2:4–6 cannot simply refer to "all kinds of men." Unless there is sufficient reason to think otherwise, it must be assumed that Paul uses the same word in the same manner when it appears in a short epistle within the same context (the context being salvation, both instances using words with a σωζω root).

Some Calvinist interpreters have argued for a universalistic understanding of 1 Timothy 2:4, but interpret the intended universalism in another manner.[7] In this approach, what Paul is describing is the universal call to repentance and faith, which is differentiated from the call to the particular number for whom the atonement was intended. Classical Calvinism affirms a universal offer of the gospel, though without a universal atonement and the *gratia universalis* (universal grace) confessed in Lutheran theology.[8] The distinction is often made between the sufficiency of Christ's work and its efficiency. The atonement is sufficient for all people, but is efficient only for the elect.[9]

With this distinction in mind, some interpreters seek to read this passage in a universalistic sense while seeking consistency with the doctrine of particular redemption. There are two manners in which this is accomplished. First, one could propose that the first use of "all men" is universal and refers to God's desire for universal salvation, but that the second refers only to a particular group. This is confessed by those who argue that there are two wills in God.[10] One is a universal will, which is a desire for salvation for all of humanity, and the second is God's effectual will, by which God

---

7. Boettner, for example, speaks of "a sense in which Christ died for mankind in general" (Boettner, *Reformed Doctrine of Predestination*, 295).

8. "The *gratia universalis* is the doctrine of the Lutheran Church. The Lutheran Confessions maintain the universality of saving grace in its full extent. They teach the threefold universalism of the love of the Father, the merit of Christ, and the efficacious operation of the Holy Ghost, through the means of grace, on all hearers of the Word" (Pieper, *Christian Dogmatics* 2:22).

9. A good discussion of this teaching is found in Nettles, *By His Grace*.

10. John Piper gives a thorough explanation and defense of this view in the article "Are There Two Wills in God? Divine Election and God's Desire for All to Be Saved," in *Pleasures of God*.

elects only some, sending Jesus to atone only for the elect. This is the meaning of the first use of "all men." The second use of the phrase "all men" then refers to all types of men. However, the inconsistency of the phrase used twice in the same context is unlikely. Thus, the second Calvinistic alternative is preferable.

In the second proposal, both of the uses of "all men" are universal. Thus it is confessed in the "two wills" concept that God desires the salvation of all, and also that there is a sense in which Christ's death was universal in nature and intention. As Lorraine Boettner writes, "Calvinists do not deny that mankind in general receive some important benefits from Christ's atonement."[11] Though Christ did not purchase saving grace on the cross, he purchased common grace for all men. Common grace is distinct from effectual saving grace in that it has reference to the general kindness of God toward all people, regenerate and unregenerate. Though a creative solution, this interpretation depends on later distinct categories that were not likely in Paul's mind while penning this epistle. There is no evidence in the New Testament that Jesus purchased a different kind of grace, other than that which saves, through the cross. Only with a preexisting conviction of the particularity of the atonement could the text be interpreted in this unlikely manner.

2 Peter 2:1

> But there were also false prophets among the people, just as there will be false teachers among you. They will secretly introduce destructive heresies, even denying the sovereign Lord who bought them—bringing swift destruction on themselves.

The initial impression of this verse is that these false teachers, according to Peter, deny Jesus Christ, who bought them through the cross. This seems to be the obvious meaning of the text. Some have argued that the reference is not to Christ's atonement but to God's general ownership of all humankind. Two arguments which have been leveled against the universalistic interpretation of this verse are as follows:[12]

---

11. Boettner, *Reformed Doctrine of Predestination*, 91.

12. These arguments are taken primarily from Long, *Definite Atonement*. James White cites these sections of Long's work in his article "2 Peter 2:1."

Part I: Predestination and Free Will

First, some have argued that the word δεσπότην is not used in reference to Jesus Christ. It is a term referring to the Father. Thus it refers to God's "ownership" or sovereignty over each individual. While it is true that this is a common term in reference to the Father in the Septuagint, it is false to assert that this is never a reference to Jesus. There is another reference in the book of Jude: "For certain men whose condemnation was written about long ago have secretly slipped in among you. They are godless men, who change the grace of our God into a license for immorality and deny Jesus Christ our only Sovereign and Lord" (Jude 4). The word translated as "Sovereign" is δεσπότην.

It is noteworthy that Peter and Jude have almost identical language in many places. They are likely confronting the same group of false teachers. Virtually all New Testament scholars agree that either Jude relied heavily on the text of 2 Peter, or 2 Peter relied on Jude.[13]

Not only is this word used in an epistle addressing the same or a similar matter; it is in fact in a parallel statement. They are both writing a warning to these false teachers who have secretly introduced heresy into the fellowship. Peter refers to those who "deny the Lord who bought them," while Jude refers to those who "deny Jesus Christ our only sovereign and Lord." If Jude wrote after Peter, which is more likely, he had Peter's epistle in mind as he used the same term. If Peter was referring to the Father, Jude most likely misread Peter.

Reformed interpreter Gary Long admits that δεσπότην is likely a reference to Jesus rather than the Father, conceding that the passage from Jude gives precedence for such a description of Christ. Long argues that this still does not give credence to a universalistic interpretation wherein Peter is discussing the atonement in this particular passage:

> This leads to the third point, namely, that *despotes* is used about thirty times in the whole of Scripture—twenty times in the Greek Septuagint translation of the Old Testament and ten times in the New Testament. But never does it refer to the Father or the Son as mediator unless II Peter 2:1 be the exception. And if this be the case, the burden of proof rests upon those who wish to make it the exception, does it not? Yet, this writer has not found a modified Calvinist attempting to do this. It is assumed. It is completely ignored that *despotês* is never used as a redemptive title for anyone, not even of Christ in Jude 4, the only other place where *despotês* is used of Christ. Rather the dominant use of *despotes* in both the

---

13. See the discussion by Barker et al. in *New Testament Speaks*, 346–60.

Old and New Testaments is of God as "absolute sovereign"; that is, as "sovereign Lord" and owner of each member of the human race. Luke's account in Acts 4:24 is a clear example of this meaning. There Luke writes of a company of believers who, upon hearing Peter and John's report, "lifted up their voice to God with one accord, and said, Lord (*despotes*), thou art God, which hast made heaven, and earth, and the sea and all that in them is." Vine's statement that *despotës* refers to one who has "absolute ownership and uncontrolled power" could find no better support.[14]

Thus Long argues that the phrase "the Lord who bought them" cannot have reference to the atonement because the term δεσπότης can never have reference to Christ as mediator, but only as Lord. Long's argument is noteworthy, but there are two reasons why it remains unconvincing. First, just because no other text utilizes the word in this sense, that does not mean that it could not be used in reference to Christ's mediatory role (though as Long points out, there would have to be a strong argument that the word *doesn't* bear its usual meaning); and second, that the context allows for both a reference to the atonement and a use of the term δεσπότην in the sense of lordship and ownership. Since Peter is specifically referencing those who depart from the gospel, and do not remain faithful to the grace received through the cross, it is understandable that Peter does not use a term which references Christ as mediator but as Lord and master. Through the cross, Christ died for the sins of all humankind. Those who, through faith, receive the benefits of the atonement have Christ as their Lord, through his atoning work. Thus it can rightly be said that they are abandoning their sovereign Lord and master, whom they had previously committed to, who bought them from the powers that held them captive. The New Testament contains various atonement motifs, including a substitutionary view emphasizing Christ as mediator, but also a *Christus victor* approach.[15] In the second approach, often utilizing the concept of ransom in the New Testament, man is under the powers of evil, including sin, the devil, and death; when Christ dies, he gives himself as a ransom, transferring humankind from being under the lordship of the devil to the lordship of Christ. It is thus unnecessary that the concept of mediator be utilized in an atonement context because the atonement also involves a transfer of lordship. Thus even if δεσπότην

---

14. Long, *Substitutionary Atonement*, 44–67.

15. The classic work on this atonement model is Aulen, *Christus Victor*. I think Aulen is right in his formulation of this model, but wrong in that he neglects the use of other atonement models.

has specific reference to Christ's lordship, a strong argument can be made that it has reference to the atonement. Christ's lordship is not an abstract concept in the New Testament, relating purely to Christ as eternal deity, but it is connected to his cross and resurrection.[16] Thus, contrary to Long's contention, it is almost certain that a reference to Christ as Lord and master would have specific reference to his atonement.

The second argument proposed against a universalistic understanding of this text is that it is claimed that the term "bought" is not a reference to the atonement. Long argues,

> First, in the Greek Septuagint *agorazō* and its related noun forms are used some twenty times to translate three Hebrew words (*sabar, qanhh,* and *laqah*); yet it is never used to translate the two great redemptive words—those translated "redeem" (*gā'al*) and "ransom" or "purchase" (*pādāh*). Second, of its thirty occurrences in the New Testament, *agorazō* is never used in a salvation context (unless II Peter 2:1 is the exception) without the technical term "price" (*times*—a technical term for the blood of Christ) or its equivalent being stated or made explicit in the context (see I Cor. 6:20; 7:23; Rev. 5:9; 14:3–4). Third, in each of the latter five references the context clearly restricts the extent of *agorazō* (regardless of what it means) to believers—never to non-believers. Fourth, a word study of *agorazō*, in both the Greek Old and New Testaments, reveals that the word itself does not include the payment price. When it is translated with a meaning "to buy," whether in a salvation or non-salvation context, a payment price is always stated or made explicit by the context. Fifth, in contexts where no payment price is stated or implied, *agorazō* may often be better translated as "acquire" or "obtain." Sixth, *agorazō* is never used in Scripture in a hypothetical sense unless II Peter 2:1 be the exception. Rather it is always used in a context where the buying or acquiring actually takes place.[17]

The primary thrust of Long's argument is that ἀγοράζω cannot refer to the atonement because it does not include the reference to a specific price which is present elsewhere. These are the five instances of the use of this word throughout the New Testament:

1 Cor 6:20—you have been bought with a price

1 Cor 7:23—you were bought with a price

---

16. Paul, for example, can speak of the crucifixion of the "Lord of glory" (1 Corinthians 2:8).

17. Long, "Redemption in II Peter 2:1."

Rev 5:9—Thou . . . didst purchase . . . men from every tribe, tongue, and people

Rev 14:3—who had been purchased from the earth

Rev 14:4—These have been purchased from among men

The phrase "with a price" is used in only two of the five contexts in reference to the atonement. The case is not as clear as Long proposes. This gives precedence for Peter's referring to the buying of men through the cross without explicitly using the phrase "for a price." Long's proposal that the other uses of the term imply the concept of a price in the context is unconvincing. Revelation 14:3–4, for example, does not make any such price explicit. There is no consistent reason why Revelation 14:3–4 should have reference to the atonement in contrast to 2 Peter 2:1 apart from the preexisting theological conviction that Christ did not buy all people on the cross, but only the elect.

Long's argument that the term ἀγοράζω in the other contexts refers only to believers is equally unconvincing. This is due simply to the context in which the concept is used in the other texts. Two of the references are to a specific Christian congregation, that of Corinth, and thus to believers; there would be no reason to discuss the nature of the atonement for the apostate in that particular context. The second set of texts is from Revelation and refers to the eschatological victory of the church; thus again there simply is no reason in the context why John would use the concept universally. The fact that the concept is used in two epistles to refer to the work of Christ for the church has no bearing on the nature of the atonement for the apostate. It is because Peter is specifically discussing apostasy in his epistle that he refers to a universal act of atonement, not because Peter is using a different concept altogether.

Long's final two arguments similarly do not prove his contention that Peter is not referring to the atonement. Long contends that the phrase ἀγοράζω can refer not only to the concept of buying and redeeming, but also to the concept of "acquiring" or "obtaining." First, note that no major English translations of the New Testament translate this phrase in such a way.[18] As I indicated above, the lack of mentioning a price does not negate such a translation as Long proposes. Second, even if the term is translated

---

18. We should be suspicious of a reading of a text which is foreign to every major translation, especially when that rendering supports our own particular theological convictions.

as "acquire" or "obtain," this would not negate a reference to the atonement. How else would Christ obtain people in time if it were not through the atonement? Since it speaks of an event in time in which one is obtained, it cannot simply refer to the relationship between creator and creation. Long's final argument does not have any merit when dealing with a Lutheran approach. Long proposes that a universal understanding of 2 Peter 2:1 makes ἀγοράζω a hypothetical event. This is not the Lutheran contention. Peter speaks of an actual redemption and of an actual apostasy by these false teachers.

Some have proposed, in light of such criticisms, that ἀγοράζω is a reference to the deliverance of the Israelites from Egypt. Wayne Grudem makes this argument, writing, "Peter is drawing an analogy between the past false prophets who arose among the Jews and those who will be false teachers within the churches."[19] Deuteronomy 32:6 refers to God as the one who "bought" them. However, the term used in the Septuagint in this verse is not ἀγοράζω, the term used by Peter. There is no direct parallel here. These verses refer to the atonement, not to deliverance in the exodus. Peter's readers would have automatically thought of the redemption bought by Christ when reading the text, rather than the exodus. Here are three reasons why:

First, Peter's audience was not exclusively Jewish. Thus, the Jews' redemption from Egypt would not have been on their mind. Second, "exodus" language was now used in early Christian tradition to refer to the death of Christ and the age of the church. Peter, for example, refers to Christians as exiles, priests, etc.[20] Paul uses the crossing of the Red Sea as a symbol of redemption bought by Christ.[21] Thus even if it did seem to refer to the exodus, the cross would still likely be a referent. Finally, the heresy that these men brought does not seem to be "denying the Father" who had redeemed Israel in the exodus, but denying Jesus who died and rose again. This is why Peter has to remind his readers that what he told them about Christ was not a "cleverly devised myth" (2 Pet 1:16). They apparently denied the majesty of Christ (2 Pet 1:17). He also needs to defend the fact that Christ is actually

---

19. Grudem, *Systematic Theology*, 600.

20. "But you are a chosen race, a royal priesthood, a holy nation, a people for his own possession, that you may proclaim the excellencies of him who called you out of darkness into his marvelous light" (1 Pet 2:9).

21. "For I do not want you to be unaware, brothers, that our fathers were all under the cloud, and all passed through the sea, and all were baptized into Moses in the cloud and in the sea, and all ate the same spiritual food" (1 Cor 10:1–3).

coming back in chapter 3, thus they also denied his return. There is simply no reason to assume that Peter is making a reference to the exodus here. It can only be read into the text because of a preexisting theological system.

1 John 2:2

> He is the propitiation for our sins, and not only for ours only but also for the sins of the whole world.

The proponents of universal atonement interpret the term "world" in this text to refer to mankind indiscriminately, while the Calvinistic interpreter limits the meaning to "types of men."[22] The Calvinist interpretation often argues that κόσμος has multiple meanings in Greek. As White argues, "we cannot help but point to the fact that John uses the term 'world' in many different ways. It cannot be assumed that 'world' means the same thing in every context."[23] This is apparent, as anyone reading the New Testament will discover. John himself has multiple uses of the term. Pointing to an ethnocentric context like Jesus' ministry or the conflict between Paul and the Judaizers, Reformed interpreters purport that in these contexts the "world" has specific reference to Gentile believers. Thus in this text, the "us" is believed to speak of Jews and the "world" to Gentiles. As A. W. Pink writes, "who are meant when John says, '*He is the propitiation for our sins*'? We answer, Jewish believers."[24]

However, there is no reason to believe that 1 John is written to ethnocentric Jews. This epistle is among the last to be written in the New Testament. At the end of the first century, the church was largely composed of Gentile converts. The council of Jerusalem was convened 40 years prior to this epistle, and Paul's writings were widely circulated. Thus, this is an unlikely interpretation. The other option is that this text teaches that Jesus died for all men. The other meanings of κόσμος do not fit this passage.

In this same chapter, John uses the word κόσμος several times. "Do not love the world or anything in the world. If anyone loves the world, the

---

22. "When it is said that Christ died 'not for our sins only but for the sins of the whole world,' 1 John 2:2, or that He came to 'save the world,' John 12:47, the meaning is that not merely Jews but Gentiles also are included in His saving work" (Boettner, *Reformed Doctrine of Predestination*, 291).

23. White, *Potter's Freedom*, 273.

24. A. W. Pink expounds upon his argument further in his pamphlet *1 John 2:2*.

love of the Father is not in him. For everything in the world—the cravings of sinful man, the lust of his eyes and the boasting of what he has and does—comes not from the Father but from the world. The world and its desires pass away, but the man who does the will of God lives forever" (1 John 1:15–17). John most often uses the term "world" in this epistle to refer to sinful humanity and the corruption of the present age. Thus, what John seems to be saying in the beginning of this epistle is "Christ died not only for our sins (the sins of believers) but also for the sins of the world (unbelieving mankind)." Who is the "our" being spoken of here? This is a catholic epistle, not written to specifically Jewish believers or even to one specific church, thus the "our" must refer to Christians in general. Therefore, the "world" is something other than the "us" being referred to. Thus, if the "us" is the church, the "world" refers those outside of the church.

Another argument in this text arises from the use of the term "propitiation" (ἱλασμός). It is argued by Reformed interpreters that since propitiation refers to the turning away of wrath rather than the potential turning away of wrath, it cannot have reference to any for whom God's wrath will become a reality. As White questions, "So, why is the non-elect person lost for eternity, if, in fact, the wrath of God was poured out on Christ *in their place*?"[25] Thus it has to have reference only to a particular group of people.[26] Two things can be said in response to this argument. First, it must be admitted that there are several metaphors describing the effects of the atonement in the New Testament. Propitiation is a relatively uncommon (though not unimportant!) one, usually overshadowed by the concepts of redemption and ransom. Propitiation is a picture which need not correspond exactly to the human conception of the term. Secondly, even the Calvinist is forced to admit that propitiation cannot necessitate that all wrath has been abolished from those for whom Christ died after the atonement. As St. Paul admits, all are by nature "children of wrath" (Eph 2:23). Even if the atonement were given for a select group, this group is still under God's wrath in some sense prior to conversion. Both of these arguments will be expounded below.

---

25. White, *Potter's Freedom*, 272.

26. This is the so-called "double jeopardy" argument made popular by John Owen's book *Death of Death*.

Conclusion

There are several verses throughout the New Testament which teach that Christ's atonement was offered for every individual indiscriminately. The three examined here are some of the most commonly cited. It has been demonstrated that the Calvinistic reading of these passages is implausible and the texts should be taken at face value. The doctrine of limited atonement is read into these texts rather than taken from their clear meaning.

THE BOOK OF HEBREWS

The book of Hebrews has the most extensive discussion of atonement in the New Testament. Drawing heavily on typology, the author of Hebrews explains the cross in light of the Old Covenant sacrificial and priestly system. Throughout the book, the author is warning his readers not to revert back to Judaism and deny Christ. If they do this, they will reject Christ for a system which does not offer actual forgiveness and they will not come back to repentance. Here are some of the warning passages that characterize Hebrews:

> Therefore we must pay much closer attention to what we have heard, lest we drift away from it. For since the message declared by angels proved to be reliable, and every transgression or disobedience received a just retribution, how shall we escape if we neglect such a great salvation? (Heb 2:1–3)

> Take care, brothers, lest there be in any of you an evil, unbelieving heart, leading you to fall away from the living God. But exhort one another every day, as long as it is called "today," that none of you may be hardened by the deceitfulness of sin. For we have come to share in Christ, if indeed we hold our original confidence firm to the end. (Heb 3:12–14)

> Therefore, while the promise of entering his rest still stands, let us fear lest any of you should seem to have failed to reach it. (Heb 4:1)

> Let us therefore strive to enter that rest, so that no one may fall by the same sort of disobedience. (Heb 4:11)

These statements could be greatly multiplied. It is clear that the author is admitting the possibility that some to whom he is writing have the ability to fall away. He is concerned that they will abandon the Christian faith. In the Lutheran approach, this would include those for whom Christ died, who have been regenerated through baptism and are justified.[27] This perspective will be further defended in the following chapter, on perseverance. The author is warning them against apostasy, which is a real possibility. For the Calvinist, one who is saved cannot be lost, thus the author is either speaking hypothetically of an impossible situation, or he is speaking to those who have the appearance of salvation but do not truly believe.[28] Christ did not die for them, and ultimately these people are reprobate.

First, let's examine the hypothetical approach. In this approach, the author is warning his readers against falling away, which is something that his readers do not have the ability to do. It seems unlikely that the author would spend so much time writing about something which is not possible. It may be plausible that small warnings would be scattered through the book urging the elect unto good works with the hint of a hypothetical warning. However, the extensive nature of these warnings warrants more than a hypothetical scenario. Hebrews 6 speaks of "those who have once been enlightened, who have tasted the heavenly gift, and have shared in the Holy Spirit, and have tasted the goodness of the word of God and the powers of the age to come, and then have fallen away" (Heb 6:4–8), and later he warns against "sinning deliberately after receiving the knowledge of the truth" because "there no longer remains a sacrifice for sins, but a fearful expectation of judgment, and a fury of fire that will consume the adversaries" (Heb 10:23–31). This continues in chapter 12, where the author warns against becoming like Esau, who, "when he desired to inherit the blessing, was rejected" (Heb 12:17).[29] The extensive and prevalent nature of such warnings makes the hypothetical approach untenable.

---

27. "Thus, many accept the word 'with joy' but thereafter they 'fall away' (Luke 8[:13]). The cause for this, however, is not that God did not want to give the grace of perseverance to those in whom he had 'begun the good work,' for that is contrary to Paul's teaching in Philippians 1[:6]. Rather, the cause is that they willfully turn themselves away again from God's holy command and grieve and embitter the Holy Spirit; they entangle themselves once again in the defilements of the world and redecorate their hearts as a haven for the devil, so that their last state is worse than the first" (FC SD XI.42).

28. Though he does not hold to either of them, these perspectives are detailed well in Allen, *Hebrews*, 534–36.

29. See also Heb 2:1–4; 3:7—4:14; 5:11–14.

There is one argument from the text itself that is often made for the hypothetical view of these warning passages.[30] It comes after the warning passage in chapter 6:

> Though we speak in this way, yet in your case, beloved, we feel sure of better things—things that belong to salvation. For God is not unjust so as to overlook your work and the love that you have shown for his name in serving the saints, as you still do. And we desire each one of you to show the same earnestness to have the full assurance of hope until the end, so that you may not be sluggish, but imitators of those who through faith and patience inherit the promises. (Heb 6:9–12)

The argument for the hypothetical approach is that the author is qualifying his warnings; he is confessing to the Hebrew believers that it is not an actual possibility that they might fall away because the author states that in their case he is "sure of better things—things that belong to salvation." However, the pastoral nature of this epistle brings forth another possibility: Being concerned that the Hebrews will live in fear of a possible future apostasy, the author, as a good pastor would, stops to give a word of encouragement. They have shown the fruits of perseverance through their love. Therefore he has confidence that they will not fall into apostasy. However, that does not negate it as a real possibility and place the multitude of warnings purely in the realm of the hypothetical. A possible interpretation of one verse does not overthrow the entirety of the author's argument, which hinges on the possibility of falling away.

There are then two possible approaches to these texts. Either the author is giving a warning to those who have been saved by the cross not to fall away, with the possibility that this could actually occur, or he is speaking to those who have false faith. They appear to be saved, but Christ did not actually die on the cross for them. Michael Horton defends this approach to these texts, writing, "The writer describes those who belong only outwardly to the covenant community."[31] This approach is, however, negated by several references in the text that Christ did die for the readers and that he is their mediator. A purely "outward membership" of the covenant is thus impossible. The author can state that "we have a great high priest who passed through the heavens . . . we do not have a high priest who is unable to sympathize with our weakness, but one who in every respect has been

---

30. On this argument, see the commentary of Phillips, *Hebrews*.
31. Horton, *For Calvinism*, 120.

tempted as we are" (Heb 4:14–16). He confesses that "Jesus has gone as a forerunner on our behalf" (Heb 6:20) and that we "have such a high priest, holy, innocent, unstained, separated from sinners, and exalted above the heavens" (Heb 7:26).[32] The author makes it abundantly clear that Christ has died for the readers of this epistle and that he is the mediator of those to whom he is writing. This could not be written only in view of false believers for whom Christ did not die because the author confesses the opposite.

It is evident that the author of Hebrews takes it for granted that Christ has sacrificed himself for all humankind. The thrust of the book is that those who are in the faith should not revert back to Judaism, because to do so would be denying the Savior who died on the cross for them and is their mediator. This admits the possibility of falling away for those who have been bought with Christ's blood.

REFUTING THE LOGICAL ARGUMENT FOR LIMITED ATONEMENT

Along with exegetical arguments, the case is often made for a logical necessity of the particularist approach to the atonement. Limited atonement is the logical conclusion to the other four points of Calvinism. One particular rational argument has been highly influential since John Owen's *The Death of Death* was published in the seventeenth century. The argument proceeds as follows:

As was described in the Calvinistic reading of 1 John 2:2, it is argued that Christ's death was a propitiation of God's wrath toward sin. The punishment of sin was laid upon the shoulders of God's Son so that those whom he represented need no longer bear the punishment themselves. ἱλασμός can only be defined by the actual turning of way of wrath rather than the potential turning away of wrath upon the condition of faith. If Christ died for the unbeliever, then God's wrath has been propitiated toward the unbeliever. Therefore, the unbeliever could not go to hell. White purports that "Evangelicals who speak of Christ dying 'for them' often hold to clearly contradictory positions on the atonement. Most have never been challenged to see the inconsistencies in their beliefs. If Christ died in the place of every single individual human being, He was dying for many who had already died in rebellion against God and who will experience God's

---

32. See also 8:1; 9:24; 10:10.

wrath for eternity."[33] In White's view, for unbelievers to end up in hell is an affront to God's justice because they would be bearing a punishment which was already paid through the cross. Thus, in order for God to be just, if the unbeliever goes to hell, his punishment could not have been paid—Christ could not possibly have died for them.

The common response of the proponent of universal atonement is that though Christ died for the sins of unbelievers, their unbelief negates a reception of that gift. But the Calvinist denies this possibility. Unbelief is a sin. If all sin has been paid for on the cross, then unbelief has also been paid for on the cross. No sin can negate the turning away of God's wrath, which has occurred through the cross. Thus, the Calvinist argues, one must either adopt total universalism, wherein everyone is saved from hell, or limited atonement.

Though this argument has been prominent since the formulation of Puritan theology, it is flawed for several reasons. First, though rational argumentation is a valid enterprise for the theologian, it should never be a final appeal to establish doctrine. In this case, the logical argument seems to take precedence over biblical evidence to the contrary. Second, the argument proves too much. The moderate infralapsarian Calvinist does not believe the statement he is trying to prove. If the cross negates that God's wrath can be placed upon those for whom Christ died, then eternal justification is a logical necessity. Eternal justification, never a mainstream Calvinist doctrine, is the teaching that man from eternity is justified through the cross.[34] Faith simply acknowledges that which is already true. However, in most Calvinist teaching, even the elect man for whom Christ died *is* under the wrath of God prior to faith. Through faith one is forgiven, not simply given the knowledge that he is forgiven already.[35] Thus even the Calvinist admits that faith is necessary for one to receive Christ's benefits. Calvinism teaches that one can be under the wrath of God due to unbelief even though God's wrath has already been propitiated on the cross for that person. It is only when faith is given that one is placed under grace and the benefit of Christ's work is applied. Thus, the argument fails.

---

33. White and Hunt, *Debating Calvinism*, 171.

34. More about the doctrine of eternal justification can be found in Berkhof, *Systematic Theology*, 517–25.

35. Bavinck, in his discussion of eternal justification, writes, "In Scripture, therefore, entry into the kingdom of heaven is made dependent upon regeneration, faith, and repentance" (Bavinck, *Reformed Dogmatics* 4:218).

Part I: Predestination and Free Will

The Argument from the Nature of the Trinity

Another common theological argument for the doctrine of limited atonement is the claim that proponents of universal atonement promote the concept that the persons of the Trinity are divided against one another. It is argued that in the universal atonement scenario, God the Father and God the Son are in conflict against each other. The Son died for all, and intercedes for all, but the Father elects only some and saves some. Thus the Father is denying the Son's requests and acting against the wishes of another Trinitarian person. This divides the unity of the Trinity and proposes different wills among the different persons. Boettner makes the argument in the following words,

> Since the work of God is never in vain, those who are chosen by the Father, those who are redeemed by the Son, and those who are sanctified by the Holy Spirit—or in other words, election, redemption and sanctification,—must include the same persons. The Arminian doctrine of a universal atonement makes these unequal and thereby destroys the perfect harmony within the Trinity. Universal redemption means universal salvation.[36]

There are a couple of points to be made in response to this.

First, no Lutheran would consciously divide the Trinitarian persons against one another. There is a unity of will among the three persons; this is an essential aspect of the Christian confession of monotheism. It is not the Lutheran proposal that the Son wills the redemption of all, and the Father wills the salvation of only some. The biblical and Lutheran approach to election proposes that God's will for the salvation of all is universal. Thus, it is the will of the Father, Son, and Holy Spirit that all be saved. None is divided against the other persons. Pieper writes that Lutheranism teaches "the threefold universalism of the love of the Father, the merit of Christ, and the efficacious operation of the Holy Ghost, through the means of grace, on all hearers of the Word."[37] At the same time it is confessed that election is particular and refers only to those who experience redemption and receive eternal life. How these two concepts work together is a mystery. One must be silent at the point of apparent tensions regarding the divine will.

Secondly, the Reformed approach to the nature of God's universal offer and particular election causes just as much—perhaps more—conflict as

---

36. Boettner, *Reformed Doctrine of Predestination*, 89.
37. Pieper, *Christian Dogmatics* 2:22.

that leveled against a universal atonement view. Calvinists often propose the theory that there are two wills in God. God has a desire for the salvation of all and thus has a universal gracious will. However, at the same time God predestines some for salvation and others for damnation.[38] This causes more confusion and division in the Godhead. In the Lutheran view, there is a unity of will which is for the salvation of all, as well as a predestination unto life, without a predestination unto death. Though this involves mystery, it does not promote the idea of contradiction in God's will. However, in the Reformed approach God has two wills in conflict with one another. One will is for the salvation of all and the other will includes the damnation of some who are simultaneously willed to be saved through God's general call. Though this does not divide the Trinitarian persons against one another, it does divide God against himself.

The other aspect of this argument is from the nature of Christ's intercession.[39] In the Reformed perspective, Christ's intercession is an act which is performed solely for the elect. Since Christ's intercession is effectual, it must always result in salvation, thus the non-elect have no intercession. It is argued that the universal atonement approach necessitates that Christ's intercession is universal, and thus either promotes the concept that Christ's intercession fails, dividing the Trinitarian persons, or that all are saved.

The concept of Christ's intercession is discussed at length in one book of the New Testament: Hebrews. It is used in contrast to the priesthood of the Old Covenant. In the Levitical priesthood, the priests were imperfect, and thus their intercession was also imperfect. Their sacrifices were made continually because they did not ultimately secure forgiveness for God's people. The author contrasts this with Christ's priestly work. Christ, in his role as both priest and sacrifice, offered himself as the perfect sacrifice. Because of his divine and sinless nature, this sacrifice perfected once for all the people of God. Christ also serves as a priest in his continual intercessory role. The typology and fulfillment discussion regarding Christ's priestly role is used as a reason to dissuade the author's audience from reverting to Judaism. This demonstrates two things: First, that Christ is the intercessor of the

---

38. There are differences within the Reformed tradition over the nature of reprobation. Infralapsarians confess a passive reprobation, whereas the supralapsarian position argues that predestination unto damnation is active. The idea of equal ultimacy is the concept that there is an exact parallel between the nature of predestination unto death and unto life.

39. James White expounds upon this argument in his article "Was Anyone Saved at the Cross?"

Hebrews. The argument that the author makes is that because in Christ the readers have a better intercessor than the Levitical priesthood, these people should not revert back to Judaism. Second, those for whom Christ is an intercessor have the possibility of falling away. It is possible, according to the argument of Hebrews, that some for whom Christ makes intercession will apostatize and will not partake of eternal life.

All of this demonstrates that Christ's intercession is not limited to the elect, who will partake of the final eschatological inheritance. The nature of Christ's intercession is not, however, described in detail. Regarding Christ's intercession for unbelievers, there is one example of this in Scripture. When going to the cross, Jesus prays the famous words, "Father, forgive them, for they know not what they do" (Luke 23:34).[40] These are unbelievers guilty of the greatest crime ever committed, yet Jesus intercedes for them. He asks the Father to grant forgiveness. These people are clearly unregenerate, and there is no reason to assume that all are elect. Thus, though the nature of Christ's intercession remains a mystery, it is clear that intercession for unbelievers is not foreign to the biblical testimony. One of the major issues with many of the Reformed critiques of universal redemption is that they are founded upon a conviction that one has access to the nature of Christ's intercession regarding the Father within the Trinitarian life. This is an aspect of the hidden God which need not be peered into except to assure the doubting Christian that Christ's intercession is continual and exists for that person.

COMMON TEXTS USED IN DEFENSE OF LIMITED ATONEMENT

Of several texts used to defend the concept of limited atonement, one of the most common is Jesus' High Priestly Prayer in John 17. It is argued that Jesus' prayer is particular, confessing before the Father the nature of particular redemption. This particularity extends to Christ's mediatory role and therefore his imminent death. Jesus says, "I am praying for them. I am not praying for the world but for those whom you have given me, for they are yours" (John 17:9). The Reformed argument is that this prayer refers specifically to the elect. Sproul writes that Jesus "explicitly excludes the

---

40. This is a textual variant, so while it supports the case, the entire argument should not hinge on such a text.

non-elect from his great High Priestly Prayer."[41] Therefore Christ is making intercession especially for those predestined to life in contrast to those predestined unto death. However, the context suggests something other than a prayer for the elect alone.

It is apparent that Jesus is speaking for a specific group of people. He prays for some to the exclusion of others. However, the group Jesus is praying for is not the elect, but the twelve disciples. He describes them as "the people whom you have given me out of the world" (John 17:6). While this could be read as a statement about all of the elect whom the Father has granted to the Son, the further description of this group in Jesus' prayer makes it apparent that the referent is more specific. Jesus describes those for whom as he prays as a group which he had spent time with.[42] He then states, "I have guarded them, and not one of them has been lost except the son of destruction, that the Scripture might be fulfilled" (John 17:12). This makes it clear that the reference in Jesus' prayer is to the twelve disciples. Those whom the Father gave the Son are the Apostles who would become the founding members of the church, along with Judas. The fact that Judas is included in the group of whom Jesus is speaking demonstrates that this prayer does not have specific reference to the elect, and even admits the possibility of those whom the Father has granted to the Son departing from him.

The prayer does later include a broader referent. Jesus asks, "I do not ask for these only, but also for those who will believe in me through their word, that they may all be one, just as you, Father, are in me, and I in you, that they also may be in us, so that the world may believe that you have sent me. The glory that you have given me I have given to them, that they may be one even as we are one" (John 17:20–22). Jesus prays for those who will become Christians throughout the history of the church. However, this does not discuss the nature of election or of the extent of the atonement. The prayer is not for forgiveness through Christ's death, or for grace which is limited in scope; rather, the prayer is for the church's unity. What Jesus prays to the Father is not that the elect alone would be impacted by his atonement, but that the unity of the church would reflect the unity of the Trinity. The entire prayer is ecclesiological rather than soteriological. Jesus first prays for the founders of the church, namely, his disciples, and then for

---

41. Sproul, *Chosen by God*, 179.

42 "While I was with them, I kept them in your name, which you have given me" (John 17:12).

the unity of the church following the life of his Apostles. To argue anything about the extent of the atonement from this passage is inconsistent with the purpose of the prayer.

Another text which is often used to defend particular redemption is also from John's gospel:

> I am the good shepherd. The good shepherd lays down his life for the sheep. He who is a hired hand and not a shepherd, who does not own the sheep, sees the wolf coming and leaves the sheep and flees, and the wolf snatches them and scatters them. He flees because he is a hired hand and cares nothing for the sheep. I am the good shepherd. I know my own and my own know me, just as the Father knows me and I know the Father; and I lay down my life for the sheep. (John 10:11–15)

It is argued that the sheep refer to Christ's elect. On the cross, Christ lays down his life specifically for the sheep, as would the good shepherd.[43] Note however that this text does not posit that Christ lays his life down for the sheep only. The only exclusivism in this text is that which is assumed by the Calvinistic interpreter.

One must not use a metaphor to narrowly define a doctrine, but must utilize the metaphor in the manner intended by the author. Christ does lay down his life for the sheep. He does lay down his life for the church. This, however, does not answer the question of the full extent of Christ's atonement. Note that the sheep aren't even explicitly defined in this text. Perhaps this metaphor does refer specifically to the elect, but perhaps it refers to all who believe including those who will depart from the faith. Ultimately the purpose of the text is not to describe the extent of the atonement but to contrast the true shepherd with false shepherds. Jesus is arguing that those who had faith in the coming Messiah had enough discernment to ignore those who preceded Jesus in claiming authority over the people of Israel. Thus, true believers (or sheep, in Jesus' metaphor) are able to hear the voice of their true shepherd, to reject the false call of the hired hand and wait for the shepherd to arrive. The extent of the atonement is irrelevant to the purpose of this text.

Another argument from Reformed interpreters is that the term "all" in the New Testament refers to "kinds of people" rather than everyone indiscriminately. This is argued on the basis of John's Apocalypse: "for you were slain, and by your blood you ransomed people for God from every

---

43. Hodge uses this argument in *Systematic Theology* 2:549.

tribe and language and people and nation."⁴⁴ Robert Peterson and Michael Williams argue from this text,

> The point is that Jesus by his substitutionary atonement redeemed a part of the human race out of the bigger whole, "every tribe, tongue, language, people, and nation." Christ's atonement here is not potential, but actual; his blood purchases people for God from among the nations. The words "tribe, language, people, and nation" refer to the same entity—humankind from the perspectives of people group, tongue, location and political entity, respectively. Here John helps us understand the meaning of Christ's dying for "the world" and "all" in Scripture. Christ ransoms people out of "every tribe and language and people and nation," that is, from out of the world. This verse does not teach a universal but a particular atonement.⁴⁵

It is argued that this verse serves as an interpretive grid regarding the seemingly universalistic passages throughout the New Testament. John makes it apparent that salvation is universal in that it is received by people of all tribes, tongues, and nations; yet salvation is also limited in that it is received only by certain people in these different ethnicities. Because the text speaks of ransom, it is argued, it defines Christ's ransom as that which was accomplished only for these specific people. However, this verse does not necessitate reference to the extent of Christ's atonement, but has specific reference to those who receive final eschatological vindication. It is only these whom Christ ransomed, who have persevered in faith, in regard to whom praise is being sung. It is unlikely that heavenly praise would include mention of Christ's death for those who rejected the grace thereby offered. The eschatological nature of John's Revelation is evidence that Christ's ransom will ultimately benefit only those who receive eternal life, but not that the offering was not universal in scope.

LIMITING THE MEANING OF THE CROSS

One of the problems that arise in Calvinistic atonement theology is the nature of its atonement theory, which is limited far beyond the broad biblical testimony. For Reformed theology, the cross is often limited to the

---

44. Rev 5:9.
45. Peterson and Williams, *Why I Am Not an Arminian*, 206.

concept of substitutionary atonement, or propitiation.[46] The doctrine of limited atonement is extrapolated from this theory to the exclusion of all others. Though at times the other atonement models are confessed, they are not central.

The Anselmian tradition regarding atonement theory has validity. There are legal metaphors in the New Testament which correspond to medieval and Reformation formulations. For example, Paul speaks about Christ "cancelling the record of debt that stood against us" (Col 2:14). On the cross, Christ takes upon himself the curse of the law,[47] which all are placed under because of their disobedience. The doctrine of propitiation is a biblical concept.[48] However, this does not exhaust the biblical testimony, and one atonement model should not be accepted to the exclusion of all others.[49]

The concept of ransom is common in the New Testament. Peter states that through the cross people are "ransomed from the futile ways inherited from your forefathers" (1 Pet 1:18). Mark states that Jesus laid down his life as a "ransom for many" (Mark 10:45). Paul writes that Christ gave himself as a "ransom for all" (1 Tim 2:6). The early church at times used the ransom model to the exclusion of all others, thus the ransom-to-Satan theory became prominent. This patristic approach is in error because it took the atonement model far beyond its biblical import. The thought was that for ransom to take place, there must be someone from whom one is ransomed. Therefore ransom must be paid to the devil. This is the same error that the Calvinistic writers engage in by extrapolating from the use of the term "propitiation" once by John, the idea that God's wrath was propitiated on the cross so as to negate hell for those whom Christ died for, therefore inferring limited atonement.

Luther takes a more realist approach to the cross which has thorough biblical support. For Luther, Christ does not merely take on a penalty imposed by the Father in a bare legal transaction. Rather, Christ bears sin itself. In Paul's writings, sin is described not only as a violation of a

---

46. For more on atonement theories, see Gustaf Aulen's classic work *Christus Victor*.

47. Gal 3:13.

48. 1 John 2:2 is the clearest text in support of the concept of propitiation.

49. Steven P. Mueller writes, "The Scriptures describe the work of Christ in many ways. Indeed these theories do not encompass everything that the word says about our Savior. It presents his work in many ways so that we will hear it, understand it better, and rejoice in what he has done for us . . . The richness of God's word allows us to present the work of our Savior in several complimentary ways" (Mueller, *Called to Believe*, 228).

commandment, but as a power which holds men captive.[50] Christ when going to the cross takes this power upon himself, making himself the "greatest sinner,"[51] in Luther's words. As Paul writes, "For our sake he made him to be sin who knew no sin" (2 Cor 5:21). In Paul's theology, Christ takes sin upon himself to such an extent that he can be identified with sin. This is also apparent in his epistle to the Galatians, wherein Paul writes that "Christ redeemed us from the curse of the law by becoming a curse for us" (Gal 3:13). Christ does not merely take the curse of God the Father given for individual sins, but he *becomes* the curse for us. Though without sin, Jesus swallowed up sin, becoming sin and becoming a curse for his sinful creation.[52]

The concept of limited atonement is based on the idea that on the cross, Jesus takes the Father's wrath upon himself for sins of specific people. However, in Luther's approach, Christ takes upon himself sin, the power which held the world captive under its grasp. It is not a question of giving his life for specific people but of Christ's taking upon himself all of the evil of the world and defeating the powers which held man captive to sin, the world, and the devil.

PRACTICAL IMPLICATIONS OF LIMITED ATONEMENT

Apart from the doctrine's lack of exegetical and theological support, there are also some practical and pastoral issues that arise in view of the Calvinistic approach to the atonement.

One who adopts a particularist approach to the atonement can never have the assurance that Christ's death was for them. Many have struggled with the question of their election. This is a pastoral issue encountered frequently. In the Lutheran tradition, one need only look to the objective means of word and sacrament, wherein God's grace is indiscriminately

---

50. Romans 6, for example, deals with sin in this manner.

51. Luther, *Table Talk*, 172.

52. We must be careful here not to argue that Christ himself actually sinned. Steven Paulson mistakenly writes, "He wants to take your sins and leave it to no one else; so he sins against the Golden Rule" (Paulson, *Lutheran Theology*, 103). Since sin is not only individual offenses, but also a power, one can speak of this power having overtaken Christ, and Christ "becoming sin" in this sense. However, we must defend Christ's sinless nature.

given.⁵³ One need only have faith and receive God's blessings. The Calvinist must point one to the fruits of conversion for there to be assurance of election and Christ's death for them. Faith can be false, and one must have a sincere faith in order to be sure of election.

According to a Reformed exegesis of Hebrews chapter 6, a false faith can still cause one to repent, taste the heavenly gift, and share in the Holy Spirit. Ultimately, one must look at the quality of one's own works to see if they are Spirit wrought. One's assurance is in one's inner transformation, not in the gospel. One ultimately never knows if Christ actually died for him or her except by the number and quality of one's good works.

Calvinists may object that they believe in a "free offer of the gospel," which is apparent in all but the hyper-Calvinistic system. Thus, one can trust in this universal offer. However, it must be asked, Is this really a universal offer? How can God offer something he has not actually paid for? Can he really tell one to accept the death of Christ while it in fact has never been paid for that person? If a man were to walk up to an Amish person and offer him a stereo system that he didn't have, it would be dishonest. Even though the Amish would never accept the gift because of their rejection of modern technology, one could still not honestly offer something one did not have regardless of the known rejection of the gift. Thus an offer of the gospel which is not intended for the unbeliever is not a true offer.

CONCLUSION

The doctrine of limited atonement fails to have exegetical support. The universalistic texts in the New Testament are clear, and Calvinistic arguments to the contrary remain unconvincing. The book of Hebrews demonstrates that Christ died for those who fall away from the faith, and that those for whom Christ died can be cut off from the promise. The logical argument for limited atonement fails because it proves too much. It proves the hyper-Calvinistic doctrine of eternal justification rather than Reformed orthodoxy. The doctrine of limited atonement is based on an over-extrapolation of one particular atonement model used in the New Testament. There are several prominent pastoral concerns which arise from Reformed teaching.

---

53. "Concerning the sacraments it is taught that the sacraments are instituted not only to be signs by which people may recognize Christians outwardly, but also as signs and testimonies of God's will toward us in order thereby to awaken and strengthen our faith" (AC XIII.1).

Overall, the doctrine of limited atonement is theologically, exegetically, and logically unconvincing.

3

Shipwrecked Faith
A Lutheran Approach to Perseverance and Apostasy

Along with disagreement over the issue of limited atonement, the fifth and final point of Calvinism is one of the central differences between the Reformed and Lutheran theological traditions. Regarding perseverance, the Westminster Confession states,

> They whom God hath accepted in his Beloved, effectually called and sanctified by his Spirit, can neither totally nor finally fall away from the state of grace: but shall certainly persevere therein to the end, and be eternally saved.
>
> This perseverance of the saints depends not upon their free will, but upon the immutability of the decree of election, flowing from the free and unchangeable love of God the Father, upon the efficacy of the merits and intercession of Jesus Christ, the abiding of the Spirit and of the seed of God within them, and the nature of the covenant of grace; from all which ariseth, also, the certainty and infallibility thereof. (WCF XIX.1)

In contrast to this Reformed perspective, Lutherans confess that salvation can be both received and forfeited. Apostasy is a real possibility for those who are in the faith. Though perseverance is solely the work of God, there is an act of falling away described in Scripture wherein one can reject grace and depart from the faith.[1]

DEFINING THE LUTHERAN DOCTRINE

Before arguing for the truth of the Lutheran approach to apostasy and perseverance, this perspective must be defined. In Lutheranism, God alone initiates salvation. When a believer is regenerated and justified, solely God can be given credit for salvation.[2] Every type of Pelagian or Semi-Pelagian doctrine is rejected.[3] Lutherans confess the doctrine of election regarding salvation, that God's predestination unto glory is unconditional.[4] Salvation is a monergistic act. Thus, faith is a gift of God; man is purely passive.[5] There is, along with imputation through justification, a process wherein one is sanctified.[6] That righteousness which one obtains through imputation is realized through God's resurrecting act wherein the old man is slain and the new rises. If one perseveres in the faith, this is also the work of God, preserving one in saving faith.[7]

Though one cannot create faith or choose faith apart from grace, it is possible to reject the gift of faith. As the Solid Declaration states, "However, if the baptized act against their conscience, permit sin to reign in them and thus grieve the Holy Spirit in themselves and lose him, then, although they may not be rebaptized, they must be converted again, as has been

---

1. "In the same vein, Holy Scripture also testifies that God, who has called us, is so faithful that when he has 'begun a good work in us,' he will also continue it to the end and complete it, if we do not turn away from him, but 'remain steadfast to the end in that which he has begun'" (FC SD XI.32).

2. "It is therefore once again obvious from the previous explanation that conversion to God is the work of God the Holy Spirit alone" (FC SD II.90).

3. FC SD II.75, 77–78.

4. "God's eternal election not only foresees and foreknows the salvation of the elect but also is a cause of our salvation and whatever pertains to it, on the basis of the gracious will and good pleasure of God in Christ Jesus" (FC SD IX.8).

5. "These testimonies tell us that we cannot come to Christ on the basis of our own powers, but God must give us his Holy Spirit, who enlightens, sanctifies, and thus brings us to Christ through faith and keeps us in Christ. Neither our will nor cooperation is mentioned in respect to these activities" (FC SD II.42).

6. "[A]s soon as the Holy Spirit has begun his work of rebirth and renewal in us through the Word and the holy sacraments, it is certain that on the basis of his power we can and should be cooperating with him, though still in great weakness" (FC SD II.65).

7. FC SD XI.20–22.

sufficiently demonstrated above." (FC SD II.69). This occurs especially as one avoids the God-given means of grace, namely, word and sacrament. This is distinct from the Wesleyan Arminian approach to perseverance, wherein one's continual cooperation with grace is instrumental.[8] It is not that the Christian is constantly falling in and out of grace, but that there is a possibility that one can lose faith and consequently, Christ. Through faith, Christ is present, giving himself to the Christian as righteousness. When faith is abandoned, Christ is lost. Faith is like a ring which grasps Christ, the jewel. However, without the ring, the jewel cannot be retained. This loss occurs solely through man's rejection of God through unbelief rather than God's predestination or allowance.[9] In contrast to this, the one who perseveres does so through grace alone.[10]

APOSTASY AND WARNING PASSAGES IN THE NEW TESTAMENT

The disagreement over the meaning of apostasy and perseverance often regards the nature of the "apostasy passages" in Scripture. Scattered throughout the New Testament are texts referring to people who departed from the faith and warning against apostasy. In the Lutheran approach, these texts are literal and refer to an actual possibility of apostasy by true Christian believers. The Calvinistic approach to these numerous texts is twofold. First, it is argued that many of the passages about apostasy refer to people who were never genuine Christians. Boettner writes, for example,

> To answer certain purposes, they make an outward profession of the Gospel, which obliges them for a time to be outwardly moral and to associate themselves with the people of God. They appear to have true faith and continue thus for a while. Then either their sheep's clothing is stripped off, or they throw it off themselves, and return again to the world. If we could see the real motives of their

---

8. For a detailed explanation of the Wesleyan approach, see Grider, *Wesleyan-Holiness Theology*.

9. "The cause for [apostasy], however, is not that God did not want to give the grace of perseverance to those in whom he had 'begun the good work,' for this is contrary to St. Paul in Philippians 1[:6]" (FC SD XI.42).

10. "He that perseveres in faith does so only through God's gracious preservation; the believer's perseverance is a work of divine grace and omnipotence" (Pieper, *Christian Dogmatics* 3:89).

hearts, we would discover that at no time were they ever actuated by a true love of God.[11]

Thus those who are described by Scripture as falling away from faith thus do not actually have faith; rather they had a false profession and the outward appearance of belief.

The second way that these texts are dealt with is to argue that many of the warnings and encouragements scattered throughout the canonical books are hypothetical. They refer to an impossible falling away, so as to urge believers unto good works.

APOSTASY IN PAULINE THEOLOGY

There are several "falling away" passages throughout the Pauline literature which promote the idea that one who has been redeemed can depart from faith. Even that great chapter of assurance, the eighth chapter of Romans, contains such admonitions: "The Spirit himself bears witness with our spirit that we are children of God, and if children, then heirs—heirs of God and fellow heirs with Christ, provided we suffer with him in order that we also may be glorified with him" (Rom 8:16–17).[12] This text has a statement of conditionality. It is necessary for one to participate in suffering that one may be glorified with Christ. This likely has reference to suffering eventual persecution in the Roman Empire. Paul was aware of the temptation of some to deny the faith to escape harm under the emperor. This, in Pauline theology, would result in the abandonment of glorification.

There are several other similar statements in the Pauline epistles. In Colossians, for example, Paul writes:

> And you, who were once alienated and hostile in mind, doing evil deeds, he has now reconciled in his body of flesh by his death, in order to present you holy and blameless and above reproach before him, if indeed you continue in the faith, stable and steadfast,

---

11. Boettner, *Reformed Doctrine of Predestination*, 191–92.

12. "As children of God we have a claim to the bliss of heaven, as God has prepared it for His only-begotten Son, for Him that was born out of the fullness of His divine essence. There is only one outward condition which is inevitable: If so be, if only we suffer with Him, in order that we may also be glorified with Him. Christians are partakers of the sufferings of Christ, they are bound to endure afflictions of many kinds for His name's sake. To attempt to evade these sufferings is equivalent to refusing to bear the cross of Christ, Mark 8, 34; Luke 9, 23" (Kretzmann, *Commentary*, Rom 8:12–17).

Part I: Predestination and Free Will

> not shifting from the hope of the gospel that you heard, which has been proclaimed in all creation under heaven, and of which I, Paul, became a minister. (Col 1:21–23)

After first proclaiming the gospel, describing the victory of Christ over the powers of evil, Paul gives an admonition to remain in the faith. According to this text, one will be presented before God as holy and blameless only if faith is not lost. It is implied by Paul that there are some who do and will shift from the hope of the gospel. A purely hypothetical approach to such texts denies the real threat which Paul is warning against, and thus is not likely what he intended.

A warning is also given in Galatians. Paul writes, "And let us not grow weary of doing good, for in due season we will reap, if we do not give up" (Gal 6:9). This is in light of the continual admonitions in Galatians not to abandon the gospel and fall into the Judaizing heresy. According to Paul, those who adopt a Torah-abiding lifestyle and reject non-observant Gentiles are "cut off from Christ" (Gal 5:4).[13] The implication is that some were believers in the gospel, recipients of Christ, but were cut off from salvation by abandoning the doctrine they had once professed.

Finally, Paul gives another warning in his first epistle to the Corinthians: "Now I would remind you, brothers, of the gospel I preached to you, which you received, in which you stand, and by which you are being saved, if you hold fast to the word I preached to you—unless you believed in vain" (1 Cor. 15:1–2). For Paul's readers, being saved is dependent upon one's remaining in the faith. If one "holds fast" to the gospel, one will receive salvation. However, those who reject the gospel and walk away will have believed in vain. Paul does not write that the belief is false, or was never present, but that it is in vain because through loss of belief, the desired result of belief—namely, eternal life—is forfeited.

Paul gives a specific example of those who have fallen prey to this danger that he consistently warns of. In 1 Timothy, Paul writes of Hymenaeus and Alexander, "By rejecting this, they have made a shipwreck of their faith, among whom are Hymenaeus and Alexander, whom I have handed over to Satan that they may learn not to blaspheme" (1 Tim 1:19–20). Paul does not write that these Christians had a "false faith" or the appearance

---

13. As Richard Lenski writes, "The moment one even tries to be justified in connection with anything in the nature of the law, this is what happens, then the terrible damage is done. It all happens in at instant: completely out with Christ and fallen from grace" (Lenski, *Epistles to the Galatians*, 257).

of faith, but states both that they had faith, and that this faith was shipwrecked. It is clear that shipwrecking one's faith is tantamount to loss of faith, as Paul even comments that they had blasphemed. This is consistent with what Paul later writes about those who will fall away from the faith: "Now the Spirit expressly says that in later times some will depart from the faith . . ." (1 Tim 4:1).[14] Paul does, however, admit the possibility of future repentance by holding out hope that God may bring them back.

It is apparent throughout the Pauline literature that apostasy is a real possibility. Paul deems it necessary to warn those who are believers to remain steadfast in their faith in the gospel which he proclaimed. If one abandons the gospel by falling into heresy or abandoning the faith, one is cut off from Christ and salvation is lost. This is demonstrated by the continual warning passages along with the example of Hymenaeus and Alexander.

Horton argues that the New Testament passages on apostasy refer to external members of the New Covenant. "Those who apostatize have been beneficiaries of the Spirit's ministry through the means of grace even as merely formal or external membership of the covenant community."[15] Thus, Paul's warnings are in view of the fact that some external members of the covenant will depart from the faith, while acknowledging that true believers don't have the ability to depart from grace. There are a few things that can be said in response to this idea. First, this argument presumes that there is such a thing as "external membership" in the New Covenant. This is precluded by Hebrews 8, which identifies membership in the new covenant with knowing the Lord, the forgiveness of sins, and having the law written on one's heart.[16] None of this would be an accurate description of someone

---

14. As Lenski writes, "'Some will apostatize' means some who at first were good church members, believers of the truth. Let us who stand be warned. All false security is dangerous" (Lenski, *Epistles to the Colossians*, 618).

15. Horton, *Systematic Theology*, 683.

16. Quoting Jeremiah 31, the author of Hebrews writes,

> For he finds fault with them when he says:
> "Behold, the days are coming, declares the Lord,
> when I will establish a new covenant with the house of Israel
> and with the house of Judah,
> not like the covenant that I made with their fathers
> on the day when I took them by the hand to bring them out of the land of Egypt.
> For they did not continue in my covenant,
> and so I showed no concern for them, declares the Lord.
> For this is the covenant that I will make with the house of Israel

Part I: Predestination and Free Will

without true faith. Secondly, this argument presupposes Reformed sacramental and covenantal theology, which separates salvation from the means of grace.[17] Finally, this approach fails to take the texts at face value and reads a preexisting theological system into them. In 1 Timothy 1:19–20, Paul talks about those who have made a "shipwreck of their faith." At face value, this reading suggests that one had faith and then lost it. In the Reformed view, they shipwrecked something that they never actually had. How can a false faith be destroyed, if it isn't real faith in the first place? The Reformed reading of the text is forced, and not tenable.

APOSTASY IN OTHER NEW TESTAMENT EPISTOLARY LITERATURE

Hebrews has perhaps been the book that presents the most problems for the Calvinistic position on perseverance. Apostasy and perseverance is a central theme to the epistle. The author, writing in a sermonic tone, is encouraging Jewish converts to remain in the Christian faith. He fears that persecution may lead some to revert back to the ceremonial aspects of Torah and reject Christ. This causes the author to expound upon the nature of typology and demonstrate the superiority of Christ over observance of the ceremonial law. The premise of the book assumes that apostasy is a real possibility and that some who have become Christians can and will reject the faith they have received.[18]

> after those days, declares the Lord:
> I will put my laws into their minds,
> and write them on their hearts,
> and I will be their God,
> and they shall be my people.
> And they shall not teach, each one his neighbor
> and each one his brother, saying, 'Know the Lord,'
> for they shall all know me,
> from the least of them to the greatest.
> For I will be merciful toward their iniquities,
> and I will remember their sins no more." (Heb 8:8–12)

17. This will be dealt with below, when I discuss baptism.

18. Martin H. Franzmann writes that "The letter is therefore basically just what the author calls it, a 'word of exhortation' (Heb. 13:22), an appeal to 'hold fast to the confession . . . without wavering' (Heb.10:23; cf. 10:38; 3:14). The author points his readers to Jesus and urges them to look at Jesus, 'the pioneer and perfecter of our faith'" (Franzmann, *Word of the Lord Grows*, 239).

Hebrews 3, for example, gives the following exhortation: "Take care, brothers, lest there be in any of you an evil, unbelieving heart, leading you to fall away from the living God. But exhort one another every day, as long as it is called 'today,' that none of you may be hardened by the deceitfulness of sin. For we have come to share in Christ, if indeed we hold our original confidence firm to the end" (Heb 3:12–14). To fall away from the living God is to assume that one was once in a relationship with the living God. The author admonishes those in the church to encourage one another so that they may not fall away. Notice that there is conditionality in final salvation similar to that found in Colossians. Both one's faith and trust must remain or salvation will be forfeited. If one does not "hold our original confidence firm to the end," then salvation is lost.

Similarly, in chapter 6 the author writes, "For it is impossible in the case of those who have once been enlightened, who have tasted the heavenly gift, and have shared in the Holy Spirit, and have tasted the goodness of the word of God and the powers of the age to come, and then have fallen away, to restore them again to repentance, since they are crucifying once again the Son of God to their own harm and holding him up to contempt" (Heb 6:4–6).[19] The author assumes that one can fall away into such a state that salvation will never be regained. One can reject the gospel and harden one's heart to such an extent that future repentance is an impossibility. Wayne Grudem argues that these are not genuine Christian believers but those who "give many external signs of conversion and may look in many ways like conversion."[20] The language in this text is stronger, however, than purely external signs. They are described by the author as those who have "shared in the Holy Spirit," have tasted eschatological blessings, and have been enlightened by the gospel. These phrases describe those who have become Christians, those who have been regenerated. Finally, Hebrews 10 contains another such admonition: "For if we go on sinning deliberately after receiving the knowledge of the truth, there no longer remains a sacrifice for sins, but a fearful expectation of judgment, and a fury of fire that will consume the adversaries" (Heb 10:26). Once again, those written of in this text are believers who have "received the knowledge of the truth." The argument also assumes that Christ was the sacrifice for the

---

19. There is an interesting volume which portrays the various approaches to these texts: Bateman et al., *Four Views*. Unfortunately, there is not enough space in a work such as this to deal with the various approaches to these texts.

20. Grudem, *Systematic Theology*, 796.

Part I: Predestination and Free Will

sins of these particular people, and that when Christ's sacrifice is rejected, no other sacrifice remains. The entirety of the purpose and argument of the book of Hebrews rests upon the fact that some who have been redeemed can depart from the faith and lose the benefits of Christ's atonement.

As was briefly discussed in the previous chapter, it is often argued that the statements in Hebrews are hypothetical because of one particular phrase in the book.[21] The author writes: "Though we speak in this way, yet in your case, beloved, we feel sure of better things—things that belong to salvation" (Heb 6:9). It is argued that the author, in this section, negates apostasy as a real possibility. Because the author is "sure of better things" for his readers, these admonitions become purely hypothetical. This is not the only possible solution to this text. Because of the sermonic tone of this epistle, it is probable that the author is giving his readers pastoral encouragement. The author is telling these Christians that they need not fear apostasy because he knows the faith and love they have demonstrated and does not believe they will apostatize. He is telling them this so as not to allow them to fall into desperation or fear that their salvation will be lost. It is not a definitive statement that none of the readers had a real possibility of falling away from the faith. To argue otherwise is to attempt to turn the entirety of the author's argument into a purely hypothetical engagement, which is unlikely. Even at the end of this section, the writer offers words of admonition that his readers "have the full assurance of hope until the very end" so that they might inherit the promise.

Ironically, Calvinist theologians Peterson and Williams back up my assertion, writing, "the writer issues a real warning to a minority of his readers whom he fears may not know Christ and may show it by committing apostasy."[22] Though still confessing the Reformed doctrine that apostasy is not possible for genuine believers, Peterson and Williams admit that this text from Hebrews does not support the assertion that the writer's messages of assurance to his readers are absolute. Though the author proclaims his unilateral confidence of preservation, this does not necessitate the final salvation of each intended reader.

In his second epistle, Peter also writes about apostasy:

> For, speaking loud boasts of folly, they entice by sensual passions of the flesh those who are barely escaping from those who live in error. They promise them freedom, but they themselves are slaves

---

21. See, for example, Williams and Peterson, *Why I Am Not an Arminian*, 83–85.
22. Ibid., 85.

> of corruption. For whatever overcomes a person, to that he is enslaved. For if, after they have escaped the defilements of the world through the knowledge of our Lord and Savior Jesus Christ, they are again entangled in them and overcome, the last state has become worse for them than the first. For it would have been better for them never to have known the way of righteousness than after knowing it to turn back from the holy commandment delivered to them. What the true proverb says has happened to them: "The dog returns to its own vomit, and the sow, after washing herself, returns to wallow in the mire." (2 Pet 2:18–22)

The Reformed response to a reading of this text which assumes the possibility of falling away is that Peter refers not to Christians, but to those who falsely profess the faith. These people are part of the Christian community and have the outward appearance of faith but inwardly are unbelievers. The clear intent of the passage suggests otherwise. Those whom Peter writes about have escaped the defilement of the world and have known Jesus Christ. Peter does not write that they "claimed to have known Jesus" or have "appeared to escape the defilement of the world." These statements denote the presence of true saving faith which has been forfeited.

James also writes of the possibility of falling away and future restoration: "My brothers, if anyone among you wanders from the truth and someone brings him back, let him know that whoever brings back a sinner from his wandering will save his soul from death and will cover a multitude of sins" (Jas 5:19–20).[23] This demonstrates that not all acts of apostasy necessitate a state of permanent departure from the faith as the book of Hebrews discusses. In this passage, James talks about those who "wander from the truth" but will be brought back to repentance and the fellowship of the church. There are certain aspects of this text which make it apparent both that this text is speaking of a true believer, and that the person described in this text has lost his salvation. First, note that James talks about a sinner being "brought back" from wandering. Thus, it is not that this person once had false faith and later gained true faith. Secondly, notice that James talks about the repentance of this person as salvation from death and the covering of sins. The assumption is that this person's soul was in a state of spiritual death, and the one who brings him back returns him to spiritual

---

23. Lenski writes, "Both subjunctives are aorists or actuality; they designate an actual erring from the truth so that it and its saving power are lost and an actual turning such a lost one back to this saving truth" (Lenski, *Hebrews and James*, 672).

life. James clearly teaches that a true Christian can depart from the faith and also be restored through repentance.

THE TEACHING OF JESUS ON APOSTASY

Jesus also speaks in a conditional manner regarding final salvation. It is not faith that is idle that saves, but a faith that endures until one's final breath: "Because lawlessness is increased, most people's love will grow cold. But the one who endures to the end, he will be saved" (Matt 24:12–14). Jesus assumes that during these last days, some who are in the faith have love that will "grow cold" and salvation will consequently be forfeited. This is not a promotion of "works righteousness" through retaining a certain level of love, or the idea that perseverance is something added to faith, but that only those who have persevering faith will continue in grace and justification. Jesus again speaks similarly in Matthew's gospel: "You will be hated by all because of my name, but it is the one who has endured to the end who will be saved" (Matt 10:22). Jesus knows of the coming persecution of the church and is aware that many will be tempted to abandon the faith to protect their own well-being. Abandoning the Christian faith in times of persecution is a rejection of grace and results in the loss of salvation.

The most prominent and extensive example of Jesus' teaching on apostasy comes from his parable of the seed and sower:

> And the ones on the rock are those who, when they hear the word, receive it with joy. But these have no root; they believe for a while, and in time of testing fall away. And as for what fell among the thorns, they are those who hear, but as they go on their way they are choked by the cares and riches and pleasures of life, and their fruit does not mature. As for that in the good soil, they are those who, hearing the word, hold it fast in an honest and good heart, and bear fruit with patience. (Luke 8:13–15)

Those who adopt the doctrine of the perseverance of the saints argue that those who have fallen away in this parable are not truly Christians. John Gill writes that "their faith is a temporary one, like that of Simon Magus; which shows it is not true faith; for that is an abiding grace, Christ, who is the author, is the finisher of it, and prays for it, that it fail not."[24] They are examples of those who have false faith and never truly have regeneration,

---

24. Gill, *Exposition of the Bible*, Luke 8:18.

justification, or any other soteriological blessings. However, the parable does not give merit to this interpretation. It can only be read in through preexisting theological convictions. The first category, those who fell on the rock, are said to "receive the word with joy." Jesus does not say that their reception of the gospel was false or insincere. It is incommensurate with the biblical state of the unregenerate that an unbeliever could receive the gospel, let alone with joy, while remaining in unbelief. Jesus says that these people do believe for a time, yet with a weak faith. The fact that faith is weak and does not have a root is not grounds for denying faith altogether contrary to Jesus' own words. Rather, because this faith is weak (though still being faith), one denies the faith in times of testing and salvation is forfeited. The second group are said to have "fruit," which is often described as a characteristic of Christians and never for unbelievers.[25] The problem with these believers is not that faith is not present, or even the fruit of faith; rather the faith is not nurtured, and fruit does not grow. Because of their lack of growth, these people become entranced by that which belongs to the present age and are led away from the faith. What differentiates the final group from the first two is that those who receive eternal salvation hold fast to the faith. They continually bear fruit because their faith is continuous and not abandoned. Jesus demonstrates that many who enter the faith, who receive the gospel and even bear fruit, will fall away and reject the gospel.

THE POSSIBILITY OF APOSTASY AND SOLA GRATIA

There is fear among Calvinist theologians that a denial of the perseverance of all believers negates a monergistic understanding of salvation, reverting to an Arminian type of synergistic system. It is contended that without God's preservation, then the duty of perseverance becomes that of the Christian. Thus, the Christian is responsible for the continual maintenance of salvation. Horton writes, for example, "How can one say that God alone saves, from beginning to end, while also affirming the possibility of losing one's salvation? It seems undeniable that this gift depends in some sense on the sinners' nonresisting, although this conclusion is rejected by Confessional Lutherans."[26] The Lutheran tradition, however inconsistent Horton may believe the position to be, has sought to retain both the belief that

---

25. Take Paul's discussion in Galatians 5 about the fruits of the Spirit, for example.
26. Horton, *For Calvinism*, 122.

apostasy is possible and is solely the fault of man, and that perseverance is a gift of God apart from one's own effort or merit. Observe what Francis Pieper states about this issue:

> What Scripture teaches on final perseverance may be summarized in these two statements: 1. He that perseveres in faith does so only through God's gracious preservation; the believer's perseverance is a work of divine grace and omnipotence. 2. He that falls away from faith does so through his own fault; the cause of apostasy in every case is rejection of God's Word and resistance to the operation of the Holy Spirit in the Word. This doctrine the Christian Church must maintain and defend on two fronts: against Calvinism and against synergism.[27]

Pieper leaves the two truths in tension without an attempt to resolve the dilemma of the nature of monergistic perseverance and the possibility of apostasy. Despite the seeming tension, Pieper's approach reflects biblical teaching regarding the subject.

It has been demonstrated above that the doctrine of apostasy is emphatically taught in New Testament literature. It remains to be shown that perseverance is a divine work, accomplished apart from merit. The biblical testimony is lucid regarding this issue as well. Look, for example, at the following statement of Jude: "Now to him who is able to keep you from stumbling and to present you blameless before the presence of his glory with great joy, to the only God, our Savior, through Jesus Christ our Lord, be glory, majesty, dominion, and authority, before all time and now and forever. Amen" (Jude 24–25). God is given credit as he who keeps the believer from stumbling, assuring one's preservation in the faith. He also is the one who will present the believer as blameless, by retaining the believer until his eschatological vindication at the resurrection.

Paul argues similarly; he writes to the Romans, "He who did not spare his own Son but gave him up for us all, how will he not also with him graciously give us all things?" (Rom 8:32). Because of God's grace and kindness shown through the cross, Paul assumes that God's grace extends to all areas of salvation. Presumably, this would include one's perseverance and inheriting eternal life. Paul assures the Philippians of this great truth as well. He gives assurance to the church by stating that "I am sure of this, that he who began a good work in you will bring it to completion at the day of Jesus Christ" (Phil 1:6). Verses such as this do not give credence to the

---

27. Pieper, *Christian Dogmatics* 3:89.

assertion that "no true believer ever loses his salvation."[28] This is apparent in that in other texts Paul admits that falling away is a true possibility for the Christian. Even so, he is able to tell the Philippians with confidence that God is working out salvation within them and that God will complete his work. This does not merit the belief that every single person in the Philippian church would be finally saved, but displays trust on Paul's part regarding the divine nature of perseverance. It is ascribed wholly to God rather than to those in the church. Paul is also able to describe his own Christian experience in similar terms: "But by the grace of God I am what I am, and his grace toward me was not in vain. On the contrary, I worked harder than any of them, though it was not I, but the grace of God that is with me" (1 Cor 15:10). Paul attributes the progress and perseverance he experiences in the Christian faith, not to his own effort, but to the work of God.

There are two things which Scripture makes clear regarding perseverance: First, it is possible for one to fall away from the faith; when this occurs it is the fault of the person rejecting grace and is in no way attributed to God's predestination. Second, God preserves his people monergistically in faith. Perseverance is wholly due to God's act of preservation. Though these concepts may not appear to be compatible, they are both taught in Scripture, and thus should be accepted as truth.

THE QUESTION OF "FALSE FAITH"

One of the primary points of disagreement between the two branches of the Reformation regarding perseverance is the nature of false faith. According to the Reformed tradition, those who fall away from the faith never had genuine belief. Thus, there are many people who seem to be regenerate but in reality remain unbelievers. Robert Reymond testifies to this, arguing that those passages which teach apostasy "teach that there is such a thing as 'temporary faith' which is not true faith in Christ at all."[29] One's faith has to be tested for genuineness so that one can distinguish true faith from false faith. Though this solves the difficulties posed by the falling-away passages, the Reformed contention of false faith results in an unintended unique theological category of "half-converts." Those who commit apostasy are neither true believers, nor do they display characteristics of unregenerate people. If one examines New Testament anthropology regarding the unre-

28. Sproul, *Chosen by God*, 157.
29. Reymond, *New Systematic Theology*, 789.

generate and the statements about those who supposedly have "false faith," the two concepts are incompatible. The description of those with false faith is not consistent with the biblical definition of an unbeliever, thus these people must either be true Christians who departed from the faith, or belong to a third category of the "half-convert" or "almost convert."

The idea of false profession and false faith is a biblical concept.[30] James writes that "even the demons believe—and shudder!" (Jas 2:19). Though demons do not possess saving faith, they do have belief in God's existence and have knowledge of the cross and resurrection of Jesus as historical events. In the same manner, there are some who believe the facts about the gospel without a heartfelt trust in Christ. The Reformation tradition developed three necessary elements of saving faith.[31] The first is *notitia*. This is a knowledge of the facts of the gospel. One hears the facts of Jesus death and resurrection for the forgiveness of sins. The second is *assensus*. This is assent that these facts are true. Like the demons, one can consent to the facts of the gospel without possessing saving faith. The final step is that which distinguishes saving faith from false faith: *fiducia*. This is a heartfelt trust in the *pro me* of the gospel. It is a personal faith and trust in Christ for forgiveness. In the Sermon on the Mount, Jesus talks about those who have a false profession of faith. Some are false prophets, preachers who cry out to God and believe themselves to have saving faith. However, when they die they will be told, "I never knew you; depart from me, you workers of lawlessness" (Matt 7:23). These people claim faith but reject the teachings of Jesus, thus demonstrating their unbelief.

Though "false faith" is a biblical category, it does not account for the many descriptions of those who depart from the Christian faith. Observe how these people are described throughout the New Testament. Hebrews 6:4–5 says about these individuals that they have "been enlightened," have "tasted the heavenly gift," "shared in the Holy Spirit," "tasted the goodness of the word of God and the powers of the age to come," and even repented.[32] There has been an epistemic change in these people's minds; "enlightenment" likely refers to a change of mind from one which does not acknowl-

---

30. The Lutheran Confessions teach this as well: "Many construct for themselves a dead faith or illusory faith, which exists without repentance or good works. As if true faith and the evil intention to remain and continue in sin could exist in a single heart at the same time! That is impossible" (FC SD IV.15).

31. On this see Sproul, *Faith Alone*, 75–88.

32. This is apparent in that the author speaks of bringing them "back to repentance," assuming that repentance had already been a reality for these believers.

edge God to one which does. This is synonymous with the scholastic doctrine of illumination.[33] Tasting the heavenly gift may have Eucharistic connotations which may not necessitate true faith and conversion, as it is possible for an unbeliever to receive the Eucharist, though for condemnation rather than blessing. Sharing in the Holy Spirit refers to some work of the Holy Spirit such as regeneration or sanctification; it is unlikely that this could refer to anything about an unbeliever.[34] Tasting of the powers of the age to come is the reception of eschatological blessings which are given to the children of God. It is unlikely that such blessing would be given to one who falsely professes faith. Finally, repentance is an act which only a believer could perform. Gill argues against this: "these apostates before described had only a show of repentance, a counterfeit one."[35] In contrast to Gill's contention, however, the author does not write about one going from false repentance to true repentance but coming back to repentance, thus admitting that one's repentance is genuine, as would be the second repentance if possible.

There are several other passages throughout the New Testament which describe these supposed "hypocritical believers." James speaks of one "wandering from the truth" (Jas 5:19), implying that one previously has understood and received the truth. Paul talks about one being "severed from Christ" (Gal 5:4), which presumes that one was previously united to Christ. There is no union with Christ that is attributed to an unrepentant sinner. According to Matthew, one can both receive the gospel message and delight in it prior to falling away (Matt 13:20). Peter speaks about some

---

33. See Hoenecke, *Evangelical Lutheran Dogmatics* 3:237–44; and Weidner, *Pneumatology*, 42–56. Hollaz defines the teaching: "Illumination is that act of applying grace by which the Holy Spirit teaches sinful man, who has been called to the Church, through the ministry of the Word, and more and more animates him with a sincere desire and purpose, that, the darkness of ignorance and error being dispelled, he may be imbued with a knowledge of the Word of God, and be led by the Law to acknowledge his sins and by the Gospel to see the divine pity which rests on the merit of Christ and thus infuses or instills a knowledge of the same" (quoted in Weidner, *Pneumatology*, 46).

34. Gill argues that "men may be said to be partakers of the Holy Ghost, to whom he gives wisdom and prudence in things natural and civil; the knowledge of things divine and evangelical, in an external way; the power of working miracles, of prophesying, of speaking with tongues, and of the interpretation of tongues; for the extraordinary gifts of the Holy Ghost seem chiefly designed, which some, in the first times of the Gospel, were partakers of, who had no share in special grace" (Gill, *Exposition of the Bible*, Heb 4:6). In response to this argument, it must be pointed out that no such qualifications are actually made in the text to distinguish an external effect from an internal effect of the Spirit.

35. Ibid., Heb 6:6.

who have apostatized, adopting heresy. He states that they had been bought by their Lord (2 Pet 2:1), they have "escaped the defilements of the world" (2 Pet 2:20), and even had "the knowledge of our Lord and Savior Jesus Christ" (2 Pet 2:20). Unbelievers are never described in the New Testament as having escaped the dangers of the world, or coming to the knowledge of Christ.

In contrast to how those who supposedly have false faith are described in the New Testament, look at how the Bible describes the unregenerate. According to Paul's epistle to the Romans, the unbeliever has a darkened heart (Rom 1:21), has futile thinking (Rom 1:21), lacks any understanding (Rom 3:11), does not seek God (Rom 3:11), does nothing good (Rom 3:12), is hostile to God (Rom 8:7), is unable to submit to God's law (Rom 8:7), is a slave to sin (Rom 6:6), and is unable to please God (Rom 8:8). In other Pauline writings, unbelievers are described as having minds that are "defiled" (Titus 1:16), as those who are alienated from Christ (Col 1:21), unable to understand the gospel (1 Cor 2:14), and blinded from seeing Christ (2 Cor 4:3–4). John expounds a similar anthropology. He writes that the unregenerate "hate the light" (John 3:20), are unable to receive the Spirit (John 14:16), and are unable to come to Christ (John 6:44).

In light of New Testament anthropology, especially as expounded upon by Paul and John, it is impossible that the supposed "false believer" and unregenerate person are one and the same. To argue otherwise is to suggest that people can receive the word with joy but be unable to understand the word, share in the Spirit but not be able to receive the Spirit, have no understanding and blinded minds but understand the truth, taste the goodness of God's word yet be unable to understand his word, be alienated from Christ yet be united to him, be enlightened but have no understanding, be in slavery to sin yet repent and escape the evils of the world, receive grace but not salvation, and know Christ but be unable to come to him.

The only way in which this group can refer to those with false faith is to propose a third group of people who are neither regenerate nor unregenerate. This, however, is inconsistent with both biblical and Reformed theology. The only conclusion is that those described in these texts as manifesting true signs of faith yet ultimately falling away are in fact earnest believers who have salvation, yet lose it through rejection of Christ.

Shipwrecked Faith

THE RELATION BETWEEN PERSEVERANCE AND ELECTION

There is a sense in which the perseverance of the saints can be confessed by Lutherans. In *The Gift of Perseverance*,[36] one of his final treatises written during the Pelagian controversy, St. Augustine expounds upon the concept that perseverance is a gift of God given to the elect, though others who are truly regenerated and saved would fall away from the faith. In its original Augustinian meaning, the doctrine of perseverance is correct. Those whom God elects unto salvation will necessarily persevere, and will do so through God's gift.[37] Paul expounds upon this in Romans 8: "For those whom he foreknew he also predestined to be conformed to the image of his Son, in order that he might be the firstborn among many brothers. And those whom he predestined he also called, and those whom he called he also justified, and those whom he justified he also glorified" (Rom 8:29–30). This has sometimes been referred to as the "golden chain of salvation" by Puritan and Reformed authors.[38] It establishes an unbroken chain beginning with foreknowledge whereby it is described how God brings about salvation for his elect people from foreknowledge to election to justification and finally to glorification. This demonstrates the truth of perseverance only in the sense that God preserves those whom he elects. Though some Reformed authors use this as a means to argue that all who are justified will be glorified, this is not necessitated by the text.[39]

With this being established, a fuller picture of the Lutheran approach to perseverance can be explained. There are three truths which have been demonstrated. First, God preserves man monergistically, through the means of word and sacrament, thus making perseverance the work of God rather than man. Second, some will fall away from the faith by rejecting the means of grace, refusing repentance, adopting heresy, and falling into unbelief. And third, all of God's elect will be finally saved, having persevered by grace alone. Thus if one perseveres it is entirely God's work; however, if someone falls away, it is entirely that person's own fault.

36. This can be found in *NPNF1* 5.

37. "The elect are only those actually saved, for Scripture teaches that without fail all elect enter life eternal, or, in other words, that none of the elect can be lost" (Pieper, *Christian Dogmatics* 3:479).

38. Boice, *Golden Chain of Five Links*.

39. The Lutheran *ordo salutis* does tend to be quite a bit "messier" than the Reformed, because steps can be repeated as one falls away and returns to the faith.

Part I: Predestination and Free Will

RESPONDING TO REFORMED ARGUMENTS

There are two manners in which the doctrine of the perseverance of the saints is generally defended in Reformed theology. First is the insistence upon the consistency of the act of election. When God elects individuals unto salvation, these individuals will necessarily persevere.[40] These arguments do not bear a response since the Lutheran position also admits that God's act of election will not fail to achieve its desired result, namely, eternal salvation. The second set of arguments refer to biblical texts which seem to deny the possibility that those who have been redeemed have the ability to reject and fall away from faith. There are several texts used in such a manner.

A common argument in favor of the Calvinistic approach is from the nature of salvation in John's theology. Jesus states in John's gospel, "Truly, truly, I say to you, whoever hears my word and believes him who sent me has eternal life. He does not come into judgment, but has passed from death to life" (John 5:24).[41] John often talks about eternal life as a present reality to those who are of faith. Since John's theology is eschatologically oriented, and one's heavenly inheritance is a present possession, it would seem inconsistent that this possession could be lost. Such is the Reformed argument. Participating in eschatological blessing, however, is not synonymous with post-resurrection life in the new heavens and earth. The time in which Christians exist is one between the ages. One is in a tension between eschatological life and righteousness, and the sinful Adamic age. One can be a participator in the present evil age, and through perseverance in faith, escape it at the resurrection. Similarly, one can participate in the eschatological blessings of the resurrection but forfeit one's place in it through rejection and adherence to the sinful ways of the world. The presence of eternal life now is not identical with that received at the resurrection. The kingdom has presently been inaugurated but remains to be consummated. It is only through the consummation of God's kingdom upon Christ's return that eternal life cannot be lost. This is made evident by the fact that

---

40. Horton states, "If our regeneration is the consequence of God's election, redemption, and effectual calling (Jn 1:12–13; 3:3, 5; 15:16; Ro 9:11–18; Eph 1:4; 2Th 2:12–13; 2Ti 1:9, etc.) rather than our decision and effort, then he will enable us to persevere to the end" (Horton, *Christian Faith*, 682).

41. See Schreiner, "Perseverance and Assurance: A Survey and Proposal," in *Believer's Baptism*, 32–62.

the author of Hebrews specifically identifies participation in eschatological blessings as something which some received who fell away from salvation.[42]

Other texts which are often utilized in the discussion are those which deal with the impossibility of earthly powers' overtaking one's status in Christ, and of the impossibility of God's letting go of one of his children. Boettner writes, "Certainly a sovereign loving God would not permit His ransomed children to thus fall away and perish."[43] Jesus states, for example, in John 6 that "those who come to me I will never cast out" (John 6:37). In chapter 10 he writes, "My Father, who has given them to me, is greater than all, and no one is able to snatch them out of the Father's hand" (John 10:29). Perhaps the lengthiest passage in this vein is from Romans:

> What then shall we say to these things? If God is for us, who can be against us? He who did not spare his own Son but gave him up for us all, how will he not also with him graciously give us all things? Who shall bring any charge against God's elect? It is God who justifies. Who is to condemn? Christ Jesus is the one who died—more than that, who was raised—who is at the right hand of God, who indeed is interceding for us. Who shall separate us from the love of Christ? Shall tribulation, or distress, or persecution, or famine, or nakedness, or danger, or sword? As it is written,
>
> > "For your sake we are being killed all the day long;
> > we are regarded as sheep to be slaughtered."
>
> No, in all these things we are more than conquerors through him who loved us. For I am sure that neither death nor life, nor angels nor rulers, nor things present nor things to come, nor powers, nor height nor depth, nor anything else in all creation, will be able to separate us from the love of God in Christ Jesus our Lord. (Rom 8:31–39)

John Murray says of Romans 8 that one "could rest the argument for the doctrine of perseverance on this one passage."[44] But notice that none of these texts speak of the impossibility of rejecting God and departing from the faith. These passages serve to give hope and encouragement to Christians when they are in doubt about God's care for them. God will never cast out his children; nor will he allow the devil to have authority over them. No

---

42. This is apparent in his description that they had "tasted the powers of the age to come" (Heb 6:5).

43. Boettner, *Reformed Doctrine of Predestination*, 183.

44. Murray, *Redemption Accomplished and Applied*, 157.

earthly circumstance, persecution, trial, or hardship can take away God's love for his people. What is not negated is the possibility that one can reject God's persevering power and walk away.

There are also passages which speak of God's continuing work within his people, which seems to negate a possibility of apostasy.[45] Paul writes to the Philippians, "And I am sure of this, that he who began a good work in you will bring it to completion at the day of Jesus Christ" (Phil 1:6). Paul writes similarly to the Corinthians, "even as the testimony about Christ was confirmed among you—so that you are not lacking in any gift, as you wait for the revealing of our Lord Jesus Christ, who will sustain you to the end, guiltless in the day of our Lord Jesus Christ" (1 Cor 1:6–8). Peter also states, "Blessed be the God and Father of our Lord Jesus Christ! According to his great mercy, he has caused us to be born again to a living hope through the resurrection of Jesus Christ from the dead, to an inheritance that is imperishable, undefiled, and unfading, kept in heaven for you, who by God's power are being guarded through faith for a salvation ready to be revealed in the last time" (1 Pet 1:3–5). This appears to be in tension with the statements of the same authors regarding the necessity of persevering and the possibility of losing one's salvation. One is left with two possibilities. Either all of the statements about the necessity of remaining in the faith and the warnings about falling away are purely hypothetical, or the promises regarding preservation are not absolute. Because of the consistency of warning passages, and the often unavoidable conclusion that they refer to real circumstances and possibilities, the second conclusion is much more probable.

The statements about God's preserving power with regard to his children are pastoral means to encourage those who are receiving the epistles. In a law-gospel context, one preaches warnings about apostasy when the hearers are seemingly content in unrepentant sin or are tempted by false doctrine. When they are confronted with sin and plagued by fear or doubt, gospel promises are to be proclaimed. This seems to be the same manner in which the Apostles utilize these concepts. Note that all of these texts occur within the context of apostolic encouragement. In the case of the two Pauline comments above, this is mentioned among several other specific comments regarding those congregations. They are thus not meant as absolute theological statements about the nature of perseverance and apostasy but as encouraging gospel promises to specific congregations.

---

45. See Boettner, *Reformed Doctrine of Predestination*, 196–201.

Shipwrecked Faith

PERSEVERANCE AND ASSURANCE

There are several pastoral concerns within this discussion of perseverance and apostasy. One of the most important and practical concerns is that of Christian assurance. It is argued on both sides of the divide that the other view lacks a sense of assurance that one can receive of final salvation.

In Reformed theology, one cannot be truly regenerate and fall away from the faith. This raises the question for many people of personal friends and acquaintances. Most Christians have known someone who claimed faith, appeared to display fruit consistent with conversion, and later fell away and rejected the faith. This brings the issue beyond that of the theoretical to relate to personal situations and dilemmas. Regarding those who have fallen away, one must conclude either one of two things: (1) That these people truly were saved and did fall away, hence the Reformed teaching is wrong; or (2) That these people were never saved in the first place. Some have "false faith," think that they are believers, but fall away from the faith. Others have true faith and persevere to the end.

Out of this arises the question of regeneration. How does one have assurance of regeneration? For a Lutheran, one can look to his or her baptism, the sacraments, and the proclamation of forgiveness in absolution. These are objective means by which God continually creates new life and brings forgiveness.[46] God's regeneration is tied to means, namely, word and sacrament. The sacraments are not mere signs of God's favor toward his people which is located elsewhere, but they are themselves acts of grace confronting sin. Thus if one departs from the faith, it need not be asked whether that faith was genuine, but confessed that they have rejected God's means of salvation and thus have cut themselves off from Christ.

For the Reformed theologian, one assesses regeneration by the nature of changed dispositions.[47] Since many who appear to have faith have fallen away, demonstrating that they had false faith, appearance of faith is not enough to guarantee regeneration. Signs must be examined to distinguish between genuine faith and hypocritical faith. Profession is not enough since both profess faith. Looking at the sacraments is not valid because regeneration does not necessarily accompany baptism, and those of both true and false faith can appear to hear and receive the word and the Eu-

---

46. For a book on this theme, see Senkbeil, *Dying to Live*.

47. Calvinistic Baptist preacher John MacArthur has gone so far as to give a list of qualifications, so that people may test whether they are among the elect; see MacArthur, *Saved without a Doubt*.

Part I: Predestination and Free Will

charist with joy. The test ultimately becomes one's works. However, those who have appeared to be Christians but have demonstrated their unbelief through apostasy also have good works, at least externally. Thus outward good works are not sufficient to establish one's regenerative state. Ultimately one is left to an act of introspection wherein one examines motives and thoughts to distinguish true from false faith. This is the problem Jonathan Edwards faced in the great awakening. With so many conversions happening, how was one to determine the true from the false? In his book *Religions Affections*, Edwards probes beyond these outward signs and asks the reader to examine his or her heart: Are your affections changed? Do you really hate sin? Do you love God for God's sake?

The defense for this idea usually comes from the book of 1 John. Calvinistic Baptist preacher Sam Storms writes, for example,

> John's primary emphasis is on the differences between the genuine Christian and the spurious and how to discern between the two. He does the latter by making application of three tests: one doctrinal (elicited by the heretical Christology of the false teachers), one moral (evoked by the licentious and unrighteous lifestyle of the false teachers), and one social (stirred by the arrogant lack of love and compassion for the Christian brethren). These tests accomplish two ends: they expose the false teachers as false, insofar as they "fail" the tests, and they confirm the genuine believers as genuine, insofar as they "pass" the tests.[48]

According to this view, John lays out a series of tests which one must compare oneself to. If one passes these tests, assurance of salvation is granted. But 1 John read in context, with an understanding of first-century protognosticism and its blatant antinomianism, does not support the concept that one must continually look to works as the primary means of assurance that one has genuine faith.[49]

John begins his epistle by stating that "if we walk in the light, as he is in the light, we have fellowship with one another, and the blood of his Son cleanses us from all sin. If we say we have no sin, we deceive ourselves, and the truth is not in us. If we confess our sins, he is faithful and just to forgive us our sins and to cleanse us from all unrighteousness. If we say we have not sinned, we make him a liar, and his word is not in us" (1 John 1:7–10). Before allowing his readers to assume that Christians are expected

---

48. Storms, *Introduction to 1 John*.
49. See Rudolph, *Gnosis*.

to live a sinless life, John reminds his readers that they are *simul iustus et peccator*—both saint and sinner. This serves as a corrective for how his later words could be misconstrued.

John does then begin to write about the necessity of works in the Christian life. He states, "whoever says 'I know him' but does not keep his commandments is a liar and the truth is not in him" (1 John 2:4). It is likely that John does not write this to tell Christians they must judge their works in order to gain assurance of saving faith, but to continue in repentance after they are in the faith. It was characteristic of many early gnostic groups to promote licentious living. Salvation is attained through knowledge, and through escaping the physical world. Therefore whatever one does with the body is irrelevant. Perpetual unrepentant sin was not seen as a barrier to the soul's salvation. John's emphasis on the physical nature of Christ (his language of seeing and touching Christ, or his insistence on Jesus' coming in flesh, for example)[50] along with the antinomianism he is fighting is evidence that he is battling early proto-gnostic groups. Thus John is not writing to doubting believers that they might have a "test" for the genuineness of faith, but rather that he might warn Christians against the early gnostic heresy.

Look, for example, at the second chapter. In verses 7–11, John tells his readers of the necessity of love in the Christian life. After he does this, he does not then tell his readers, "see if you measure up," but something very different. He writes, "I am writing to you, little children, because your sins are forgiven for his name's sake." He does not say "so that you may know *if* your sins are forgiven," but "*because* your sins are forgiven." He then mentions that he is writing to those who "know him" and "have overcome the evil one." This is a use of the indicative and imperative.

John, like the rest of the New Testament authors, assures his readers that through confession of sin and repentance they are forgiven and loved by God. However, he is warning that those who live unrepentant lives, deny the flesh of Christ, and hate their brothers are not of the fold. As Luther's first of the 95 Theses states, "the entire life of the believers [is] to be one of repentance."[51] John is warning his readers against falling away from the true faith into this gnostic heresy, adopting licentious living and denying the humanity of Christ, which he refers to as the "sin that leads to death" (1 John 5:16).

---

50. 1 John 1:1–2.
51. *LW* 31:25.

Part I: Predestination and Free Will

The book of 1 John does not promote the concept that looking to the quality of one's works is necessary to gain assurance of faith. Rather, the message of 1 John is that sin should be confessed, resulting in forgiveness, and that one should not abandon repentance, the church, and the doctrine of the gospel. Works are a necessary fruit of conversion, and can even serve as *a* sign of assurance, but they never become the sole basis by which one judges the genuineness of faith and conversion.

The dilemma regarding assurance stems from the Reformed view of election. When election becomes the primary soteriological motif, the question of salvation becomes "how do I know if I am elect?" One cannot point to the objective work of Christ, because of the exclusive nature of his atonement. Thus, before assurance of Christ's atonement can be achieved, one must look to works as evidence of the Spirit's work. It is only then, when assurance is gained through introspection, that one can look to the objective work of the cross as a means of assurance. Whether or not it is the intention of Calvinistic theology, one is ultimately pointed to one's own works. This traps one in the Augustinian plague which denies assurance to anyone. Though not the intention of most Calvinists, when election becomes central and the cross is put in a secondary position, this is inevitable. If one looks inside oneself for assurance, that person will be driven to despair and doubt. Even the regenerate heart is not completely cleansed from sin. Instead, one must look to Christ, the author and finisher of our faith.

CONCLUSION

The testimony of the New Testament regarding perseverance and apostasy leads to the conclusion that the Lutheran perspective on the issue is correct. It takes the continual warnings in the epistolary literature and the gospels at face value, rather than arguing for a purely hypothetical reading. The Reformed texts and arguments used to defend the perseverance of the saints fail to be ultimately convincing. They neglect considering the pastoral context in which God's promises are given, and they read more into other passages than is actually stated. The Lutheran teaching on perseverance does not make *sola gratia* and the possibility of falling away mutually exclusive claims, but seeks to confess both, though the manner of harmony between the two doctrines is left a mystery. Finally, the Lutheran approach to perseverance is the most pastorally sensitive, giving Christians objective assurance of grace rather than pointing people to their own works.

PART II

Worship and the Sacraments

4

Praising the Triune God
The Nature and Essence of Worship

BEYOND THE DOCTRINAL DIFFERENCES between the Lutheran and Reformed traditions, there are vast differences regarding the nature of corporate worship. The Lutheran Reformation, as a conservative reformation, retained much of the liturgy and piety of the medieval church, whereas the Reformed tradition developed its own unique liturgy and practice.[1] The Reformed adopted a strict form of worship, following only that which the New Testament expressly commands; the Lutheran church practiced the use of liturgy, vestments, hymnody, and art.[2]

THE REGULATIVE PRINCIPLE OF WORSHIP

Central to the disagreements over the nature of worship in the church is the discussion surrounding the regulative principle of worship. This position, maintained by the Reformed, claims that God must be worshiped only in specific ways which are commanded in Scripture.[3] In both the Old and

---

1. See Krauth, *Conservative Reformation*.
2. See Sundberg, *Worship as Repentance*, and Zeedon and Walker, *Faith and Act*.
3. The strictest of the adherents to the regulative principle hold to exclusive Psalmody, neglect the use of instruments in worship due to their supposed connection to the Levitical sacrificial system, and won't celebrate any holy day, including Christmas and Easter. Perhaps the best representative of this strict view is Bushell, *Songs of Zion*.

Part II: Worship and the Sacraments

New Testaments, God gives instructions regarding how worship is to be done, and those instructions must never be violated.[4] This is sometimes called the "regulative principle." The Westminster Confession upholds this principle:

> The light of nature shows that there is a God, who has lordship and sovereignty over all, is good, and does good unto all, and is therefore to be feared, loved, praised, called upon, trusted in, and served, with all the heart, and with all the soul, and with all the might. But the acceptable way of worshiping the true God is instituted by himself, and so limited by his own revealed will, that he may not be worshiped according to the imaginations and devices of men, or the suggestions of Satan, under any visible representation, or any other way not prescribed in the holy Scripture. (WCF XXI.1)

It is only special revelation which is to be the guide in worship, rather than the light of nature. The *sola scriptura* principle relates not only to the formulation of doctrine, but also to the institution and practice of worship.

This principle has been implemented in various ways, the most extreme of which rejects the singing of any songs apart from the Psalms and the use of instruments in worship.[5] Worship was altered early in Zwingli's Reformation.[6] Preaching was at the center of the Swiss worship service; Zwingli displaced the centrality of the Eucharist and at first abolished all music during worship. Eventually singing was reinstated in the Swiss church, albeit in a simplistic fashion without instrumentation. Calvin followed Zwingli's rejection of instrumentation in worship, instituting a service with a simplified liturgy and Psalm singing. In Calvin's approach, a strict observance of biblical commands regarding worship is necessary. Without holding to the regulative principle, one is in danger of adopting medieval Roman Catholic practices which Calvin viewed as idolatrous and superstitious. This resulted in the abolition of traditional vestments, images, instrumentation, the observance of holy days, and hymnody.

---

4. However, the Anglican branch of the Reformation, sometimes labeled as Reformed, rejects this principle in favor of liturgical worship.

5. This is the practice of the Reformed Presbyterian Church of North America.

6. A helpful compilation of essays on the history of Reformed worship can be found in Vischer et al., *Christian Worship in Reformed Churches*.

Praising the Triune God

The Lutheran approach to worship has at times been labeled the "normative principle" of worship.[7] It is proposed that in the normative principle, whatever is not condemned is allowed during worship.[8] This description is somewhat simplistic as it may give the impression that the Lutheran church grants absolute freedom in worship. Lutheran theology necessitates certain elements in worship and denies others, even if these practices are not expressly condemned in Scripture.[9]

The discussion of the nature of divine command in worship in Lutheranism largely revolves around the adiaphoristic controversy in the sixteenth century.[10] Emperor Charles V made several attempts to unite the Roman Catholic and Lutheran churches in his territories.[11] He first proposed the Augsburg Interim, which demanded that Lutherans adopt certain Roman beliefs, practices, and rituals, to which the response was universal rejection. There was however a second attempt known as the Leipzig Interim, which was better received. The Leipzig Interim proposed similar concessions on behalf of the Lutheran church. Melanchthon this time conceded along with other pastors and theologians, arguing that the concessions referred to adiaphora (indifferent matters) rather than to central theological claims. Thus, these elements of worship could be compromised based on their indifferent nature. The Gnesio Lutheran party opposed the Interim and especially Melanchthon's approval of it. The Gnesio party argued that this unnecessarily burdened consciences, forcing Christians to adopt practices which should remain in the realm of Christian freedom. Whatever practices are considered adiaphora can be either accepted or rejected based on preference in one's spirituality. The Formula of Concord states,

> Therefore we believe, teach, and confess that the community of God in every time and place has the right, power, and authority to change, reduce, or expand such practices according to circumstances in an orderly and appropriate manner, without frivolity or offense, as seems most useful, beneficial, and best for good order,

---

7. For more information on worship in the Lutheran tradition, see Just, *Heaven on Earth*. Just expertly examines and explains practically and theologically the various elements of the Lutheran worship service. Another classic on the topic of worship from a Lutheran view is Brunner, *Worship in the Name of Jesus*.

8. Calvinistic Baptist preacher Mark Driscoll discusses this in *Religion Saves*.

9. Anglicans use a similar principle. See Luoma, *Primitive Church*.

10. On this controversy, see Kurt Marquart, "Confessions and Ceremonies," in Preus et al., *Contemporary Look*, 260–70.

11. See Gritsch, *History of Lutheranism*.

> Christian discipline, evangelical decorum, and the building up of the church. Paul teaches how one may yield and make concessions to the weak in faith in such external matters of indifference with good conscience (Rom. 14[:1–23]), and he demonstrates this with his own example (Acts 16[:3] and 21[:26]; 1 Cor. 9[:10]. (FC SD X.9)

Those things which aren't commanded directly by God need not be uniform. The church cannot command certain liturgical practices, because each congregation has freedom to adopt its own liturgy and traditions. Though these things are different, they can be more or less beneficial in differing circumstances. For example, it would be unwise to use ornate liturgy infused with Latin in an inner city church where this culture is utterly foreign. There has to be some pastoral sensitivity. While the use of images in worship can be helpful as a means of instruction, it would be irresponsible to adorn churches with images in a culture particularly prone to idolizing images in a superstitious manner.

This principle does not allow for absolute freedom in worship. Worship is meant to be orderly rather than chaotic, to have elements which edify rather than entertain, and to magnify the gospel rather than obscure it.[12] The type of worship practiced in modern Pentecostalism, often akin to that of Anabaptism, would be condemned by the Lutheran Confessional tradition as an instance of disorderly and distracting worship. This is the case with many movements in the modern church. Though some have argued otherwise, it is not the intent of the Confessions to promote liturgical worship as one option among many, but to allow freedom in the nature of the liturgy.

The so-called normative principle approach promotes worship that is biblically saturated.[13] The liturgy is primarily a combination of biblical statements and theology, along with thoughtful Trinitarian prayer and praise. The central elements commanded in Scripture to be involved in the worship service—prayer, singing, preaching, absolution, and the Eucharist—are the primary tenants of historic liturgical worship. Despite what advocates of the regulative principle may argue, liturgical worship is thoroughly biblically centered and infused.

---

12. Marshall, *Beyond the Bible*, 40–42.
13. See Brauer, *Lutheran Worship*.

Praising the Triune God

ARGUMENTS FOR THE REGULATIVE PRINCIPLE

Much of the argument in support of a strict regulative principle is from the nature of worship from the Old Testament. Derek Thomas outlines some of the basic contentions of the typical Reformed approach to worship:

> Where does the Bible teach this? In more places than is commonly imagined, including the constant stipulation of the book of Exodus with respect to the building of the tabernacle that everything be done "after the pattern . . . shown you" (Ex. 25:40); the judgment pronounced upon Cain's offering, suggestive as it is that his offering (or his heart) was deficient according to God's requirement (Gen. 4:3–8); the first and second commandments showing God's particular care with regard to worship (Ex. 20:2–6); the incident of the golden calf, teaching as it does that worship cannot be offered merely in accord with our own values and tastes; the story of Nadab and Abihu and the offering of "strange fire" (Lev. 10); God's rejection of Saul's non-prescribed worship—God said, "to obey is better than sacrifice" (1 Sam. 15:22); and Jesus' rejection of Pharisaical worship according to the "tradition of the elders" (Matt. 15:1–14). All of these indicate a rejection of worship offered according to values and directions other than those specified in Scripture.[14]

Thomas' arguments come primarily from the nature of worship in the Old Testament. God gave his people specific regulations regarding worship; when those principles were violated, the perpetrator was punished. It is often argued by Calvinists that the giving of the second commandment (part of the first commandment for Lutherans) promotes a view of worship in which human creativity is negated:

> You shall not make for yourself a carved image, or any likeness of anything that is in heaven above, or that is in the earth beneath, or that is in the water under the earth. You shall not bow down to them or serve them, for I the Lord your God am a jealous God, visiting the iniquity of the fathers on the children to the third and the fourth generation of those who hate me, but showing steadfast love to thousands of those who love me and keep my commandments. (Exod 20:4–6)

---

14. Thomas, "Regulative Principle of Worship."

Part II: Worship and the Sacraments

Many conservative Reformed theologians argue that this text forbids the use of any images in worship.[15] This includes especially images of God, including that of Christ. The nature of God expressed in this commandment as "jealous," it is argued, negates possible innovation such as using art or other imagery. God is jealous for worship in his own prescribed manner, thus one should worship only in the way that he commands. God's holiness is so great that one cannot hope to approach him in any human-created manner, but only as he expressly gives instruction. This applies not only to idol making, but to all elements of worship.

As Thomas writes, this is defended by demonstrating that God's judgment was placed upon those who did not obey his strict instructions regarding worship. The book of Leviticus tells of Nadab and Abihu, who attempted to worship God in a manner incommensurate with God's express command.[16] They offered God a fire in his name, but because this act was not authorized by the law, God killed both of them. Many argue that this is also the sin of Cain, who, unlike Abel, worshiped God with a sacrifice that had not been prescribed. There is another similar story in the book of Samuel, wherein Saul gives a sacrifice to God which was not commanded.[17] Instead of waiting for the prophet Samuel, as Saul was instructed to, Saul appointed his own time of sacrifice. This act caused Samuel to pronounce curses on Saul and eventually led to his dethronement and the installation of David as king. It is argued that in these circumstances, even if one's heart is genuine and a desire to serve God is present, neglecting God's express command regarding worship brings judgment.

The Old Testament gives hundreds of details regarding the nature of worship. It gives the proper dimensions of the temple, the location of worship, the nature of priesthood, the clothing to be worn by priests, the appointed times of worship, specific sacrifices, and even an inspired Psalter. All of this demonstrates God's concern with his own glory through specific acts of human worship. Due to the unity of the Testaments, this principle is extended through the church and necessitates the same strict adherence to God's appointed manner of worship.[18]

15. See, for example, Packer, *Knowing God*.

16. Lev 10:1–3.

17. 1 Sam 13:1–14.

18. This is due to the influence of Presbyterian covenant theology, which emphasizes the unity of the covenants, viewing all of Scripture as comprising the covenant of works and covenant of grace. A good introduction to covenant theology can be found in Horton, *God of Promise*. It is to be noted that there are various strands of covenant

Praising the Triune God

Another argument used in favor of the regulative principle, one which does not arise directly from Old Testament revelation, is from human propensity for idolatry. This is apparent throughout church history. Practices began in the early church which may have been initiated with good intentions but eventually led to idolatry. For example, the church decided in the first few centuries to honor its martyrs by keeping bones and venerating their memory.[19] Though this may have begun innocently, it led to the development of the medieval concept of relics and the abuses on indulgences which led to the Reformation. This type of development has been demonstrated since the Old Testament, wherein the people sought to worship God through the means of a golden calf. This was condemned by God as pure idolatry. Because of the fallen nature of humankind, people have a propensity to invent their own ways of worship which are directly contrary to God's express purpose. To follow only God's specific commands in worship protects one from the temptation toward idolatrous worship.

There are several reasons why these Reformed arguments are unconvincing. First, the regulative principle fails to distinguish between the nature of the Old and New Covenants. Mosaic worship was typological, prefiguring the priesthood and sacrifice of Christ, as well as the nature of eschatological life. The principles of Levitical worship are not to be applied to the New Covenant church. The types and shadows have faded as Christ came as the antitype, negating the necessity of Mosaic modes of worship. The assumption of the Reformed is that while certain forms of worship have passed away, the strict nature of worship has not. The form has changed, but the essence remains. However, there is no justification for this approach in New Testament worship. The Old Testament contained specific commands regarding worship, such that the nature and character of worship is unambiguous. Along with this were specific punishments and examples of judgment for disobedience. The New Testament does not contain such commands. There is no guide to worship in the New Covenant as there was for the Old. There are passing references in the New Testament to the structure of the church and the nature of the worship service, though no order of service or explanation of how these elements cohere is present. This implies a freedom which was not present in Levitical worship.

---

theology, thus Horton is not representative of the entire federal tradition.

19. As Peter Brown has demonstrated in *Cult of the Saints*, the veneration of martyrs had more to do with the Christian insistence on resurrection than adopting pagan practices, as many often argue.

Part II: Worship and the Sacraments

Second, Jesus himself does not follow a strict regulative principle. The prevalence of the synagogue in the New Testament is not a reflection of God's express command for Levitical worship, but is a later development. The synagogue is an intertestamental institution, created as a means by which those separated from the temple would have access to worship, public Scripture reading, and an educational facility.[20] The synagogue was led by elders and had its own structure of worship. According to the regulative principle, this would be an example of human innovation in worship. Yet Jesus, rather than rebuking the leaders of the synagogue for their innovations in worship, went to the synagogue and taught there. This is an implicit approval of its existence. This allows for the development of worship practices throughout time, so long as they are in accord with sound doctrine. It also demonstrates that different liturgical practices and customs can be developed to handle specific situations which develop in time.[21]

Finally, a strict adherence to the regulative principle is not even practiced by those who profess to adopt it. This does not necessarily prove that the idea is wrong, but it demonstrates the fact that it is a hard principle to adopt in practicality. Many Reformed churches still utilize elements in worship which are not explicitly commanded. For example, it is common to practice the recitation of the ecumenical creeds or elements of the Reformed Confessions. Reformed churches make choices regarding worship each Sunday apart from that which is directly commanded in Scripture. For example, churches make a decision as to how they should look, how the minister is dressed, the sound of their music, the length of sermons, the order of the different elements of worship, etc. It is argued by proponents of the regulative principle that these "circumstances" in worship are different from the substance, or elements, of worship.[22] There is freedom to make de-

---

20. See Bender, *Into the Temple Courts*.

21. This is also apparent in that the apostolic church merely adopted the synagogal structure of authority until such time as the church grew, and in that new situation it adopted an episcopal system.

22. Some recent Reformed interpreters have also recognized that this distinction is largely arbitrary. See Gore, *Covenantal Worship*. John Frame has also utilized the same critiques. See his essay, Frame, "Fresh Look at the Regulative Principle." This article was written for a book on the subject which was never released, and gives a comprehensive Reformed critique of the typical understanding of the Puritanical regulative principle. Particularly important is Frame's contention that the elements/circumstances distinction is Aristotelian, deriving from the substance/accidence distinction of Aristotle.

Another source which is helpful is Frame's email debate with Darryl Hart on the issue. Hart takes the traditional view and Frame takes the modified view: Frame and

cisions regarding things indifferent, such as the time of a worship service. This, however, is distinct from the nature of the service itself. But this divide seems forced and unnecessary. The so-called "circumstances" of worship have as much effect on the worship life of a congregation as other elements. Since people are holistic, they are affected not only by what is heard in a sermon, but also by the looks of the church building and sanctuary, the smells of the building, the clothing of the minister, and the furnishings in the building. The Old Testament law recognizes the importance of such elements and thus prescribes specific visuals, surroundings, clothing, and smells. If the New Testament had constructed a similar concept limiting worship to specific elements, it would have also contained such commands. In reality, all churches must make decisions regarding the nature of a worship service and even the look of the church building and the appearance of the minister. The distinction between the circumstances and essence of worship is arbitrary.

CONFESSION AND ABSOLUTION

A central element of the Lutheran worship service is the "third sacrament" of Holy Absolution.[23] In the beginning of the Divine Service, the congregation confesses their sinfulness and how they have dishonored God in their actions throughout the week. The minister then declares God's forgiveness over the congregation. The Reformed have, since Calvin, adopted a similar confession of sins at the beginning of the worship service. One example of such a confession is from Calvin:

> Lord God, eternal and almighty Father: We acknowledge before your holy majesty that we are poor sinners, conceived and born in guilt and in corruption, prone to do evil, unable of our own power to do good. Because of our sin, we endlessly violate your holy commandments. But, O Lord, with heartfelt sorrow we repent and turn away from all our offenses. We condemn ourselves and our evil ways, with true sorrow asking that your grace will relieve our distress. Have compassion on us, most gracious God, Father of mercies, for the sake of your son Jesus Christ our Lord. And in removing our guilt, also grant us daily increase of the grace of your Holy Spirit, and produce in us the fruits of holiness and

---

Hart, "Regulative Principle."

23. Fred L. Precht, "Confession and Absolution: Sin and Forgiveness," in *Lutheran Worship*, 322–86.

of righteousness pleasing in your sight: Through Jesus Christ our Lord. *Amen.*[24]

There is unity between the two traditions regarding the necessity of corporate confession of guilt. However, there is a difference in the nature of absolution. When the pastor speaks words of absolution in a Reformed congregation following the corporate confession of sin, they are reminders of God's grace and forgiveness toward those who have confessed. The minister might point to the many promises in Scripture regarding God's mercy and his promise to forgive those who are penitent.[25] In the Lutheran tradition, absolution is more than a description or a reminder of God's mercy. A common form of absolution in Lutheranism involves the pastor declaring unto the repentant sinner, "In the stead and by the command of my Lord Jesus Christ I forgive you all your sins in the name of the Father and of the Son and of the Holy Spirit."[26] Absolution comes to the sinner as a declarative word, bringing the forgiveness it proclaims.[27] It may be objected that this follows a Roman Catholic view of the sacrament, and of the nature of the priestly office. If the pastor declares forgiveness, the minister becomes a *de facto* priest and intercessor between God and the congregation, obscuring the mediatory role of Christ. There are a few things to be said in response to this claim.

First, a distinction needs to be made between a Lutheran and Roman view of ordination. In Roman Catholic theology, ordination is a sacrament. When the priest is ordained, there is an ontological change; there is indelible mark placed onto the individual's character. He is declared an "*alter Christus*," meaning "another Christ." The man who is ordained becomes a priest and is able to offer up sacrifices to God on behalf of the congregation and to re-present Christ's sacrifice during the mass.[28]

In a Lutheran view of ordination, there is no indelible mark placed on the individual. Ordination is not a sacrament, and there is no special grace thereby received by the one ordained. However, ordination is a divine call. It is a call from God, enacted through the church, which places one into a specific office in the church. In this office, one is to preach the word

---

24. This, along with several other historic Reformed liturgical elements, can be found online at *Reformed Worship Resources*.

25. 1 John 1:9 is probably the most common.

26. This is the absolution used throughout the *Lutheran Service Book*.

27. See Chemnitz, *Loci Theologici* 3:1198–200.

28. See Baker, *Fundamentals of Catholicism* 2:316–33.

and administer the sacraments. The pastor's calling is not higher than other essential roles in the church; it is merely different. Thus all roles in the body of Christ are significant, and no one needs to be placed above another as if a pastor is on a higher spiritual plane than other members of the church. But because of the divine nature of the call, the pastoral office should not and cannot be usurped by the laity, and the pastor should not usurp the role of the laity either.[29]

It is apparent that the Roman and Lutheran views of ordination are different. What Luther feared about the priesthood's laying claim to aspects of Christ's own unique priesthood was done away with during the Reformation. However, Luther still promoted the pastoral office as one in which God acts to forgive sins. This may still open the Lutheran view to the charge that the pastor becomes a co-mediator and obscures Christ's own intercessory role, thereby denying the central tenant of the Reformation.

This dilemma can easily be solved if one examines the concept of mediator and thinks about what Paul means by describing Christ as sole mediator.[30] A mediator is a go-between, acting in an intercessory role between two parties. Technically, if you pray for someone else, you are acting as a mediator. If my brother falls into sin and I pray for his repentance and forgiveness, I am interceding for my brother, being a mediator between him and God. The point is that Christ has a unique mediatory role which does not negate others as mediators in a lesser sense. Unless one is willing to deny the necessity of intercessory prayer, Paul's meaning cannot exclude mediation in a lesser sense. In the instance of confession and absolution, Christ's mediatory role is not being violated. Rather, it is being emphasized and enacted. This is apparent in the fact that Christ himself commands the leaders of the church to absolve and retain sins. This is apparent in the following two texts:

> "I will give you the keys of the kingdom of heaven, and whatever you bind on earth shall be bound in heaven, and whatever you loose on earth shall be loosed in heaven." (Matt 16:19)

> "If you forgive the sins of any, they are forgiven them; if you withhold forgiveness from any, it is withheld." (John 20:23)

---

29. See Wengert, *Priesthood, Pastors, and Bishops*.
30. 1 Tim 2:5.

Part II: Worship and the Sacraments

John commands his disciples, the leaders of the first-century church, to forgive sins. He does not tell them to talk about the forgiveness of sins as in the common Reformed practice, or tell them where to receive the forgiveness of sins; rather, Jesus commands the actual forgiving of sins by his disciples.[31] One can only arrive at another meaning of this text by severely distorting its plain meaning. Remember that it is the same John who writes the epistle wherein he commands personal confession to God for forgiveness,[32] who also writes of the forgiveness that the disciples could offer those in the church. The two concepts are not mutually exclusive. God does forgive sins through confession in prayer. However, he has also instituted a means by which the forgiveness that we receive can be heard and received visibly. This does not mean that Christ is obscured, but that when the minister proclaims forgiveness, it is the act of God coming through the pastor to bring forgiveness. It does not point away from Christ's mediatory role but points to the one who continues to be the church's intercessor. It is not the pastoral office that makes the word effective. It is not that the pastor's words and actions have magical powers. Rather, it is the word itself which is effective; the minister is merely a means to bring that word to people's ears, and forgiveness to sinful saints.

Though the Reformed have a consistent tradition of corporate confession which reflects the New Testament and patristic teaching, it neglects the biblical doctrine of absolution. Through the institution of absolution, Jesus grants the church a means whereby forgiveness is granted corporately to the church.[33] The minister is a tool to bring God's forgiveness, not a co-mediator with Christ. Absolution emphasizes Christ's role as mediator rather than obscuring it.

THE USE OF IMAGES IN WORSHIP

Among the various practical elements affected by the adoption of the regulative principle of worship is the nature of images and art. The Reformed

---

31. Forde makes a distinction between two modes of discourse: One talks about a thing; the other is a direct address. This is helpful when discussing absolution. See Forde, *Theology Is for Proclamation*.

32. 1 John 1:9.

33. Many Lutherans are also recently promoting the ancient practice of private confession as well, which has much pastoral wisdom and patristic backing. I am unaware if such a practice exists in any Reformed churches.

have argued that the use of images in worship is a violation of the second commandment and encourages idolatry.[34] Lutherans have used images liberally in worship, viewing them as powerful tools to bring the gospel message to people through a visible means.[35] Before arguing for the correctness of the Lutheran view, some misconceptions must be addressed.

Lutherans do not venerate icons. At the second council of Nicea in 787, the issue of images was at hand. One side, known as the iconoclasts, was against the use of images altogether. For the iconoclasts, churches should not be adorned at all with pictures of Jesus or the saints. The other position, represented most adequately by John of Damascus, argued that icons of Jesus, Mary, the angels, and the saints should be displayed in churches and homes. One could venerate (in distinction from worship) the icons.[36] When one venerates the icon, he is not venerating the picture, but what it represents. This distinction between veneration (*dulia* in Latin) and worship (*latria*) remains the means by which it is explained in the Roman Catholic and Eastern Orthodox churches that the adoration of saints does not necessitate idolatry because it is not worship.

While the Reformed have traditionally accepted the iconoclast position, Lutherans have not adopted either position in the debate. The Lutheran fathers rejected the abuse of images in medieval piety as well as the strict iconoclasm of the Reformed and Anabaptist churches.[37] There are several reasons why the Damascene position has not been adopted in the sense in which the Orthodox Church has defined it.[38]

First, Lutherans do not venerate the saints in the same manner as the Eastern church. The saints should be commended and remembered for their great faith and example in this life.[39] It is not uncommon to see icons of saints in Lutheran households and churches. Many Lutherans also adopt a historic church calendar wherein certain feast days are held in remembrance of great saints. This includes both biblical saints as well as venerable

---

34. See Eire, *War against the Idols*, and Wandel, *Voracious Idols and Violent Hands*.

35. Kretzmann, *Christian Art*.

36. Writings of John of Damascus on this topic have been helpfully compiled in John of Damascus, *On the Divine Images*.

37. The best treatment of this subject is from Chemnitz, *Examination* 4:55–141.

38. For a short introduction to the Orthodox perspective on this, see Cavarnos, *Orthodox Iconography*.

39. This is the purpose of Hebrews 11, for example, a favorite text to use on All Saints Day. For the Confessional basis for this, see Apol XXI.4–6.

figures in church history.[40] However, Lutherans do not pray to or perform any act which could be conceived as worship to the saints. While the veneration/worship distinction is valuable in that it stops the Roman and Orthodox churches from blatant idolatry, it is somewhat arbitrary. Scripture does not make such a distinction. Acts of adoration such as prayer and prostrating oneself are limited to one's worship of God. Performing these acts to anyone else, whether a saint, the blessed virgin, or an angel, detracts from acts which should be reserved for God alone. Second, Scripture does not imply that icons are a window into the heavenly realms. This is the rationale behind the Eastern Orthodox view of icons, wherein the physical picture becomes a window into the spiritual realm. While this idea promotes an incarnational and sacramental view of reality which is in accord with the Lutheran insistence on the principle that the finite *is* capable of the infinite, this concept is not taught in Scripture. Believing in *sola scriptura*, one cannot adopt this approach.

There is a positive use of images which does not necessitate adopting the abuses of some which lead to unintended idolatry. Lutherans use images, icons, and statues as tools to instruct and remind people of central elements of their faith. The crucifix is a constant reminder of the gospel. It is often placed in the sanctuary to remind both the pastor and the congregation that Christ and his cross are the center of the church's worship life. Churches use images of saints to remind the congregation of the great faith of those who have come before them, and to remind them of the unity of the church in heaven and on earth. It is a valuable picture of the communion of saints as expressed in the creed.

Though the Reformed claim to adopt the scriptural position on the issue and that any other position necessitates idolatry, there are a few reasons why the Reformed approach is untenable. The primary argument used by iconoclasts is from the same text used in reference to the regulative principle of worship. It is the second (first for Lutherans) commandment.[41]

> You shall not make for yourself a carved image, or any likeness of anything that is in heaven above, or that is in the earth beneath, or that is in the water under the earth. You shall not bow down to

---

40. The *Lutheran Service Book* contains a list of celebrated feast days in the Lutheran Church—Missouri Synod (*Lutheran Service Book*, xxii–xxiii).

41. The numbering of the commandments in the two respective traditions likely affects the piety of the people. The Reformed, having a separate commandment regarding the worship of images, tend to be much more sensitive to images, whereas the rejection of image worship is included within the first commandment in Lutheran catechesis.

them or serve them, for I the Lord your God am a jealous God, visiting the iniquity of the fathers on the children to the third and the fourth generation of those who hate me, but showing steadfast love to thousands of those who love me and keep my commandments. (Exod 20:4)

The Reformed have typically utilized this commandment in reference, not only to portrayals of God the Father, or to the Holy Trinity, but also to images of the incarnate Christ. The second commandment forbids images of God, and Jesus is God; therefore, the commandment forbids images of Christ. In the most extreme circumstances, some even reject imaging Christ with one's mind as idolatrous. J. I. Packer writes,

> The realization that images and pictures of God affect our thoughts of God points to a further realm in which the prohibition of the second commandment applies. Just as it forbids us to manufacture molten images of God, so it forbids us to dream up mental images of him. Imagining God in our heads can be just as real a breach of the second commandment as imagining him by the work of our hands.[42]

The focus of the text of the second commandment (first for Lutherans) is the negation of idolatrous worship through the use of images and statues. In the ancient Near East, it was common for religions to venerate statues of false gods. As did many other laws given to Israel, this law served to protect the people of Israel from the corruption of the false religions of surrounding nations. Contrary to the Reformed insistence, it does not oppose using images for any purpose whatsoever. This is clear from the fact that Israel was actually commanded to make images in other texts; for example:

> You shall make a mercy seat of pure gold. Two cubits and a half shall be its length, and a cubit and a half its breadth. And you shall make two cherubim of gold; of hammered work shall you make them, on the two ends of the mercy seat. Make one cherub on the one end, and one cherub on the other end. Of one piece with the mercy seat shall you make the cherubim on its two ends. The cherubim shall spread out their wings above, overshadowing the mercy seat with their wings, their faces one to another; toward the mercy seat shall the faces of the cherubim be. And you shall put the mercy seat on the top of the ark, and in the ark you shall put the testimony that I shall give you. There I will meet with you, and

---

42. J. I. Packer, *Knowing God*, 48.

from above the mercy seat, from between the two cherubim that are on the ark of the testimony, I will speak with you about all that I will give you in commandment for the people of Israel. (Exod 25:17–22)

This command to create images was not for pure decoration but for religious purposes. These images were commanded to be placed at the location of the ark, the most holy place in Jewish piety. Thus, the moderated use of images in a worship setting is admissible. If God commanded the use of images in the Old Testament, it is a valid practice for the church; though it ought to be moderated so as to avoid idolatry.

One may object that images of saints and angels are permissible, but images of God are not. John of Damascus refuted this argument by discussing the nature of the incarnation.[43] Icons do not show the Holy Trinity in majesty (though Andrei Rublev's famous painting of the Trinity is admissible because it pictures the Trinity in a specific form explained in Scripture through the story of Abraham), but they portray the incarnated God. In taking an image upon himself, Christ unites the divine to that which is created and can be viewed. To argue otherwise denies the worldliness of the incarnation. Jesus had a face which could be seen, remembered, and (if the technology had existed) photographed. Some more extreme forms of the regulative principle argue that it is idolatrous even to picture Jesus in one's mind as a specific person; one does not know the actual look of Jesus, so one will be picturing a man as God. This argument so radically divorces the divine from humanity that it almost becomes a denial of the incarnation. One cannot think about a person without imagining a body and even a face and hair in a vague sense. To do otherwise is to make Christ into a mere idea, an abstraction. It may be objected that Christ is often visually portrayed as a white male, and thus these images are invalid because they are distinct from the Jewish man that Jesus actually was. This is not necessarily a flaw, however. Each culture pictures Jesus as being of the same ethnicity of that culture. There are African, Asian, and Indian paintings of Christ. This is not idolatrous, but is a recognition that in becoming incarnate as an individual, Jesus unites himself to all humankind, redeeming people of all races. Thus paintings of Jesus through different ethnicities demonstrate the universality of his redemption. They need to be viewed as symbolic rather than literal representations of Christ. One does, however, need to be careful not to extract from this that Jesus is a universal principle of deity becoming

---

43 John of Damascus, *On the Divine Images*.

united to humanity. Jesus was a concrete individual in a Jewish culture. In another sense, Jesus is united to all in that he redeems people from all ethnicities and cultures.

THE NATURE AND PURPOSE OF PREACHING

Both the Zwinglian and Lutheran reformations can rightly be called reformations of the word. Tantamount to the various reform movements in the sixteenth century was a recovery of the importance of Scripture. This focus on the importance of the Bible led to the practice of exegetical preaching, liturgy in the vernacular, and Bible translations. This word-centric focus is also demonstrated through the hymnody of both branches of the Reformation. However, despite the agreements on the importance of the word and of preaching, the meaning and purpose of preaching differs in both reform movements.

For the Reformed, preaching has typically taken the form of extended exposition and Bible study. Zwingli, when he began his reformation in Zurich, preached directly through the New Testament beginning with the gospel of Matthew. Calvin followed the same tradition in preaching through specific books of the Bible.[44] Reformed sermons are typically composed of verse-by-verse exposition, wherein the preacher expounds upon the historical background of the text, discussing textual issues and explaining the meaning of Greek and Hebrew vocabulary. Interspersed within this exposition are practical applications and theological claims. Essentially, preaching takes the form of an extended study of Scripture. It is appropriate that the typical vestment of the Reformed preacher is the "Geneva gown," which is a doctoral robe. Preaching in Calvinistic congregations is lengthy, and is essentially an academic exercise with practical application.

A distinction must be made, however, between different preaching traditions within the Reformed movement. Puritan preaching laid a heavy emphasis on Christian living, the nature of good works, and the experiential nature of grace.[45] It has sometimes been said that the Puritans "have the theology of Augustine but preach like Pelagius." This reflects the emphasis on the third use of the law in Puritan preaching. It is common for these sermons to contain extended discussions of specific sins which infect the lives of the congregants, along with practical advice as to how one

---

44. See Parker, *Calvin's Preaching*, and Lawson, *Expository Genius of John Calvin*.
45. See Gangi, *Great Themes in Puritan Preaching*.

should stop committing these particular sins. In later Puritan preaching, especially as Puritanism was formulated in early America, the focus soon became Christian experience.[46] Preaching challenged the authenticity of one's conversion experience and encouraged extensive introspection to gain assurance of one's regenerate state.

The Dutch Reformed tradition typically avoided the moralism of the Puritan model of preaching, instead emphasizing redemptive history.[47] In this perspective, preaching takes the form of narrating biblical events in view of Christological typology. Covenant theology is central to this movement, wherein the Bible is studied as a progressive narrative about various covenants which God makes with mankind. These covenants culminate in the life, death, and resurrection of Christ. Soteriology became more central to this movement than the heavy third-use-of-the-law emphasis of Puritanism. Despite the severe differences between the two Reformed methodologies of preaching, there are some important points of agreement. Both movements utilize an expositional method of preaching and preach through books of the Bible, often expounding upon a single verse for a lengthy sermon.

Gerhard Forde distinguishes between two modes of theological discourse.[48] The first is that which talks *about* God. It describes the nature of God, salvation, and the sacraments. This is distinct from the second form of address, which is that of direct address. Rather than speaking *about* theology, this is an act of proclamation which delivers a message that requires a response. It is not descriptive, but proclamatory.[49] Though this idea has sometimes been taken to an unhelpful extreme, his distinction helps to formulate some of the differences between a typical Reformed and generally Protestant approach to preaching, and that of Luther.[50]

---

46. Stout, *New England Soul*.

47. The best modern treatment of this approach to preaching is Clowney, *Preaching Christ in All of Scripture*.

48. This is expounded upon in Forde, *Theology Is for Proclamation*.

49. Forde does, however, divorce these two modes of speech from each other in a manner that is not tenable. In a sense, no statement is purely active without any content behind the statement. Such a phrase as "you are forgiven," has several presuppositions behind it about sin, grace, Christ, and the cross. Thus "secondary discourse" is more important than Forde is willing to admit.

50. In conversations with pastors, I have sometimes been told that preaching is not catechetical but simply proclamatory. This idea gives precedence to the "speech-act" or forgiveness over the objective facts of theology, which is ultimately a false dichotomy.

Praising the Triune God

In the Lutheran tradition, preaching is distinct from Bible study.[51] The first mode of theologizing is important, and expositional Bible study is necessary and should be practiced. However, the pulpit involves something beyond a simple descriptive exposition of a text. Preaching serves also as proclamation. God's word is to be delivered in two forms: law and gospel.[52] This models the prophetic mode of speech, wherein theology is not merely descriptive, but the prophets proclaim both judgment and salvation to their readers. Similarly, the pastor declares God's judgment over sin. The preaching of the law does not merely tell people of their sins, but the law itself crushes them under the weight of their sins. The word of God's law convicts; it shuts the mouths of those who listen as they are confronted with their sin. The minister also proclaims the gospel. The message that one's sins are forgiven does not just describe something which is true, but itself *delivers* that forgiveness. God calls by means of his word.

Exposition of a text in a sermon is helpful and necessary, and giving some background to what the author is saying is beneficial to the congregation. The sermon should also contain catechetical instruction, so that the congregants learn about Christian doctrine through preaching. However, preaching must still be strongly distinguished from Bible study. Preaching takes the form of proclamation wherein law and gospel are declared, crushing the old sinful selves of the listeners and granting forgiveness and raising the new self through proclamation of the gospel. The third use of the law does have implications for preaching as well. It is important for the minister to exhort his listeners unto love for their neighbors and other good works. A distinction must be made here between one's righteousness *coram Deo* (before God), and one's righteousness *coram mundo* (before the world). In the vertical realm, before God, the law always accuses. It is here that one sees the insufficiency of one's own works and is pointed to the all-sufficiency of Christ. In the horizontal realm, before others, the law serves as a guide by which Christians are taught how to love and serve those around them. In this way, both the second and third uses of the law are at work in preaching. Exhortations to obedience must, however, always be proclaimed in light of the gospel. One's active righteousness in the world flows from the passive righteousness that God gives in Christ.[53]

---

51. A great early manual of Lutheran preaching can be found in Hendrix, *Preaching the Reformation*.

52. The classic text on this is Walther, *Proper Distinction between Law and Gospel*.

53. This is often labeled the "two kinds of righteousness." Faith ascends to heaven

Part II: Worship and the Sacraments

CONCLUSION

It has been shown that there are several differences between the Reformed and Lutheran traditions regarding the nature of worship. The Reformed hold to the regulative principle of worship, promoting the idea that there is a specific worship model in the New Testament which must be followed exclusively. The Lutheran tradition has adopted historic liturgical practices as valid and helpful means by which the church has expressed her praise throughout the centuries. The Reformed approach has been demonstrated to be arbitrary, making the unfounded distinction between the circumstances and essence of worship. The New Testament does not forbid the use of images, but only of idolizing images. Thus, the Reformed argument that images of Christ are idolatrous is unfounded. Finally, there are important differences regarding the nature of preaching. In the Calvinistic tradition, preaching is primarily exposition, a lengthy Bible study; in the Lutheran tradition, preaching is the proclamation of law and gospel.

---

and receives Christ's righteousness. This is passive righteousness, or justification. Faith also extends itself outward in love toward the neighbor. This is active righteousness. Joel Biermann expounds upon this in *Case for Character*.

5

The Washing of Regeneration
The Sacrament of Baptism

THE LUTHERAN CHURCH HAS differentiated itself from the broader Protestant world by its sacramental nature. While the Reformed and Anabaptist traditions sought to differentiate themselves from medieval tradition by holding to the primacy of the word over the sacraments, the Lutheran tradition formed itself in a patristic manner, giving the word *and* sacraments primacy in the church. The difference between these approaches has demonstrated itself in how the Lutheran tradition and the broader Protestant tradition have approached the doctrine of baptism. This is apparent in modern church history through the de-sacramentalizing nature of the contemporary church. In the broader Evangelical movement, baptism does not hold a significant place in Christian life apart from use as a symbol of one's conversion experience. In the Presbyterian and Reformed tradition, infant baptism is practiced, but the doctrine of baptismal regeneration is neglected.

LUTHER AND CALVIN ON BAPTISM

While agreeing on the necessity of baptizing infants in contradistinction to the radical Anabaptist movement, the sixteenth-century Reform movements of Luther and Calvin differed in their approach to the purpose and meaning of baptism.[1] While Luther retained the patristic teaching of baptismal regeneration—while rejecting the medieval *ex opere operato* approach to it—Calvin followed Zwingli in promoting a covenantal view of baptism which negates a full-orbed doctrine of baptismal regeneration.

Luther's approach to baptism is apparent in his catechetical writings.[2] He states that baptism "works the forgiveness of sins, rescues from death and the devil, and gives all eternal salvation who believe this, as the words and promises of God declare" (SC IV). Luther adopts a literal reading of baptismal passages, assuming that when Scripture speaks of the soteriological benefits of baptism, it speaks literally rather than symbolically or analogously. In Luther's approach, baptism saves. As the Augsburg Confession states, "Concerning baptism, our churches teach that baptism is necessary for salvation and that God's grace is offered through baptism" (AC IX). Baptism is not purely a symbol of grace that is received through faith. Baptism genuinely offers and gives grace to the recipient. Though some might confuse the Lutheran view of baptism with the Roman *ex opere operato* approach, there are significant differences. In the Roman system, one who is baptized is placed in a state of grace regardless of one's personal faith. This grace is lost through committing a mortal sin, at which point one must perform penance, which is the second plank of salvation.[3] Commensurate with Luther's contention of the primacy of faith in salvation, baptismal regeneration is dependent upon faith. Since faith is a gift, God gives the gift of faith to the recipient, even as an infant.[4] For Luther, the benefits of the sacrament are given indiscriminately, but faith must be present to receive these benefits. Unbelief does not negate the sacrament but rejects its blessings.[5]

---

1. See Spinks, *Reformation and Modern Rituals*; and Fisher, *Christian Initiation*.

2. On Luther's view of baptism see Trigg, *Baptism in the Theology of Martin Luther*; Stjerna, *No Greater Jewel*; Althaus, *Theology of Martin Luther*, 353–74; and Lohse, *Martin Luther's Theology*, 298–305.

3. See *Catechism of the Catholic Church* 1213–85, 342–58.

4. As Althaus says, "Children must believe for themselves and must believe at the time of baptism. The fact that they do so is not to be doubted. Since Christ both promises the kingdom of heaven to children and says, 'He who does not believe will be condemned,' who can maintain that the children he receives into his kingdom so not believe? If the church seriously practices infant baptism as a means of salvation, it thereby necessarily confesses that children can believe" (*Theology of Martin Luther*, 365).

5. "Hence it follows that whoever rejects baptism rejects God's word, faith, and Christ, who directs and binds us to baptism" (LC 29).

The Washing of Regeneration

Calvin's approach to baptism serves as a mediating view between Luther and the pure symbolism of Anabaptism. He writes that "Baptism is the sign of initiation by which we are received into the society of the church, in order that, engrafted in Christ, we may be reckoned among God's children."[6] This is not pure symbolism. In Calvin's view, baptism is not a work of man which serves as a public profession of faith; he expressly states in the same chapter, "they who regard baptism as nothing but a token and a mark by which we confess our religion before men . . . have not weighed what was the chief point of baptism. It is to receive baptism with this promise: 'He who believes and is baptized will be saved.'"[7] While demonstrating the broad chasm between Calvin's view of the sacrament and some contemporary Reformed theology, these quotes highlight a difference between Calvin's and Luther's approaches. For Luther, the grace given to the recipient in baptism, including infants, is the Holy Spirit himself.[8] For Calvin, the gift given is grace, but this grace comes through entrance into the ecclesial community. There is a connection between one's relation to the Spirit and baptism, but only as the Spirit is present with the church. Calvin's approach to election negates Luther's approach to baptismal regeneration. For Calvin, saving grace is irresistible and necessarily results in both conversion and preservation. Thus, unless Calvin is willing to grant final salvation to all of the baptized, there must be a divide between the sacramental act and the grace received.

The Reformed tradition has not yet arrived at a consensus regarding the purpose and effect of baptism.[9] Many in Reformed churches unknowingly adopt a Zwinglian approach, wherein infant baptism is a symbol given in hope of future faith.[10] Others hold to the doctrine of presumptive regeneration,[11] wherein it is professed that after baptism an infant should be presumed regenerate and treated as a Christian believer. However, with

---

6. Calvin, *Institutes* IV.XV.

7. Ibid. Scripture cited from Mark 16:16.

8. "Christians always have enough to do to believe firmly what baptism promises and brings—victory over death and the devil, forgiveness of sin, God's grace, the entire Christ, and the Holy Spirit with his gifts" (LC IV.31).

9. What I have found to be the best Reformed treatment of baptism is Murray, *Christian Baptism*. Unfortunately, Murray does not treat the subject of baptismal regeneration in any depth in this volume. He points to Hodge's *Systematic Theology* on the issue, though Hodge's criticism is of the Roman rather than the Lutheran view.

10. Charles Hodge being a notable example; see *Systematic Theology*, 526–611.

11. Most famously, Abraham Kuyper.

the uncertainty apparent in the doctrine of predestination, one can never have certainty of the recipient's regeneration. More recently, some have promoted a view which is similar to baptismal regeneration,[12] though the broader Reformed community has often rejected this as radical and inconsistent with the Calvinistic tradition.

THE LUTHERAN APPROACH TO BAPTISM

Though the Calvinistic tradition has greatly diverged from Calvin in its approach to the sacraments, the Lutheran church has adopted the structure of Luther's own writings on the subject. In the Lutheran tradition, baptism is essentially a means by which God brings forgiveness of sins, union with Christ's death and resurrection, and the gift of the Spirit. This is tethered to the incarnational theology of the Lutheran Reformation. Since the sixteenth century, Lutheran theology has emphasized the "ordinary" or earthly nature of the means by which God communicates himself to his creation.[13] For the Lutheran tradition, the finite is capable of containing the infinite. This understanding frames several of the primary differences between the two strands of Reformation thought. In the Lutheran tradition, grace is not abstract and spontaneous but is tied to specific earthly means by which God communicates himself. This includes the word preached, Holy Absolution, the Eucharist, and Holy Baptism.

Because of this incarnational emphasis, the Lutheran church teaches baptismal regeneration. God's connection to this means of grace is analogous to his presence in the word as confessed by non-sacramental churches. As the Spirit has tied himself to the word in such a way as to ensure both its inspiration and efficacy upon the hearer, he has tied himself to baptism as a means of regeneration. The Reformed tradition often confesses the preached word as a means of regeneration but fails to recognize the efficacious nature of the sacraments.[14] For the Reformed, a strict tie between baptism and regeneration would negate the spontaneous nature of regeneration. For the Lutheran church, both word and sacrament are means which God uses to bring his promise to his people.[15] The gospel is not separate

---

12. See, for example, Lusk, *Paedofaith*, and Leithart, *Baptized Body*.

13. See Scaer, *Law and Gospel*, 156–66.

14. This is consistent with the Reformed insistence on the free and spontaneous nature of the Spirit's work of regeneration.

15. "Word and sacrament both work the forgiveness of sins, but each is distinct

The Washing of Regeneration

from, but is communicated through the sacraments. Baptism is the gospel in visible form, thus it delivers the benefits of the gospel.

In contrast to the Anabaptist and American Evangelical traditions, the Lutheran church has continued to profess and practice infant baptism.[16] Due to their inability to comprehend the preached word, baptism is the only means by which young children can receive the blessing of regeneration. Through baptism, God grants the gift of faith. This is framed by the Lutheran distinction between law and gospel; in the Lutheran tradition, baptism is placed under the rubric of gospel rather than law. In various Baptist and Barthian[17] theologies, baptism is viewed primarily as an act of the recipient. When one is baptized, one is making a public statement about oneself and is performing an act of obedience to God. This promotes baptism as law—as an act of duty. However, in the Lutheran tradition, the passive nature of the sacrament is emphasized. In baptism, one is inactive. It is the minister who acts in the stead of Christ pouring water on the passive Christian. There is no greater picture and example of man's pure passivity regarding grace than an infant's receiving the Spirit and the forgiveness of sins through baptism.

This is distinct from the Reformed argument for infant baptism, which stems from covenant theology.[18] The Calvinistic argument for paedo-baptism is based largely on the concept of the unity of the biblical covenants as well as the concept of a familial covenant within Christian households.[19] In Reformed federal, or covenant, theology, there is a covenant of grace which extends from the *proto evangelion* (first gospel) given to Adam,[20] to the end of the church age and the consummation of God's kingdom. The Abrahamic covenant and the New Covenant are different administrations of the

---

from the other. Preaching has to do with hearing even though the Word can be read . . . Sacraments have to do with what is touched and handled" (Scaer, *Law and Gospel*, 139).

16. Even the best recent work on the subject of credo-baptism fails to be convincing. The best work I have found supporting the credo-baptist position is Schreiner et al., *Believer's Baptism*.

17. Look at the final volume of Barth's *Dogmatics*: Barth, *CD* 4.

18. There are several books written on this topic. One that is particularly helpful is Strawbridge et al., *Case for Covenantal Infant Baptism*. Some of the writers have federal vision leanings and thus do not always represent the mainstream Calvinistic position. Despite that, this book offers a consistent argument which is as convincing as any other Reformed work on the subject.

19. See Hodge's argument in *Systematic Theology* 3:546–58.

20. Gen 3:15.

one covenant of grace. Thus, there are many similarities. In the Abrahamic covenant, circumcision—the sign of the covenant—was given to the children of covenant members. The New Covenant, similarly, includes children and administers its covenant sign, baptism, to children as well. This can be inferred from the similarities of the two covenants as well as the fact that baptism is a replacement for circumcision.[21] This leads to the concept that there is a covenant within each Christian family. If one parent is of the faith, the whole household is covenantally deemed holy, and the children can participate in the church's covenantal life through baptism.[22]

Though the Lutheran tradition has identified baptism as a relative necessity for salvation, it is not an absolute necessity. Since God works through both word and sacrament, the word is sufficient to regenerate and save. However, neglect of the reception of God's gift is refusal of the gospel itself, and thus is damning. If one refuses to receive baptism, it is evidence of unbelief and a rejection of God's commands.[23] True faith will always result in baptism if possible. That baptism does not carry absolute necessity is demonstrated by the thief on the cross. Without an opportunity to receive baptism, he was promised entrance into paradise based on his faith. This is the only example of such a scenario in the New Testament because all others who become believers have the opportunity to receive baptism. Bernard of Clairvaux distinguishes between a baptism with water and a baptism of desire.[24] Though God ordinarily ties himself to the means of the sacrament, if one desires baptism but is unable to receive it prior to death, God counts one's desire as sufficient for the grace given.

A common charge from Evangelicals and Reformed theologians is that baptismal regeneration is incompatible with *sola fide*. If faith alone saves, then baptism cannot.[25] It is argued that Luther's inconsistency was

21. This is argued by pointing to the parallel Paul makes between the two in Col 2:11–13.

22. The idea of covenant households is defended by 1 Cor 7:14, wherein Paul talks about an unbelieving spouse being "sanctified" by the one who believes.

23. "Baptism is not a matter of choice (an adiaphoron), but a divine ordinance; still one may not assert an absolute necessity of Baptism or say that one can obtain remission of sins and be saved without Baptism" (Pieper, *Christian Dogmatics* 3:280).

24. See Bernard's *Epistola* 77 in James, *Letters of Saint Bernard*.

25. Look at the claim from James White: "He [Paul], as all the other Apostles, believed that we are redeemed, cleansed, forgiven, in the blood of Jesus Christ. Yet, there are many today who would replace the blood of Christ with the water of a baptistery" (White, *Brief Rebuttal of Baptismal Regeneration*). White pits both *sola fide* and the sufficiency of the atonement of Christ against the concept of baptismal regeneration contrary

unfortunate and solved by other reformers by rejecting baptismal regeneration. However, the Lutheran church has consistently argued that this seeming tension is imagined rather than real. Baptism and faith are not to be separated. Baptism gives and strengthens faith. It does not "add to" faith or give different soteriological blessings than faith. It is baptism which delivers the promise that faith clings to.[26]

The issue of the benefits of baptism for the adult convert is a more complex question than that of infant baptism. For the infant, faith is given for the first time to the infant through baptism. Baptism is one's initiation into the Christian faith and into the church. However, for the adult, faith is already present. For Luther in the sixteenth century, everyone in Germany was baptized as an infant. Luther didn't face the question of adult baptisms as is common in modern culture. Charles Hodge argues that the Lutheran scholastic tradition is muddled on this question as well, sometimes seeming to promote baptismal regeneration for infants only, and baptism as a sign and assurance of faith for others. This is a primary argument against a Lutheran view of baptismal regeneration, because it has no consistent doctrine of baptism for both infants and believers.[27]

Despite the supposed inconsistencies of the scholastic tradition, it is exegetically and theologically sensible to assert that baptism gives the gospel promise in a concrete way for the believer, seals him with the Holy Spirit, and brings the forgiveness of sins. These things are present through the word but are sealed, confirmed, and strengthened through baptism. Hoenecke notes that "the effect it has as it continually works on those who are already reborn is basically the same effect it has in rebirth. It is always producing faith in them."[28] It is unambiguous in the book of Acts, and of the way Paul speaks of baptism, that the presence of the Spirit is increased through baptism.[29] He is present in a way he was not beforehand. It is also

---

to Paul's contention that baptism is the means by which Christ's death and resurrection are applied to believers (Rom 6:1).

26. As David P. Scaer notes, "Lutherans . . . recognize that the New Testament requires faith for Baptism, though the Baptists have no tolerance for Luther's view of infant faith" (Scaer, *Confessional Lutheran Dogmatics*, 147).

27. "From this it follows that in the case of adults, faith and therefore regeneration must precede baptism. And consequently in their case the design and effect of baptism cannot be to convey the remission of sin and renovation of the heart, but simply to confirm and strengthen a faith already possessed" (Hodge, *Systematic Theology* 3:607–08).

28. Hoenecke, *Evangelical Lutheran Dogmatics* 3:97.

29. It is to be noted that Paul speaks of the efficacy of baptism to congregations

Part II: Worship and the Sacraments

possible to speak of regeneration as more than a one-time act. In contradistinction to the Reformed *ordo salutis*, Luther speaks of the Christian life as continual repentance and renewal.[30] Thus it is valid to argue that one was regenerated both through the word and through baptism.

EVIDENCE FOR THE VALIDITY OF THE LUTHERAN DOCTRINE

1 Peter 3

> For Christ also suffered once for sins, the righteous for the unrighteous, that he might bring us to God, being put to death in the flesh but made alive in the spirit, in which he went and proclaimed to the spirits in prison, because they formerly did not obey, when God's patience waited in the days of Noah, while the ark was being prepared, in which a few, that is, eight persons, were brought safely through water. Baptism, which corresponds to this, now saves you, not as a removal of dirt from the body but as an appeal to God for a good conscience, through the resurrection of Jesus Christ, who has gone into heaven and is at the right hand of God, with angels, authorities, and powers having been subjected to him. (1 Pet 3:18–22)

Some theologians point to the obscurity of this text as a means to dismiss a sacramental interpretation. Popular Calvinistic Baptist preacher John Piper concludes about this passage that "Peter is saying, 'Baptism is the God-ordained, symbolic expression of that call to God. It is an appeal to God—either in the form of repentance or in the form of commitment.'"[31] It takes an extensive amount of explanation and obscuring of Peter's clear words to arrive at such a conclusion. In a straightforward reading, Peter's epistle unambiguously promotes the perspective that baptism saves. According to Peter, in contradistinction to the claim of Piper, baptism is not

---

who were primarily converts to the Christian faith, rather than those baptized as infants. Thus, Paul views baptism as efficacious for those who receive it after already receiving the word.

30. See Carry, "*Sola Fide*." I do not mean to imply that the Reformed tradition does not view repentance as a continual necessity, but the steps in the *ordo salutis* are generally viewed as one-time acts which cannot be lost or repeated.

31. John Piper, *What Is Baptism and Does It Save?*

The Washing of Regeneration

a mere symbol or a profession of faith, but it is an act of God wherein soteriological benefits are applied to the recipient.

Peter states directly that "baptism now saves you." Despite arguments to the contrary, these words bear their obvious meaning. Peter makes this apparent by his analogy from the Old Testament. In the deluvian narrative of Noah's ark, Noah and his family were saved from God's wrath on the earth by means of water. Analogously, the Christian is saved from God's wrath through the waters of baptism. A symbolic approach is negated by the fact that Noah was saved by real water in a real flood. Noah, through the water, was actually saved. It would make an inconsistent parallel to compare the flood by which Noah was actually saved to a symbolic act which points to something that saves apart from water. The nature of typology also negates this interpretation. Peter, in calling the flood a prefiguration of baptism, is professing that the benefits of baptism as the antitype are greater than those of the flood as the type. In biblical theology, the type is always pointing toward something greater than itself. The book of Hebrews, for example, points toward Christ as a greater priest, temple, and sacrifice. The fulfillment is always greater than the type. The argument that Peter is making is that the water saved Noah from God's temporal wrath; baptism is greater because it saves men from God's eternal eschatological wrath.

The argument most commonly proposed against the seemingly obvious interpretation of the passage is that because Peter qualifies his statement by writing, "not the removal of dirt from the body," he must not be referring to water baptism since water baptism does indeed remove dirt from the body. As Piper writes,

> Now the problem with this is that Peter seems very aware that his words are open to dangerous misuse. This is why, as soon as they are out of his mouth, as it were, he qualifies them lest we take them the wrong way. In verse 21 he does say, "Baptism now saves you"—that sounds like the water has a saving effect in and of itself apart from faith. He knows that is what it sounds like and so he adds immediately, "Not the removal of dirt from the flesh, but an appeal to God for a good conscience—through the resurrection of Jesus Christ." (Or your version might have: "the pledge of a good conscience toward God"). [*sic*]
>
> But the point seems to be this: When I speak of baptism saving, Peter says, I don't mean that the water, immersing the body and cleansing the flesh, is of any saving effect; what I mean is that, insofar as baptism is "an appeal to God for a good conscience,"

[*sic*] (or is "a pledge of a good conscience toward God"), it saves. Paul said in Romans 10:13, "Everyone who calls on the name of the Lord—everyone who appeals to the Lord—will be saved." Paul does not mean that faith alone fails to save. He means that faith calls on God. That's what faith does.[32]

First, the Lutheran position regarding this text does not imply that baptism saves apart from faith or that baptismal efficacy negates *sola fide*. Piper seems to assume that a belief in baptismal efficacy necessarily denies *sola fide*. Second, Piper's critique misses the purpose of Peter's argument. The reason Peter uses the flood as an example is because water is the means by which Noah was delivered. If Peter were arguing that "God saved Noah through water, which symbolizes your salvation through baptism—but not water baptism, but baptism by the Spirit," the analogy would fall apart. Piper's argument is quite a stretch. The argument put forward by Peter is that it is not the physical act of washing which makes one clean, but it is the spiritual benefits given through the sacrament which cleanse the soul, giving one a clean conscience before God.

It must be noted that Piper's interpretation of passages such as that in 1 Peter 3 are not universal in Reformed theology. While most of the "new Calvinist" movement and many Puritanical Reformed movements argue for a purely symbolic approach to these texts, some argue for baptismal efficacy in a sense. Michael Horton defines the effect of baptism with the following words:

> In the administration of a sacrament, the Father ratifies his pledge toward us in the Son by the Spirit. As a sign, it objectively witnesses to our inclusion in the covenant of grace; as a seal, it is the means by which the Spirit brings about within us the "amen" to God's promise and command, not only once but throughout our pilgrimage. Baptism itself does not effect this in an *ex opere operato* fashion, but achieves its perlocutionary effect when and where the Spirit chooses. "The efficacy of baptism is not tied to that moment wherein it is administered," according to the Westminster Confession (28.7), "yet, notwithstanding, by the right use of this ordinance, the grace promised is not only offered, but really exhibited and conferred, by the Holy Ghost, to such (whether of age or infants) as that grace belongeth unto, according to the counsel of God's own will in His appointed time." (WCF 28.7)[33]

32. Ibid.
33. Horton, *Christian Faith*, 192.

The Washing of Regeneration

In this way, Horton tries to argue for baptismal efficacy *in a sense*, but he denies the Lutheran approach to baptismal regeneration. He does this in covenantal terms, defining baptism as a "seal" of the gospel promise, though not necessarily effecting the gospel promise itself. As Horton cites from the Westminster Confession, baptism can be said to be efficacious, though the effect of the sacrament is not necessarily tied to a specific time. It is only if one is elect that regeneration is effected, and when applied to the elect, it occurs only when the Spirit freely chooses to apply the benefits.

The problem with Horton's approach is that it reads Calvinistic convictions into texts such as 1 Peter 3. Horton seeks both to accept the conviction that "baptism saves" in some covenantal sense, while also accepting the Reformed conviction that regeneration is spontaneous and external. However, the New Testament does not make such distinctions. Peter does not argue for Horton's approach, which amounts to this: baptism saves, but not necessarily, unless one is elect, and while it saves it does not do so through the actual act but may do so any time before or afterward. Such distinctions are confusing and would rob Peter's words of any comfort to his readers. For how would his readers know whether or not baptism actually saved them if it only did so in certain circumstances and not necessarily through the actual act? Peter is making a more simple point. As Noah was saved through water, his readers were saved through the waters of baptism. Peter does not argue from such a convoluted perspective as several Reformed interpreters make it to be.

An honest interpretation of 1 Peter 3 which takes the text at face value and analyzes the analogy made by Peter with reference to the nature of typology must come to the conclusion that the Petrine view of baptism is akin to baptismal regeneration. Baptism, like the flood, saves from God's wrath through the means of water. It does so not because of its physical effect but because it cleanses one's conscience.

Baptism with the Holy Spirit and with Fire

In non-sacramental church traditions, there is often a distinction made between baptism of the Holy Spirit and water baptism. Baptism with water, beginning with John's baptism prior to the beginning of Jesus' ministry, is a symbolic act wherein one's conversion is symbolized through immersion. It is a sign of dying to the old self and rising to the new. There is a separate baptism identified with the Holy Spirit, which is a Spirit-wrought act separate from the water applied. In the Reformed tradition, the Spirit's work of regeneration is symbolized and sealed through water but is enacted by the Holy Spirit apart from the sacramental act. In contemporary Pentecostal theology, baptism with the Holy Spirit is a separate action from both water baptism and regeneration, often identified with the manifestation of glossalalia.[34]

The exegetical evidence does not support a division between water baptism and a later baptism with the Holy Spirit. In the New Testament, water baptism, regeneration, and baptism with the Spirit are synonymous acts. Severing the link between these acts of God is unwarranted and unfaithful to the text.

All three synoptic gospels record the account of John the Baptist and the distinction he makes between his own baptism and a later baptism. In the Matthean account it is written, "I baptize you with water for repentance, but he who is coming after me is mightier than I, whose sandals I am not worthy to carry. He will baptize you with the Holy Spirit and fire" (Matt 3:11). Some interpreters promote the view that this text is making a distinction between water and Spirit baptisms.[35] However, this approach does not take Matthew's entire gospel into account regarding how Matthew himself writes of the fulfillment of John's statement. The distinction is not between a symbolic baptism by water and a spiritual baptism by the Holy Spirit, but between John's baptism of repentance and the church's Trinitarian baptism.

Baptism serves in a chiastic structure in Matthew's gospel. Prior to the beginning of Jesus' ministry is the account of John's baptism of repentance. The theme of repentance characterizes both the ministry of John and Jesus' ministry prior to the crucifixion. By accepting John's baptism, Jesus identifies himself as a member of sinful Israel in need of repentance, though without personal sin. Identifying himself with Israel, Jesus proclaims repentance and forgiveness until his crucifixion. After the resurrection, the ministry of Jesus is to be carried out through the church, empowered by the sending of the Paraclete. Matthew summarizes the mission of the church in

---

34. See Duffield and Van Cleave, *Foundations of Pentecostal Theology*, 304–23.

35. John Gill writes that baptism with fire is "referring, either to the extraordinary gifts of the Spirit, to be bestowed on the disciples on the day of Pentecost, of which the cloven tongues, like as of fire, which appeared unto them, and sat upon them, were the symbols; which was an instance of the great power and grace of Christ, and of his exaltation at the Father's right hand. Or rather, this phrase is expressive of the awful judgments which should be inflicted by him on the Jewish nation; when he by his Spirit should 'reprove' them for the sin of rejecting him" (Gill, *Exposition of the Bible*, Matt 3:11).

The Washing of Regeneration

these familiar words: "Go therefore and make disciples of all nations, baptizing them in the name of the Father and of the Son and of the Holy Spirit, teaching them to observe all that I have commanded you. And behold, I am with you always, to the end of the age" (Matt 28:19–20). Baptism is of the essence of the church and characterizes its mission.

Matthew introduces Jesus' ministry with John's baptism, a baptism of repentance. He points his readers forward to a greater baptism, which he calls one of the Holy Spirit and fire. As Jesus rises from the dead and prepares to leave his disciples at his ascension, he gives the command to baptize in the Triune name. This baptism is to characterize the ministry of the church. By placing the introduction of Triune baptism at the end of Jesus' ministry, Matthew intends this as the fulfillment of John's prediction that the church would baptize with the Holy Spirit. Both baptisms serve as bookends to Jesus' ministry. John's baptism of repentance characterizes and initiates Jesus' earthly ministry. Jesus then ends his ministry with the command to baptize in the Triune name, characterizing the mission of the church.

The division between John's baptism and baptism with the Holy Spirit is redemptive-historical rather than existential. It is a *historia salutis* issue rather than an *ordo salutis* one. The baptism of the Holy Spirit which John predicts is not a baptism devoid of water, but occurs through the means of water, by which the Holy Spirit is delivered.[36]

John 3

> Now there was a man of the Pharisees named Nicodemus, a ruler of the Jews. This man came to Jesus by night and said to him, "Rabbi, we know that you are a teacher come from God, for no one can do these signs that you do unless God is with him." Jesus answered him, "Truly, truly, I say to you, unless one is born again he cannot see the kingdom of God." Nicodemus said to him, "How

---

36. Richard Lenski writes, "The idea that even our present baptism is only water, a mere sign and symbol without the Spirit, only a confessional act and work of obedience on our part; and that the only baptism that gives us the Spirit is the so-called 'Baptism of the Spirit' by which the Spirit is thought to seize a man suddenly without the use of divine means . . . is a fanatical view which casts aspersions upon the very means of grace by which the Spirit does come to us and substitutes for these means human emotions, imaginings, and dreams by which the Spirit never comes" (*Interpretation of St. Matthew*, 115–16).

Part II: Worship and the Sacraments

can a man be born when he is old? Can he enter a second time into his mother's womb and be born?" Jesus answered, "Truly, truly, I say to you, unless one is born of water and the Spirit, he cannot enter the kingdom of God. That which is born of the flesh is flesh, and that which is born of the Spirit is spirit. Do not marvel that I said to you, 'You must be born again.' The wind blows where it wishes, and you hear its sound, but you do not know where it comes from or where it goes. So it is with everyone who is born of the Spirit." (John 3:1–8)

This text in John's gospel demonstrates the unity between baptism by water and regeneration. In conversation with Nicodemus, Jesus stresses the importance of a second birth. Jesus describes this birth as the result of water and the Spirit. The seemingly obvious meaning of the text is that Jesus is speaking of water baptism accompanied by the regenerative work of the Holy Spirit.

However, several interpreters have rejected the view that this text refers to baptism. According to Reformed and other Protestant interpreters, the water in reference is not baptism. There are two primary Protestant perspectives on the content of the water which Jesus speaks of.[37] First is the view that states that Jesus is speaking of natural birth. By discussing birth by water and the Spirit, Jesus is proposing that first one must be born naturally, through water, and sometime later a birth through the Spirit occurs. The second view is that the water spoken of is a reference to something other than baptism which has regenerative power; this has been viewed as either the Spirit or the word.

The first approach argues that the flesh/spirit births respectively mentioned in the same text clarifies the distinction between water and Spirit.[38]

37. In many of these interpretations, the obvious meaning of the text is dismissed without any textual consideration, simply because it contradicts the writer's preexisting theological system. Look at Gill's interpretation, for example: "by 'water,' is not meant material water, or baptismal water; for water baptism is never expressed by water only, without some additional word, which shows, that the ordinance of water baptism is intended: nor has baptism any regenerating influence in it; a person may be baptized, as Simon Magus was, and yet not born again; and it is so far from having any such virtue, that a person ought to be born again, before he is admitted to that ordinance: and though submission to it is necessary ... it is not necessary to the kingdom of heaven, or to eternal life and salvation" (Gill, *Exposition of the Bible*, John 3:5).

38. This view is generally not adopted by Reformed interpreters, but by some evangelicals. Evangelical apologist Matthew Slick writes, for example, "The implication is that the first birth is the natural birth and the second birth is the spiritual birth. In other words, the water refers to the water of the womb—the first birth. This seems to have

The Washing of Regeneration

By discussing natural birth and spiritual birth, Jesus is making the contrast between that which is "born of the flesh" and that which is "born of the Spirit." While there may be some validity to this argument, it is more contextually probable that Jesus is including both water and the Spirit as means of entrance into the kingdom of God. This is likely because the question which Jesus is answering is related to the nature of the new birth. For Jesus to be saying that one must first be born physically before entrance into the kingdom through the Spirit would be an unnecessary and obvious claim.

The second approach purports that Jesus speaks of being born of the Spirit and water, which symbolizes either the Spirit or the word.[39] Grudem is a proponent of this approach, writing, "Although some have understood this as a reference to baptism, it is better understood against the background of the promise of the New Covenant of Ezekiel 36."[40] Grudem presumes that Ezekiel 36 does not refer to baptism. However, it is likely that the language of sprinkling with water, and the spiritual nature of that cleansing, is precisely a promise of baptism. Grudem's argument is circular. He first presumes that Ezekiel 36 (which speaks directly about water being efficacious in regeneration) does not refer to baptism. He then interprets John 3 in light of its reference to this previous text, of which his interpretation has not been demonstrated. Grudem's argument fails to be convincing.

If John is using water as a reference to the Spirit in his gospel, the text becomes both redundant and confusing. If Jesus already attributes rebirth to the Spirit, it is unnecessary to then connect the Spirit with an unclear analogy. Further, there are no references in the New Testament to the Spirit as water, and the texts which do connect the two concepts have reference to baptism. The proposal that water refers to the word is equally untenable. The word is never described as water. The one text used to propose that the cleansing nature of the word merits a description as water is from Paul's epistle to the Ephesians: "Husbands, love your wives, as Christ loved the church and gave himself up for her, that he might sanctify her, having cleansed her by the washing of water with the word" (Eph 5:25–26). It is likely that this text also has reference to baptism. If it doesn't, there is still no merit for the interpretation of John 3:5 as a reference to the word. Paul

---

support in the understanding of Nicodemus about entering into the womb to be born a second time" (Slick, *Baptism and John 3:5*).

39. Hodge writes, "to be born of water and of the Spirit, is to experience a cleansing of the soul analogous to that effected for the body by water. This is the interpretation generally adopted by the Reformed Theologians" (Hodge, *Systematic Theology* 3:593).

40. Ibid., 573.

makes it clear in Ephesians that the word is also present and a means by which the church is "washed." John does not make this apparent. It is also exegetically unwise to interpret a reference to water by one possible conflation of the word with the concept of water rather than baptism, which is consistently tethered to the use of water throughout the New Testament.

In the first century, the church grew rapidly and exponentially. As the church expanded, each new convert was received into the Christian faith through baptism. Baptisms were seen often, and they would have likely been a recent occurrence for John's readers. Thus when John wrote the words of Jesus regarding water and the Spirit, baptism would naturally come to mind for his readers. Being aware of this, had John meant something else he would have clarified his meaning. Also, the context in which John places this discussion supports the sacramental interpretation of John 3:5. Jesus' discussion with Nicodemus comes only two chapters after John's baptisms. As the reader gets to chapter 3, he still is thinking about the significance of John's baptism. This is likely what Nicodemus is asking about and what Jesus is referencing as he points forward to the church's Trinitarian baptism.

There is no reason to interpret John 3:5 in any manner other than the obvious reference to baptism. Baptism is the one act of the church which is consistently emphasized in reference to water. It is an act which John's readers were seeing on a regular basis. Unless evidence is sufficient to negate the clear meaning of the text, the baptismal reference stands as the most plausible reading.[41]

1 Corinthians 1:10–17

> I appeal to you, brothers, by the name of our Lord Jesus Christ, that all of you agree, and that there be no divisions among you, but that you be united in the same mind and the same judgment. For it has been reported to me by Chloe's people that there is quarreling among you, my brothers. What I mean is that each one of you says, "I follow Paul," or "I follow Apollos," or "I follow Cephas," or "I follow Christ." Is Christ divided? Was Paul crucified for you? Or were you baptized in the name of Paul? I thank God that I baptized none of you except Crispus and Gaius, so that no one may say that you were baptized in my name. (I did baptize also the household of Stephanas. Beyond that, I do not know whether

---

41. For a more detailed exposition of this text, see Scaer, *Confessional Lutheran Dogmatics*, 61–67.

I baptized anyone else.) For Christ did not send me to baptize but to preach the gospel, and not with words of eloquent wisdom, lest the cross of Christ be emptied of its power.

Though this text has often been used to argue against the doctrine of baptismal regeneration, a careful reading confirms the effectual nature of the sacrament. The argument to the contrary is promoted through the following syllogism: Paul went to Corinth to save those who were lost. Paul preached the gospel but did not baptize. Therefore, Paul viewed the preaching of the gospel as saving but not the act of baptism. Thomas Nettles argues in the following words:

> If Paul were sent not to baptize, but nevertheless those to whom he preached were established by his gospel and if his preaching of the "revelation of the mystery" subdued nations to the "obedience of faith" (Rom 1:5 NASB), he cannot have seen faith as incomplete without baptism. He certainly does not minimize baptism in its proper place as an expression of the relationship established by faith, but he views it as separate from faith and adding nothing to that which can be gained by faith only.[42]

First, in response to this argument, it must be stated that the text does not directly address the effect of baptism; to infer from this text that baptism serves a symbolic, covenantal, or representative purpose is stretching the text beyond what is exegetically tenable. Second, if anything is to be inferred from this text, it seems that Paul's writing necessitates something beyond a purely symbolic approach. Paul is assuming that those who baptized the individual in the congregation would be so identified with the one receiving the sacrament that those receiving baptism would attribute their Christian life to the hands of the baptizer.

It is apparent that Paul assumes a saving efficacy in the baptismal act because he states that those who were baptized would view their baptizer as a savior. If one were baptized by Paul, he fears that the baptized might place in Christ's own role the baptizer as instrumental in one's salvation. This is apparently the reason why Paul denied baptizing in Corinth. Paul demonstrates this misunderstanding of the Corinthian church by rhetorically asking, "Was Paul crucified for you?" Apparently some in the congregation were claiming to be followers of the one who performed the sacramental act, negating Christ's role in their conversion. It is highly unlikely that a practice considered a symbol or sign without soteriological efficacy would

42. Nettles et al., *Understanding Four Views*, 34.

cause such division, allowing one to be so identified with the baptizer as to neglect Christ's role in salvation.

There is further evidence of the Corinthians' belief in baptismal efficacy in their obscure practice of baptizing the dead.[43] Paul asks, "Otherwise, what do people mean by being baptized on behalf of the dead? If the dead are not raised at all, why are people baptized on their behalf?" (1 Cor 15:29). This question is asked in the midst of Paul's great discussion of resurrection, which details both Christ's resurrection and the resurrection of humankind upon Christ's return. The purpose of Paul's question is to demonstrate that the Corinthians presuppose the doctrine of resurrection when baptizing on behalf of the dead. When the Corinthians baptize the dead, they do so with a view to resurrection. If baptism were a purely symbolic act, demonstrating one's faith, there would have been no purpose in baptizing on behalf of the dead. If baptism brings one into the covenant community of the church apart from regeneration as in Calvin's approach, baptizing for the dead is also logically incoherent. However, if the Corinthians viewed baptism as a means of salvation, the reason for baptizing the dead is apparent. Seemingly the Corinthians assumed that baptism on behalf of either an unbeliever or a Christian who had not received baptism would assure that person's resurrection. This is the only context in which Paul's rhetoric is sensible in arguing that the concept of baptism for the dead presupposes a doctrine of resurrection.

Paul's letter to the Corinthians presupposes that the gathered church views baptism as a means of salvation. This is demonstrated in their willingness to attribute their salvation to and follow the one who administered their baptism. It is also apparent in the obscure practice of baptizing on behalf the dead, wherein the Corinthians sought to assure the redemption of those who had passed on through being baptized on their behalf.

Acts 2:38

As an ecclesiological text, the book of Acts contains several references to the sacrament of baptism. During Pentecost, the arrival of the Spirit fulfills the promises of Jesus that a comforter would come to guide the church after his ascension. Peter and the Apostles begin to preach and are miraculously heard by those who speak various languages. Luke writes that the hearers

---

43. See Scaer's discussion on this point: Scaer, *Confessional Lutheran Dogmatics*, 54–59.

The Washing of Regeneration

were "cut to the heart" (Acts 2:37). Those who were aware of their guilt asked the Apostles what to do. Peter gives the following answer: "Repent and be baptized every one of you in the name of Jesus Christ for the forgiveness of your sins, and you will receive the gift of the Holy Spirit. For the promise is for you and for your children and for all who are far off, everyone whom the Lord our God calls to himself" (Acts 2:38–39). This is as succinct and comprehensive a statement regarding baptism as can be found in the New Testament.

Peter states that baptism is "for the forgiveness of sins." The Greek phrase is εἰς ἄφεσιν τῶν ἁμαρτιῶν ὑμῶν. The term εἰς is usually translated in this context as "into," "unto," or "for." Those who deny baptismal regeneration have argued that in this context εἰς is not instrumental; rather it is to be understood as meaning "in reference to." A. T. Robertson defends this approach:

> This phrase is the subject of endless controversy as men look at it from the standpoint of sacramental or of evangelical theology. In themselves the words can express aim or purpose for that use of "εἰς" does exist as in 1 Cor. 2:7 . . . But then another usage exists which is just as good Greek as the use of "εἰς" for aim or purpose. It is seen in Matt. 10:41 in three examples "εἰς ονομα προπητου, διακαιου, ματητου" where it cannot be purpose or aim, but rather the basis or ground, on the basis of the name of prophet, righteous man, disciple, because one is, etc. It is seen again in Matt. 12:41 about the preaching of Jonah . . . They repented because of (or at) the preaching of Jonah. The illustrations of both usages are numerous in the N.T. and the Koine generally.[44]

Thus, Peter is simply stating that one should be baptized with reference to the forgiveness of sins which occurs apart from baptism. Hodge also takes this approach, writing, "The remission of sins was that to which baptism was related; that of which it was the sign and seal."[45] However, this translation is not usually defended by contextual arguments but by the preconceived conviction that baptism can never have soteric import in New Testament theology. Robertson admits his bias, stating, "One will decide the use here according as he believes that baptism is essential to the remission of sins or not. My view is decidedly against the idea that Peter, Paul, or any one in the

---

44. A. T. Robertson, *A Grammar of Greek New Testament in Light of Historical Research*, 592, as cited by White, *Brief Rebuttal*.
45. Hodge, *Systematic Theology* 3:599.

Part II: Worship and the Sacraments

New Testament taught baptism as essential to the remission of sins or the means of securing such remission."[46] In the text, the listeners are cut to the heart, they are convicted of sin. When they are asking the Apostles, "What should we do?" they are asking in reference specifically to their guilt. Peter gives them the solution by telling them of repentance and baptism for the remission of sins. All of this is the answer to their guilty consciences. There is no contextual evidence to assume that Peter is giving the solution to guilt through repentance and forgiveness and then consequently commanding obedience to a symbolic act. Rather, repentance and baptism for the forgiveness of sins is the solution for guilt.

It is also to be noted that virtually every major translation has rendered this phrase in such a manner that baptism is instrumental in one's receiving forgiveness. This is likely contrary to the theological leanings of several translators. Look at the following translations:

> "Then Peter said to them, 'Repent, and let every one of you be baptized in the name of Jesus Christ for the remission of sins; and you shall receive the gift of the Holy Spirit.'" (NKJV)

> "Then Peter said unto them, Repent, and be baptized every one of you in the name of Jesus Christ for the remission of sins, and ye shall receive the gift of the Holy Ghost." (KJV)

> "Peter replied, 'Repent and be baptized, every one of you, in the name of Jesus Christ for the forgiveness of your sins. And you will receive the gift of the Holy Spirit.'" (NIV)

> "And Peter said to them, 'Repent and be baptized every one of you in the name of Jesus Christ for the forgiveness of your sins, and you will receive the gift of the Holy Spirit.'" (ESV)

> "Peter said to them, 'Repent, and each of you be baptized in the name of Jesus Christ for the forgiveness of your sins; and you will receive the gift of the Holy Spirit.'" (NASB)

Luke also ties baptism to the reception of the Holy Spirit. This is consistent with the synoptic description of a baptism with the Holy Spirit which would occur after Jesus' earthly ministry. It is significant that even though the Spirit works miraculously in the midst of the preachers and

---

46. Robertson, *Word Pictures* 3:35.

hearers at Pentecost, it is only through baptism that the listeners are said to "receive the gift of the Holy Spirit." This demonstrates that Luke views water baptism rather than speaking in tongues as the fulfillment of John's prediction of a baptism with the Spirit as the first instance of conversion and baptism in Acts, and this serves as the ongoing pattern of ecclesiastical life.

Baptism in Pauline Theology

Though Paul does not offer an extensive treatment of baptism, various references to the sacrament are scattered throughout his letters, which are perspicuous enough to construct a Pauline baptismal theology. For Paul, baptism has profound soteriological significance. It connects one to Christ, uniting the believer to Christ's death and resurrection. Through baptism, the believer dies to sin, and baptism then becomes the foundation for Christian living.

In Romans 6, Paul writes,

> What shall we say then? Are we to continue in sin that grace may abound? By no means! How can we who died to sin still live in it? Do you not know that all of us who have been baptized into Christ Jesus were baptized into his death? We were buried therefore with him by baptism into death, in order that, just as Christ was raised from the dead by the glory of the Father, we too might walk in newness of life. (Rom 6:1–3)

In this text, Paul is responding to the question of sin in Christian living. After having expounded upon the doctrine of justification by grace through faith, Paul assumes that his hearers might question the role of good works if justification is received apart from works. Paul's response is to expound upon the nature of baptism. Through baptism, one has "died to sin." This occurs because through baptism, one is placed into Christ and participates in Christ's death. Consequently, having died to sin, one is united to Christ's resurrection and, through union with Christ's resurrection, walks in newness of life.[47]

---

47. Some Reformed interpreters have recognized the sacramental import of this text. Matthew Henry says, "Baptism binds us to Christ, it binds us apprentice to Christ as our teacher, it is our allegiance to Christ as our sovereign. Baptism is *externa ansa Christi—the external handle of Christ,* by which Christ lays hold on men, and men offer themselves to Christ. Particularly, we were baptized into his death, into a participation of the privileges purchased by his death, and into an obligation both to comply with the design of his death, which was to redeem us from all iniquity, and to conform to the

Part II: Worship and the Sacraments

Paul does not expound upon baptism as pure symbolism.[48] His argument is not that baptism symbolizes death from sin and is a sign of one's union with Christ. To the contrary, according to Paul through baptism one is placed *into* Christ and dies, participating in Christ's own death and resurrection.

In Colossians, Paul expresses a similar pattern of thought: "In him also you were circumcised with a circumcision made without hands, by putting off the body of the flesh, by the circumcision of Christ, having been buried with him in baptism, in which you were also raised with him through faith in the powerful working of God, who raised him from the dead" (Col 2:11–12). As in Romans, Paul argues that through baptism, one dies to sin through the death of Christ, and one is subsequently raised to newness of life through union with Christ's resurrection. Similarly, the language is realist rather than symbolic.

---

pattern of his death, that, as Christ died for sin, so we should die to sin. This was the profession and promise of our baptism, and we do not do well if we do not answer this profession, and make good this promise" (Henry, *Commentary on the Whole Bible*, Rom. 6:1–21; emphasis in the original).

48. This is contrary to the claim of Gill, who expounds on this verse, saying, "This does not suppose, that some of this church were baptized persons, and others not; but that some might be baptized in water who were not baptized into Christ: there is a difference between being baptized in water in the name of Christ, and being baptized into Christ, which believers in their baptism are; by which is meant, not a being brought by it into union with Christ, which is either secretly from eternity, or openly at conversion, and both before the baptism of true believers; nor a being brought by it into the mystical body of Christ the church, for this also is before it; but rather it designs a being baptized, or a being brought by baptism into more communion with Christ, into a participation of his grace and benefits; or into the doctrine of Christ, and a more distinct knowledge of it: the power of which they feel upon their hearts, and so have really believed in Christ, heartily love him, and make a sincere profession of him; though rather the true meaning of the phrase 'baptized into Christ,' I take to be, is to be baptized purely for the sake of Christ, in imitation of him, who has set us an example, and because baptism is an ordinance of his; it is to submit to it with a view to his glory, to testify our affection for him, and subjection to him, without laying any stress or dependence on it for salvation; such who are thus baptized, are 'baptized into his death'; they not only resemble Christ in his sufferings and death, by being immersed in water, but they declare their faith in the death of Christ, and also share in the benefits of his death; such as peace, pardon, righteousness, and atonement: now this proves, that such persons are dead to sin, who are so baptized; for by the death of Christ, into which they are baptized, they are justified from sin; by the death of Christ, their old man is crucified, and the body of sin destroyed; besides, believers in baptism profess themselves to be dead to sin and the world, and their baptism is an obligation upon them to live unto righteousness" (Gill, *Exposition of the Bible*, Rom 6:3).

The Washing of Regeneration

Galatians also contains similar references, stating that one is baptized "into Christ" (Gal 3:26). Through baptism one "put[s] on Christ" (Gal 3:26). The concept of baptism into Christ can be expounded upon by the analogy Paul makes between Christ and Moses. He writes, "For I do not want you to be unaware, brothers, that our fathers were all under the cloud, and all passed through the sea, and all were baptized into Moses in the cloud and in the sea" (1 Cor 10:1–2). The exodus was the most significant redemptive event in the Old Testament and was the foundation of the Mosaic covenant. In this event, Moses acted as a mediator to the people of Israel, defending the nation against Pharaoh. Moses served as a type of Christ, and as a representative figure, he was the instrument through whom salvation was procured. As Moses split the sea and crossed, the Israelites were saved through participating in Moses' act of redemption. The blessings God gave to Moses were communicated to the people of Israel through the corporate act of crossing the Red Sea. Similarly, the Christian participates in Christ's act of redemption as one is received into him through baptism.

One final text which needs to be examined in the Pauline literature is from 1 Corinthians chapter 6:

> Or do you not know that the unrighteous will not inherit the kingdom of God? Do not be deceived: neither the sexually immoral, nor idolaters, nor adulterers, nor men who practice homosexuality, nor thieves, nor the greedy, nor drunkards, nor revilers, nor swindlers will inherit the kingdom of God. And such were some of you. But you were washed, you were sanctified, you were justified in the name of the Lord Jesus Christ and by the Spirit of our God. (1 Cor 6:9–11)

In this text, Paul is contrasting the Christian's identity prior to conversion and after conversion. That which identifies the unregenerate is their sinful nature and desires. However, after conversion, one is renewed, forgiven, and imputed righteous; sin no longer defines redeemed people. Rather, they are defined by the Triune name. In describing conversion, Paul uses three distinct terms: sanctified, justified, and washed. The term "washed" most likely has reference to baptism. This is probable for a few reasons. First, the concept of washing is most often linked with the sacrament of baptism. Without qualifying the term, washing would have immediately brought one's baptism to mind in the Corinthian congregation. Second, this act is said to be done "in the name of the Lord Jesus Christ and by the Spirit of our God." This is likely a reference to baptism in the name of

Jesus as is expressed in the Acts formula. The phrase "by the Spirit of our God" also has reference to baptism; in the New Testament it is the Spirit who is described as the active Trinitarian person in baptism. Finally, this would give concretion to Paul's argument and is consistent with how he argues elsewhere. Paul is not pointing to an abstract *ordo salutis* for the Corinthians, but is reminding them of a concrete event which defines their identity as Christians. This occurs in baptism. This is also consistent with how Paul argues in Romans 6. In this chapter, Paul reminds his readers of their identity in Christ through baptism, thus giving them a reason to live as renewed people rather than according to their sinful flesh. The old man was drowned through baptism. Similarly, Paul is also telling the Corinthians that they should not live according to their old nature because that nature has died in baptism, and they have been made new creations. If this verse does refer to baptism, as is almost certain, then Paul connects his common theological categories of both justification and sanctification to the baptismal act.

It is clear in Pauline theology that baptism is more than a symbolic act. It does not simply demonstrate Christ's death and resurrection or bring entrance into the church. Through baptism one dies and is raised to new life. When one is baptized, one is united to Christ's death and resurrection and receives all that Christ won on the cross. This then becomes the foundation for the Christian life and motivates ethical living.

Old Testament Typology of Baptism

The New Covenant doctrine of baptism is connected to several statements and stories regarding purification and water in the Old Testament. It was shown above, for example, that Peter points to the flood as a type of Christian baptism, and Paul discusses the crossing of the Red Sea as a baptism. Though other references may not be as explicit, there are several other instances of baptismal language and typology in the Old Covenant.

Let's examine the story of the flood, which Peter draws upon to make his parallel. The connection is not merely that water is involved in both events, as is salvation from God's punishment. The story also portrays water as that which cleanses and purifies. The flood not only saved Noah through the ark, but it also wiped evil out of the world. It had a purifying effect, cleansing the world from paganism and allowing a new world to begin with a faithful family. This is, in a sense, the first renewal of the earth, a picture

The Washing of Regeneration

of eschatological re-creation.[49] Commensurate with the eschaton, God's people would be spared judgment, and the wicked would face judgment. Both salvation and condemnation are simultaneous realities. In light of this approach to the flood, one's baptism is an instance of re-creation. Through it one participates in eschatological restoration and redemption. As the flood purified by the destruction of evil and salvation of the righteous, the waters of baptism cleanse the recipient from the evils of the Adamic age, delivering that person into the age to come.

The exodus through the Red Sea, as described by Paul, is also a redemptive event. It brought both the salvation of the Israelites and the destruction of Pharaoh, Israel's enemy. Commensurate with the flood, evil and unrighteousness were cleansed as the righteous were delivered. This represents the deliverance from sin, death, and the devil that the New Covenant people receive and the cleansing and death of the old self, which occurs simultaneously.

There were several cleansing rituals in the Levitical law which served the purpose of purification and cleansing. Eleazer says the following regarding cleansing for soldiers:

> This is the statute of the law that the Lord has commanded Moses: only the gold, the silver, the bronze, the iron, the tin, and the lead, everything that can stand the fire, you shall pass through the fire, and it shall be clean. Nevertheless, it shall also be purified with the water for impurity. And whatever cannot stand the fire, you shall pass through the water. You must wash your clothes on the seventh day, and you shall be clean. And afterward you may come into the camp. (Num 31:21–24)

This served as an act of cleansing. As the Israelites returned from battling the Midianites, washing with water was used as a ceremony of cleansing. It is only after such cleansing that one is permitted to go back to the camp.

The book of 2 Kings tells the story of Naaman and his cleansing through water. Naaman is described as a "commander of the army of the king of Syria" (2 Kgs 5:1). Having been struck with leprosy, Naaman is sent to the king of Israel so that he may be cured. Elisha sends a messenger to Naaman, who tells him to dip himself into the Jordan River seven times. Initially Naaman refuses, but he is finally convinced to do so by his servants. When he does, Naaman is instantly healed of his leprosy. This story demonstrates that God uses means to bring about healing. Though some might call this

---

49. Meredith Kline expounds upon this point: Kline, *Kingdom Prologue*, 220–25.

"magic," as some are wont to do regarding baptismal regeneration, it is a legitimate form of God's work, whereby he uses earthly elements to bring salvation—in this instance, physical salvation from a debilitating disease. Further, it demonstrates the cleansing nature of water. The cleansing in this instance is beyond that of a ceremonial and representative function, but the water actually cures Naaman of his disease. This is a type, a picture, of baptism, which cleanses people from their spiritual disease of sin.

Perhaps the most direct statement regarding the cleansing nature of water is a prophecy which relates directly to baptism. It comes from the prophet Ezekiel:

> I will sprinkle clean water on you, and you shall be clean from all your uncleannesses, and from all your idols I will cleanse you. And I will give you a new heart, and a new spirit I will put within you. And I will remove the heart of stone from your flesh and give you a heart of flesh. And I will put my Spirit within you, and cause you to walk in my statutes and be careful to obey my rules. You shall dwell in the land that I gave to your fathers, and you shall be my people, and I will be your God. And I will deliver you from all your uncleannesses. And I will summon the grain and make it abundant and lay no famine upon you. (Ezek 36:25–29)

In this text, Ezekiel is giving a prophecy about the New Covenant. He refers both to the gift of regeneration with the language of replacing a heart of stone with flesh, and to the inheritance of the new heavens and earth, which belong to the people of God. The event which brings this about occurs through God's sprinkling clean water onto his people. This is a reference to baptism. It is not a coincidence that the language of water is used in the most explicit Old Testament text about regeneration. Through the waters of baptism, one is made clean, given a new heart, granted the indwelling of the Holy Spirit, and given the inheritance that Christ won for his people through the resurrection.

CONCLUSION

It has been demonstrated that the Lutheran doctrine of baptism is exegetically supported. Other approaches are forced onto the text by preconceived theological systems and ignore the plain meaning of the text. In Petrine theology, baptism saves one from God's eschatological wrath as Noah was saved from God's temporal wrath at the time of the flood. Baptism with the

The Washing of Regeneration

Holy Spirit has been shown to refer, not to a blessing separate from water baptism, but Trinitarian baptism in the church. Through that Trinitarian baptism one receives the Spirit. John, through Jesus' conversation with Nicodemus, also demonstrates that the new birth is connected to baptism. Lucan theology places emphasis on baptism as a means of both forgiveness and reception of the Spirit. In Paul's theology, baptism unites one to Christ and delivers his benefits to the recipient. Paul's correspondence with the Corinthians demonstrates an understanding of baptismal efficacy in the Corinthian church. New Testament theology is a sacramental theology. Baptism is not a mere sign and symbol, but is a means by which God brings salvation to his people.

6

The Medicine of Immortality
The Lutheran Doctrine of Holy Communion

THE DEBATE BETWEEN LUTHER AND ZWINGLI

MARTIN LUTHER'S HOSTILITY TOWARD the Swiss branch of the Reformation, due to their diverging approaches to the Lord's Supper, is well known. Luther was a conservative reformer, retaining the sacramental emphasis of the patristic and medieval church. However, Zwingli's humanistic tendencies led to an abandonment of several patristic and medieval approaches to theology and worship, including the sacramental nature of the church. Luther's Reformation arose from within the church, while Zwingli abandoned medieval ceremonies and beliefs without much struggle.[1] This allowed for Zwingli to adopt a symbolic view of the Lord's Supper. According to Zwingli, the bread and wine simply represent Christ's body and blood.[2] For Luther, in line with patristic and medieval thought, Christ's body and blood are truly communicated to the recipient.[3]

   1. See Vischer et al., *Christian Worship*.
   2. See Richardson, *Zwingli and Cranmer on the Eucharist*, 63–78.
   3. The best treatment of the Zwingli-Luther debate remains Sasse, *This Is My Body*. See also Althaus, *Theology of Martin Luther*, 375–403; Lohse, *Martin Luther's Theology*, 306–13.

The Medicine of Immortality

Behind the discussion of the nature of the sacrament were deeper convictions about the human nature of Christ. Zwingli argued that Christ's human nature has a limited locality.[4] For Christ to be true man, he must take on the physical limitations of mankind. Therefore, Christ's human nature is at the right hand of the Father and nowhere else. Zwingli rejected the patristic approach to the two natures of Christ wherein divine attributes are communicated to Christ's human nature. According to Luther, Zwingli's denial of the *communicatio idiomatum* (the communication of attributes) was a profound Christological error. Ancient Chalcedonian Christology had emphasized not only the separation of the two natures, but also the unity of the person of Christ. Since Zwingli denied that an action performed by one nature could be attributed to the other, Luther accused him of Nestorianism. The Nestorian heresy denied that Mary was to be called *theotokos* (Mother of God), because technically speaking, Mary is the mother of the human nature of Christ, not the divine. Patristic theologians argued that this separated the natures unnecessarily, resulting in a schizophrenic Christ with a human person divided from the divine.[5] The Nestorian view was condemned at the Council of Ephesus in 431 under the leadership of Cyril of Alexandria.[6]

Luther believed that Zwingli adopted the Nestorian heresy by his denial of the *communicatio idiomatum*. Luther argued that the human nature of Christ is omnipresent through the communication of the attributes of his divine nature. This allows for Christ's presence in the Supper. Zwingli denied this, proposing that the finite is not capable of the infinite. In Luther's view, this principle necessitates a denial of the incarnation, wherein the infinite God united himself to a finite human nature. He argued that Zwingli's perspective of the sacrament was arrived at through misused human reason rather than honest exegesis.

---

4. "Jesus Christ, in his human nature, cannot possibly be in heaven and in the eucharistic bread at the same time. It is irrelevant to look for him where he is not. Present in his divine nature both in heaven and on earth, Christ in his human nature is in heaven alone" (Courvoisier, *Zwingli*, 71).

5. For primary texts on the Nestorian and related Christological debates, see Norris, *Christological Controversy*.

6. Cyril's Christology remains highly influential for Lutheran theology. The best book on the topic is John Anthony McGuckin's edition of Cyril of Alexandria, *On the Unity of Christ*.

Part II: Worship and the Sacraments

Representatives of both the Lutheran and Swiss theological camps met at the Colloquy of Marburg to discuss their theological differences.[7] Out of fourteen issues discussed, thirteen were agreed upon. The only contentious point was that of the Supper. After hours of intense discussion, Luther resorted to writing and repeating only the words, "*Hoc est corpus meum!*" ("This is my body!"), not allowing further discussion on the subject. For Luther, these words of Christ were decisive. There was to be no debate over the clear words of Jesus. After the colloquy had ended unsuccessfully, Luther famously rejected a handshake from Zwingli, giving the message that fellowship was not possible between the two parties due to their different approaches to the sacrament. The issue of the Lord's Supper was too essential to be compromised on.

CALVIN'S DOCTRINE OF THE SUPPER

After Zwingli's death, John Calvin became the leader of the Reformed branch of the Reformation. Calvin had an intense admiration for Luther and freely disagreed with many elements of Zwingli's theology. Calvin was willing to align himself with Lutherans, at times taking the label upon himself while debating Roman Catholic theologians.[8] Calvin's loyalty to both Luther and the Swiss Reformation led him to attempt a mediating approach to several of the divisive issues between the two parties. Essential to this mediating task was a view of the Lord's Supper which both transcended pure memorialism and rejected Luther's patent realism.[9] Calvin attempted to communicate these issues with Luther in his early theological career; however, Melanchthon refused to allow Luther to read Calvin's writings due to fear of his growing hostility toward the Swiss party.

Calvin outlines his position thoroughly in his magnum opus, the *Institutes of the Christian Religion*. Commensurate with both the Swiss and German parties of the Reformation, Calvin rejects the Roman view of transubstantiation. For Calvin, as well as the other reformers, the doctrine of transubstantiation was exegetically untenable and depended upon flawed philosophical presuppositions.[10] Calvin begins his discussion of the Supper

---

7. Kittleson, *Luther the Reformer*, 195–212, 265–68.

8. For example, in his response to Sadoleto; see Olin, *John Calvin and Jacopo Sadoleto*.

9. On Calvin's doctrine of the Supper, see Mathison, *Given for You*.

10. Namely, the Aristotelian distinction between substance and accidents, which

by shifting the focus from the nature of Christ's presence to what he viewed as the primary purpose of the sacrament: "It is not the chief function of the Sacrament simply and without higher consideration to extend to us the body of Christ. Rather, it is to seal and confirm that promise by which he testifies that his flesh is blood indeed and his food is drink that leads us to eternal life."[11] The Lutheran reformers, in contrast with Calvin, argued that God testifies to his promise *by* giving the church his body. These purposes are part of one unified reality.

Calvin attempts an explanation of the Supper which allows for both Christ's local restriction to the right hand of the Father and a true participation in Christ's body and blood in the Eucharist:

> Even though it seems unbelievable that Christ's flesh, separated from us by such great distance, penetrates to us, so that it becomes our food, let us remember how far the secret power of the Holy Spirit towers above all our senses, and how foolish it is to wish to measure his immeasurableness by our measure.[12]

Calvin introduces a third element into this discussion which was not before present: the role of the Holy Spirit. In Calvin's theology, one participates in Christ not through a local communicated presence of Christ's human nature, but through a mysterious work of the Holy Spirit, who mediates between Christ and his church. The Spirit causes the Christian's soul to ascend to heaven to partake of the whole person of Christ. In this way, Calvin attempts to retain some of Luther's realism. "For why should the Lord put in your hand the symbol of his body except to assure you of a true participation in it?"[13]

Calvin denies the doctrine proposed by Luther that the attribute of omnipresence is communicated to the human nature of Christ by the divine nature.

> For as we do not doubt that Christ's body is limited by the general characteristics common to all human bodies, and is contained in heaven (where it was once for all received) until Christ return in judgment [Acts 3:21], so we deem it utterly unlawful to draw it

---

Aquinas modified to explain transubstantiation.

11. Calvin, *Institutes,* 4:XI.32.
12. Ibid., 4:XVII.10.
13. Ibid., 4:XVII.10.

back under these corruptible elements or to imagine it be present everywhere.[14]

For Calvin, Christ at the ascension was seated at the right hand of the Father and would remain there until he returned. This refers to a locality rather than a statement of role and authority. Thus Christ's body is unable to be located anywhere else. It is of the essence of humanity to have physical limitations. Therefore, to promote a Lutheran perspective of the two natures of Christ lends itself to a denial of Christ's true humanity. Calvin feared that Luther steered in the direction of monophysitism, conflating the two natures and obscuring Jesus' humanity through an overemphasis on divinity. As Luther feared that Zwingli adopted an ancient Christological heresy through his Nestorian tendencies, Calvin feared that Luther adopted the tenants of another ancient Christological heresy, namely, monophysitism.

Calvin purported that Christ's words of institution at the Last Supper were symbolic. Jesus did not intend the phrase "this is my body" to be understood in a literalistic sense; rather, Christ's words are to be understood symbolically. The words are sacramental rather than literal. "Christ's words are not subject to the common rule and ought not to be tested by grammar."[15] Calvin supports this figurative view of the words of institution by demonstrating that figurative language is a common literary tool in Scripture. For example, Paul writes that the rock the Israelites drank from "was Christ." He also points to the commonality of anthropomorphisms in the Old Testament.

Calvin promotes Zwingli's contention that Christ's human nature is located in heaven alone. He demonstrates this principle through the words of Christ prior to the ascension, wherein he tells his disciples that he will depart from the world. Calvin claims that the Lutheran party unintentionally makes Christ's human body into a phantom in a Docetic manner. Calvin argues that in the Supper, the movement is upward rather than downward. Christ does not come down to the church to feast; rather the partakers of the Eucharist are lifted up to him.

Finally, Calvin disagreed with Luther on the nature of Christ's presence for the unbeliever who partakes of the Eucharist. In Luther's view, Christ's presence in the sacrament was not tied to the faith of the person partaking of the Supper. The validity of the sacrament depends upon the proclaimed word, not on the faith of the administrator or recipient. The

14. Ibid., 4:XVII.12.
15. Ibid., 4:XVII.20.

unbeliever who receives the Eucharist does partake of Christ's true body and blood. However, in contradistinction to the blessing received by the believer, judgment instead is being communicated. Calvin denied this approach to the Supper. He writes that "all those who are devoid of Christ's Spirit can no more eat Christ's flesh than drink wine that has no taste."[16] In Calvin's view, faith is necessary to give the sacrament validity. Without faith, there is no sacrament, but an empty sign.

AN EXEGETICAL AND THEOLOGICAL RESPONSE TO CALVIN

While Zwingli's pure symbolism might remain easily dismissible, Calvin's doctrine of the Eucharist contains a level of theological sophistication and logical rigor that merits serious attention. Rather than dismissing the Supper as an ordinance, or only a memorial meal, Calvin fought for an elevated view of the sacrament while essentially retaining the Swiss criticism of the Lutheran approach to the Lord's Supper. The two primary theological differences in the Lutheran and Calvinist divide over the Eucharist are the question of the omnipresence of Christ's human nature and the meaning of the words of institution.

Before beginning a defense of Luther's approach to the Eucharist, some common misconceptions of Lutheran sacramental theology should be corrected. First, it is often the contention of various critics of Luther that the Lutheran church teaches the doctrine of consubstantiation.[17] This argument has been proposed since the Reformation and continues to be leveled against Lutheran theology today. The word "consubstantiation" in itself is not necessarily problematic, and a few Lutheran dogmaticians have used it. However, most Lutherans have rejected using the term due to possible misunderstandings of Lutheran Eucharistic theology. This misunderstanding arises from the fact that there was a medieval Eucharistic doctrine of consubstantiation which differs from that of Luther. This view, called "consubstantiation" along with "impanation," asserts that the physical body and

---

16 Ibid., 4:XVII.33.

17. "This presence of the body and blood of Christ in, with, and under the bread and wine has been generally expressed by non-Lutherans by the word consubstantiation, as distinguished from the Romish doctrine of transubstantiation" (Hodge, *Systematic Theology* 3:672).

blood of Christ are implanted into or alongside the sacramental elements.[18] Though affirming, along with Luther, both the real sacramental presence of Christ and that the earthly elements remain, consubstantiation's explanation of the nature of Christ's presence was rejected by the Lutheran Reformation. The Lutheran church has never tried to explain *how* the whole Jesus is present in bread and wine, but *that* he is. The words "in, with, and under" commonly used in Lutheran theology are an imprecise means by which the church professes its belief that in some manner, Christ is present.

Another charge which is often leveled against the Lutheran church is that it teaches the *necessary* or *local* omnipresence of the body of Christ. If Christ's human nature had omnipresence through itself, that would negate his true humanity.[19] Lutherans have rejected the contention of Menno Simons[20] that Christ had a heavenly human nature differentiated from ordinary humanity. Thus, Christ's humanity is not of itself omnipresent. However, due to the unified person of Christ, the attributes of the divine nature are *communicated* to the human nature. Whatever attributes of divinity are attributed to humanity are given as gift through communication rather than by nature.

There are different modes of presence which can be spoken of. The body of Christ was on earth before the ascension in a local manner, which is different from the manner in which he is present subsequently in the church.[21] Jesus testifies that though he would ascend, his presence with the church is continuous in a manner different from his local earthly ministry. He states, "And behold I am with you always, to the end of the age" (Matt 28:20). The Lutheran divines viewed this statement as a confession by Jesus that there are two modes of presence. One would be lost through the ascension (the local), while another presence would carry the church (the sacramental). It is the contention of the Reformed that this continuous presence is through the divine nature alone, while Christ's human nature has only one mode of presence. However, this is not exegetically or logically

18. Pieper rejects the terms "*localis inclusio, impanatio, consubstantantiatio*" (Pieper, *Christian Dogmatics* 3:362) as a misrepresentation of the Lutheran view.

19. Though Horton acknowledges the distinction of different modes of presence, he contends, "Although the intention of the Lutheran view is to affirm the closest possible union of God and humanity in Christ, the idea that the divine attributes can be predicates not merely of the person but of the human nature of Christ threatens his genuine humanity" (*Christian Faith*, 478).

20. See George, *Theology of the Reformers*, 280–85.

21. These distinctions are primarily taken from Chemnitz, *Two Natures in Christ*.

The Medicine of Immortality

defensible in light of this text. The Jesus standing before his disciples was a human Jesus; he was the one whom they had followed the past three years and with whom they had eaten and fellowshipped. It is thus implausible that the disciples would have understood this statement as a reference only to Christ's divine nature. The subject of the sentence is the person of Christ, not a nature.

If the Reformed contention is correct that the divine nature of Christ is omnipresent while his human nature remains locally fixed, the incarnation is incomplete. In the Calvinistic scenario, the majority of Christ's personhood is without a human nature.[22] Where one encounters Christ, other than at the right hand of the Father in heaven, one encounters deity rather than the incarnate God. It is the Lutheran contention that if Jesus was truly incarnated, all of Jesus was incarnated; thus wherever he is, there is both his human and divine nature. As Paul states, "For in him was all the fullness of God pleased to dwell" (Col 1:10). This assumes a robust incarnational theology in which Christ's deity is not to be encountered apart from his humanity. It is not part of God, but the fullness of God, which is incarnated. This is further demonstrated by Paul's statement in Ephesians 4, "He who descended is the one who also ascended far above all the heavens, that he might fill all things" (Eph 4:10). According to Paul, Christ's ascension involves not only a departure of Christ, but an arrival, a filling of the earth which takes place through the ascension. Some have argued that this refers to Christ's influence through the church or the sending of the Holy Spirit rather than a filling by Christ's person. Matthew Henry argues that Christ's filling refers to "all the members of his church, with gifts and graces suitable to their several conditions and stations."[23] This, however, ignores the context of Paul's statement. Paul is speaking specifically about Christ's person rather than his influence or Trinitarian relations. Because Christ's person and location are the topic of this thought, it is most likely that it refers to a filling of all things by Christ. One could object that this refers only to Christ's divine nature rather than the human. However, this is not sensible if one accepts the classically defined attributes of divinity. If this were Paul's point, then he would be promoting the idea that Christ lacked omnipresence according to his divine nature prior to the ascension. Unless one is willing to adopt an extreme form of kenoticism,[24] this is untenable.

22. This is often labeled the *extracalvinisticum* (Horton, *Christian Faith*, 478).
23. Henry, *Commentary on the Whole Bible*, Eph 4:10–16.
24. The belief that Christ divested himself of his divinity in the incarnation.

Part II: Worship and the Sacraments

The doctrine of Christ's omnipresence is part of a larger belief in the communication of Christ's divine attributes to his human nature. For the Lutheran tradition, the human nature receives several attributes of divinity in time.[25] The Reformed and broader Protestant tradition has rejected this definition of the *communicatio idiomatum*. Thus the Lutheran reformers developed a system by which different aspects of the *communicatio* could be discussed. This occurred through a division of three *genera* of modes of attribution between natures.[26]

The first class is the *genus idiomaticum*. This means that what is attributed to one nature can be attributed to the whole person. Thus one can say "the Son of God died" without having to clarify by saying, "the human nature of Christ died." The second *genus* will be treated below. The third class is the *genus apotelesmaticum*. This is an affirmation that whatever work Christ performs for the salvation of mankind is performed by both natures. One nature does not perform without the other. The Reformed could confess these two aspects of the *communicatio idiomatum*, at least in some sense; however, the second *genus* divided, and continues to divide, the two Reformation traditions.[27]

The divisive issue during the Reformation was the *genus maiestaticum*. This refers to the communication of divine attributes to Jesus' human nature. According to the second *genus*, the majesty of divinity is communicated to the human nature. This is demonstrated by the fact that Christ is said many times in Scripture to gain attributes of deity *in time*. Unless one adopts a Hegelian model of divinity wherein divine attributes develop through a cosmic process, one must admit the impossibility of these texts' referring to the divine nature since Christ's divine nature already had these attributes prior to the incarnation. Thus, they must have been given in time to Christ's human nature. For example, in Philippians 2:9, Paul speaks of Christ gaining a name that is above every name by his death on the cross rather than possessing it by nature.[28] Jesus was exalted *because of his obedi-*

---

25. Hoenecke, *Evangelical Lutheran Dogmatics* 3:79–102.

26. The numbering of the *genera* of the *communicatio idiomatum* differs within the various schools of the scholastic tradition. Earlier writers called the *genus apotelesmaticum* the second *genus*, whereas the later scholastics called it the third. Some of the later scholastics added a fourth *genus* relating specifically to Christ's presence in the Supper. On this, see Schmid, *Doctrinal Theology*, 313–37.

27. Pieper's defense of Lutheran Christology remains unsurpassed; see Pieper, *Christian Dogmatics* 3:85–330.

28. "Therefore God has highly exalted him and bestowed on him the name that is

The Medicine of Immortality

ence. Jesus speaks similarly in John 3:35 by confessing that he had been given all things by the Father. Parallel expressions are found in Matthew 11:27 and Luke 10:22. If Jesus has truly been given *all things*, then he must be, according to his whole person, omnipotent. This cannot refer to his divine nature unless one resorts to some type of subordinationism. As American Lutheran theologian Charles Krauth says, "Christ, then, has received according to one nature, to wit, the human, what He intrinsically possessed in the other, to wit, in the divine, or, as it has been expressed, Whatever Christ has in the one nature by essence, He partakes of in the other by grace—and this is the doctrine of our Church."[29] These are attributes, not of humanity, but of deity. They must have been communicated to the human nature. Jesus confessed before his disciples, "All authority in heaven and on earth has been given to me" (Matt 28:18). The man Jesus said this to his disciples. There is no reason to believe this refers to his divine nature alone.

Scripture also teaches the communication of Christ's omniscience to his human nature. John writes, "He did not need man's testimony about man, for he knew what was in a man" (John 2:25). This statement assumes that Jesus was able to gain knowledge of people's thoughts, even as a man. Jesus also demonstrates supernatural knowledge in his encounter with Nathanael wherein he testifies having knowledge of Nathanael's whereabouts even though absent from the scene.[30] The testimony of Scripture regarding the communication of divine honor along with divine omniscience confirms the Lutheran understanding of the *communicatio idiomatum* and places the omnipresence of Christ's human nature in an exegetically supportable theological context.

The doctrine of the communication of attributes is not only a Reformation teaching but can be found in several church fathers. For example, Athanasius writes, "Whatever the scripture declares that Christ had received in time, it affirms with reference to his humanity, not with reference to his deity."[31] This also is in accord with Cyril of Alexandria's concept of a divinization of Christ's human nature.[32] The authors of the Book of Con-

---

above every name, so that at the name of Jesus every knee should bow, in heaven and on earth and under the earth, and every tongue confess that Jesus Christ is Lord, to the glory of God the Father" (Phil 2:9–11).

29. Krauth, *Conservative Reformation*, 503.

30. John 1:48.

31. As cited in the catalogue of testimonies in McCain, *Concordia*, 509.

32. There is a great discussion of this topic in Ivan V. Popov, "The Idea of Deification in the Early Eastern Church," in Kharlamov, *Theosis*, 42–82.

cord compiled a catalog of patristic testimonies regarding the doctrine of the communication of attributes.

Interpreting the Words of Institution

Having demonstrated the exegetical backing of the Lutheran concept of the *communicatio idiomatum*, it remains to be demonstrated that this Christology has relevance for the sacrament. It must be demonstrated not only that Christ communicated omnipresence to his humanity, but also that this humanity is specially present in the Supper.

The words of institution are some of the most debated words of the New Testament. Interpreting the phrase "this is my body" is often decisive in the debate over the nature of the Eucharist. Luther's one-time pupil Andreas Carlstadt argued that when Jesus said these words, he was pointing to his literal body, not to the bread.[33] The absurdity of this interpretation caused it to be abandoned early in the Reformation era. Though disagreeing on the nature of the Eucharist, both the Reformed and Anabaptist parties argued that Christ's words at the Last Supper bore a symbolic meaning. This brings about the question of which word or phrase in the statement "this is my body" is symbolic. It has at times been proposed that the word "body" is representative. By "body," Jesus means bread. Thus, Jesus' words are conveying the message that this bread is broken for the forgiveness of sins. This brings about more confusion because it also necessitates a symbolic meaning of "broken for you," unless one is willing to argue that the breaking of physical bread brings the forgiveness of sins.

The majority Reformed position on Jesus' words is that the word "is" is symbolic, meaning "represents." Jesus' intention is to say, "this represents my body."[34] Lutheran theologians argued that unless there is sufficient reason to think otherwise, the plain meaning of the text stands.

The question which naturally arises is that of analogous statements. Did Jesus ever use this type of language symbolically in other circumstances? Some argue that the symbolic nature of phrases such as "I am the vine" are analogous figures of speech and allow for a symbolic reading of

---

33. Courvoisier, *Zwingli*, 72.

34. "The real problem with this passage, therefore, is not with the word 'this' but with the word 'is.' 'Is' here must be synonymous with 'signifies'" (Courvoisier, *Zwingli*, 73).

the words of institution.³⁵ Webster purports, "He speaks in physical terms but we are not meant to take his words in a literal, physical sense. Precisely the same is true with his teaching in John 6 and his words at the institution of the Lord's Supper. To interpret all his words in those passages literally would adopt an interpretation which directly contradicts the teaching of Scripture."³⁶ What is apparent in these phrases is that Jesus utilizes symbolic language and does so frequently. However, the words of institution are not parallel to the other symbolic phrases used throughout the gospel. Take the statement "I am the vine" (John 15:5), for example. It is clear that this statement is not intended as literal. Jesus is not calling himself a plant. However, it is still not directly parallel to the words of institution. One does not interpret this phrase in the same manner that many Protestants interpret Jesus' words at the Last Supper. In the phrase "I am the vine," it is not the word "am" that is symbolic, but the word "vine." A parallel statement would have to mean that Jesus is saying "I represent the vine." But the point Jesus is making is that he is like a vine. There is something about a vine which Jesus is pointing out to make an analogy about himself.

One text which has been alleged to contain a similar use of "is" to the Zwinglian approach to the Supper is not from the mouth of Jesus, but from the Apostle Paul. Paul writes to the Corinthians, "and all drank the same spiritual drink. For they drank from the spiritual Rock that followed them, and the Rock was Christ" (1 Cor 10:4).³⁷ Paul, in this text, is referring to the Israelite period of wandering wherein the Jews were miraculously given water through rocks. The argument some interpreters have made is that this text cannot be literal, and "was" has a purely symbolic meaning. The argument that Paul is making is that the rock is a picture of Christ, who now feeds the church spiritually. The rock represents Christ as the bread represents Christ's body.

There are two points to be made in response to this argument. First, to prove that a term could be used in a certain sense in a rare occasion does not prove that it must have that meaning in other texts. If this use of the word "is" means "represents," it is an isolated incident of this in the New Testament. The words of institution should still be read in the most plain and obvious manner unless sufficient textual evidence suggests otherwise.

---

35. As Hodge writes, "There is no more necessity for understanding those words literally than, 'I am the true bread,' or, 'I am the door'" (Hodge, *Systematic Theology* 3:683).

36. Webster, "Eucharist."

37. See Rosenthal, *Defense of the Classical Reformed View*.

Part II: Worship and the Sacraments

Second, the text does *not* necessitate a purely symbolic and representative approach. Look at the entire argument of the passage:

> For I do not want you to be unaware, brothers, that our fathers were all under the cloud, and all passed through the sea, and all were baptized into Moses in the cloud and in the sea, and all ate the same spiritual food, and all drank the same spiritual drink. For they drank from the spiritual Rock that followed them, and the Rock was Christ. Nevertheless, with most of them God was not pleased, for they were overthrown in the wilderness. (1 Cor 10:1–5)

Paul is paralleling the Israelite experience in the wilderness to the church's sacramental life. As Christians experience baptism, the Israelites experienced salvation through water under the leadership of Moses. As Christians partake of Christ, the Jews partook of Christ as their spiritual food.

Paul is not identifying these Old Covenant acts with New Covenant sacraments but is making parallels. The Jews were not "baptized" in the same sense that Christians are. However, in some sense the Jews experienced baptism into Moses. This does not mean that this act of crossing the Red Sea is merely a picture of what baptism would be in the New Covenant, as some with a Zwinglian or Calvinistic approach might argue; the parallel runs deeper. Paul often parallels baptism with incorporation into Christ. Through baptism, one is united to Christ's death and resurrection, and subsequently one is spiritually resurrected and Jesus' victory becomes the possession of the baptized. This is similar to the nature of the exodus. Moses acted as a mediator in the Israelites' redemption from Egypt. God gave him the authority over against Pharaoh. In his mediatory role, Moses becomes the "savior" of Israel by parting the Red Sea and leading his people away from their captors. Water thus became an instrument of redemption for Israel. That which Moses did in his role as a mediator and representative of the people was given to the Hebrews as they crossed dry land. Those who are baptized "into Christ" receive Christ's victory over sin, death, and the devil. Those who were baptized "into Moses" received his victory over Pharaoh and slavery in Egypt. Thus the parallel is not that the crossing of the sea "represents" baptism, but that it was a baptism of a lesser sort.

Commensurate with his baptismal parallel, Paul makes a parallel with the Lord's Supper. As Christians partake of the Eucharistic meal and receive Christ, the Israelites had Christ as their spiritual food and drink in the wilderness. One may be tempted to believe that this leads back to symbolism. The water and manna that the Israelites drank is representative of the Eucharist. Paul is saying, "the rock represents Christ." However, this does not seem to be the most obvious interpretation. In the Moses parallel, there is an actual "baptism" of sorts that occurs, though of a lesser nature. In the same manner there is a "partaking of Christ" as food and drink, though in a lesser sense than in the church. Note that Paul includes the terms "spiritual rock" and "spiritual food." This differentiates this food and drink from the physical manna and water that the Israelites received. The point Paul is making is that their spiritual sustenance came from the same source, from Christ.

This is further demonstrated by the argument that Paul draws from these parallels. He writes,

> Now these things took place as examples for us, that we might not desire evil as they did. Do not be idolaters as some of them were; as it is written, "The people sat down to eat and drink and rose up to play." We must not indulge in sexual immorality as some of them did, and twenty-three thousand fell in a single day. We must not put Christ to the test, as some of them did and were destroyed by serpents, nor grumble, as some of them did and were destroyed by the Destroyer. Now these things happened to them as an example, but they were written down for our instruction, on whom the end of the ages has come. Therefore let anyone who thinks that he stands take heed lest he fall. (1 Cor 10:6–12)

Paul uses the Israelites as an example for ethical exhortation. Just as the Israelites fell into idolatry and were "destroyed," the Christians who abuse the Lord's Supper and fall into licentious living and heresy also have the possibility of destruction. The parallels between the spiritual rock in the wilderness and the Eucharist are used to identify the faith of Old Testament Israel as a Christological one, thus tying the punishments of those who broke the Mosaic covenant to those who abandon Christ for heresy or unrepentant sin. There is no reason in this text to assume that the word "was" can be translated as "represented." Rather, the concept of bread and drink is what is symbolic of the Jews' faith in their coming Messiah. There is no reason to assume that "is" means anything other than "is."

One argument often proposed against Luther's approach to the sacrament is the claim that if Jesus means that the bread literally *is* his body, this would support a doctrine of transubstantiation rather than sacramental union.[38] According to Luther's reading, Jesus must have meant, "my body is in, with, and under this bread." However, it is not the case that for Jesus to admit that his body is present, it would deny that the bread is also present. It is a common figure of speech, for example, to hold a glass filled with water and say "this is water"; this figure of speech is known as a synecdoche. This would not in any way deny the fact that the glass also remains present. It would be absurd to argue that the statement "I am holding water" translates to the concept that the entire glass has been transubstantiated into water. The argument does not account for the way speech works.

1 Corinthians 10

The most widely contested passage in the Eucharistic debate during the Reformation, apart from the words of institution, is Paul's words from 1 Corinthians 10:16, "Is not the cup of thanksgiving for which we give thanks a participation in the blood of Christ? And is not the bread that we break a participation in the body of Christ?" This text is highly relevant because it delves into the nature of the Christian's relation to Christ during the Eucharistic celebration. According to Paul, through the cup one participates in Christ's blood, and through the bread one participates in the body of Christ. This text demonstrates both a realism by which one truly encounters Christ's body and blood, and also the contention that the bread and wine remain what they are. They are vehicles which bring Christ's body and blood. As the incarnation is a joining of the earthly and the heavenly by God's taking on flesh, the Eucharist involves a union of heaven and earth wherein Jesus approaches his people through the material elements of bread and wine.

Zwingli argues that the body spoken of by Paul refers not to God's actual incarnate body, but to the church: "For when you offer thanks with the cup and the bread, eating and drinking together, you signify thereby that you are one body and one bread, namely, the body which is the church of Christ, which in this sacrament confesses its faith in the Lord Jesus Christ, who gave his body and blood on our behalf."[39] There is some justification for this interpretation because Paul does stress the unity of the church in the following text. However, the language of participation in Christ's blood

---

38. Pieper cites many who make this argument and gives an extensive response; see Pieper, *Christian Dogmatics* 3:298–336.

39. Ulrich Zwingli, "On the Lord's Supper," in Bromiley, *Zwingli and Bullinger*, 237.

negates this reading. While language of the body of Christ in reference to the church is common in Pauline theology, language of Christ's blood as referring to the church is not. Zwingli proposed that this also is a reference to the church because the ecclesiastical community is identified by and covered by the blood of Christ.[40] Though a creative solution, this reading is based on an interpretation of the phrase "blood of Christ" foreign to both the New Testament and the patristic testimony.

Calvin saw the implausibility of Zwingli's reading of this text and proposed that Paul speaks of an actual participation in Christ's body and blood. However, being committed to Zwingli's Christology, Calvin denied the bodily presence within bread and wine. Thus, he developed a new explanation of the manner in which participation occurs: one participates in Christ's person through an act of the Spirit which causes one's soul to ascend to heaven with Christ and commune with his whole person.[41] There are three primary reasons why this approach is in error. First, biblical testimony is lacking regarding a work of the Spirit which causes the believer to commune with Christ. There is no New Testament language referring to the Spirit's role as being instrumental to one's participation in Christ. Secondly, the nature of one's ascension to God is contrary to the incarnational leanings of New Testament theology. In Lutheran sacramental theology, the Eucharist is God's downward movement toward creation, bringing the spiritual to the earthly. The Reformed position denies this by proposing that the nature of participation is man's ascent to God, rather than God's descent to man. Finally, this reading is based on a false Christology which negates the communication of omnipresence to the human nature of Christ.

John 6

The bread of life discourse in John 6 is a highly debated passage. Roman Catholic interpreters have typically viewed these texts as Eucharistic. Jesus is speaking of his sacramental body and blood as a means of bringing life. The Reformed have argued that there are Eucharistic principles in this text,

---

40. "And Paul calls believers the community of the blood of Christ" (ibid.).

41. "Although Christ has not yet returned bodily to earth, we are 'seated with Christ in heavenly places' (Col 3:1–4; Eph 1:20; 2:6). Christ is not seated with us on earth, but we are seated with him in the heavenlies—in a semirealized manner now, but one day face to face. Even now, the Spirit takes that which is Christ's and makes both him and his gifts our own" (Horton, *Christian Faith*, 815).

Part II: Worship and the Sacraments

namely, that "the flesh profits nothing" (John 6:33), though denying the sacramental interpretation of Rome.[42] Orthodox Lutherans used this text to make a distinction between a spiritual eating and drinking and a physical eating and drinking.[43] The believer spiritually feeds on Christ's body and blood through faith and physically receives Christ's body and blood through the sacramental elements. This interpretation stems from Luther's denial of a Eucharistic reading of the passage due to his fear of Zwingli's argument regarding Christ's distinction between flesh and spirit.

There are reasons to deny a sacramental reading of John 6, unlike the words of institution. The figure of speech Jesus uses in this text does approach the symbolic structure of other phrases in the gospels. If the text is symbolic, it is not that the word "is" means represents, but that he is using bread as a picture of himself; this is similar to how he uses "vine" as a picture of himself as the root of unity among believers. Thus, grammatically, the position is not secure in either direction.

However, in contradistinction to Luther's argument, there are sufficient reasons to adopt a Eucharistic reading of this text. First, remember the context of John's writing. John is the last gospel to be written, or at least compiled in its final form, near the end of the first century. The church had been established and saw exponential growth in a relatively short period of time. Baptism was a common occurrence in the church for those who were catechized. The anticipation of the catechumen was for baptism so that one might enter into the communion service. In the second-century church, it is clear that all non-baptized attendees of a worship service were dismissed prior to the Eucharistic celebration.[44] Partaking of Holy Communion was seen as the height of the worship service, the moment when the baptized would partake of the body and blood of their Lord, confessing their unity of faith in the cross. The Supper was received weekly, if not daily.[45] In light of the centrality of the Eucharist in the early church, it is likely that a sacramental reading of John 6 would have been obvious to his first-century readers. Surely a text about eating Christ's body and drinking Christ's blood

---

42. Francis Turretin expounds upon this argument: Turretin, *Against Consubstantiation*. Also look at Zwingli's argument in "On the Lord's Supper," in Bromiley, *Zwingli and Bullinger*, 190.

43. Hoenecke, *Evangelical Lutheran Dogmatics* 4:127–28.

44. This is the reason why certain authors accused Christians of cannibalism—because of the mysterious nature of the communion rite, which didn't allow outsiders to partake or observe.

45. See Just, *Ongoing Feast*.

cannot be anything other than a reference to the church's central practice, which utilizes the same language.

There is some evidence in the text, however, which points to a symbolic understanding of Christ's words. John writes, "I am the bread of life; whoever comes to me shall not hunger, and whoever believes in me shall never thirst" (John 6:45). Jesus equates coming to him as that which satisfies as a drink, and believing in him as an act which satisfies hunger. This justifies the distinction between a spiritual and physical partaking of Christ. However, John negates a *purely* figurative reading of Jesus' words in the bread of life discourse. While Jesus is speaking of faith as that which satisfies one spiritually through partaking in him, he also speaks of a real eating and drinking. John writes that those listening to Jesus were confused and asked, "How can this man give us his flesh to eat?" (John 6:52). Rather than correcting a false understanding of his words, Jesus says, "Truly, truly, I say to you, unless you eat the flesh of the Son of Man and drink his blood, you have no life in you. Whoever feeds on my flesh and drinks my blood has eternal life, and I will raise him up on the last day. For my flesh is true food, and my blood is true drink" (John 6:53–55). Jesus affirms the seemingly absurd statement that his flesh and blood are able to be eaten and drunk by identifying his flesh as "true food" and his blood as "true drink." If John was not intending an explanation of the Eucharist in this discourse, he would have put some indication in the text that this did not refer to the sacrament.

It is also significant that John does not include a narrative of the Last Supper in his gospel. For a writer who spends the majority of his book dealing with the last few days of Jesus' life, it is odd that one of the most significant events of Christ's ministry on the night of his betrayal is absent. It is likely that the bread of life discourse is intended as John's Last Supper narrative. Rather than explaining the story as it happened, John discusses the theological aspects of the Supper in terms of a discourse of Jesus so as not to repeat the story of the synoptics; instead John speaks in theological discourse, as is common in the fourth gospel.

Practical Theological and Pastoral Issues

Though it has been demonstrated that the Lutheran approach to the sacrament is exegetically preferable to the Calvinistic alternative, it may be objected that this debate is a purely scholastic one. Perhaps the nature of

Part II: Worship and the Sacraments

Christ's presence in the Eucharist has no practical import, but is a medieval debate which is irrelevant for the lay person in the average parish. This has been the opinion of various unionist movements since the Reformation. Usually it is the Reformed who have contended that the differences, while important, are not significant enough to break fellowship, while the Lutherans have more rigidly defended their Eucharistic orthodoxy. There is a reason why this is the case. The Lutheran approach to the Lord's Supper has several important pastoral implications which are lost through a Reformed approach to the Eucharist.

First, it reflects and influences the nature of the worship service. Lutheranism, with its emphasis on the condemnatory use of the law and its privileging justification over sanctification, has a downward focus. Many Lutherans have adopted the term "Divine Service" to refer to the corporate worship service.[46] The gathering of the church is primarily an assembly wherein God distributes gifts to his people. The service follows a pattern of forgiveness and grace given from God, and a response of praise from the congregation. Ethical exhortation does have a necessary role in the worshiping community; however, this is always in view of God's grace. For the Lutheran tradition, an incarnational approach to worship is adopted. The direction of the Christian life is downward. It is a continual act of God condescending to humanity. This is displayed in the Eucharist, wherein God-enfleshed joins himself to ordinary, earthly food, descending toward his people, offering himself to those gathered to receive him. The stance of pure passivity and reception is the continual stance of the Christian before God, as a beggar receiving gold.

In the Reformed tradition, there is a heavier emphasis on the third use of the law. Justification and sanctification are viewed as twin benefits of union with Christ, and one does not hold priority over the other.[47] Ethical exhortation has a more prominent place in the worship service. This is reflected in the Calvinistic contention that church discipline is a mark of the church.[48] Though important and practiced in Lutheranism, church discipline does not have the prominence that word and sacrament do in demonstrating the presence of Christ's church. The Reformed approaches to the Eucharist reflect this ethical focus. The Zwinglian approach to the Supper removes the action from God and places it into the hands of the church.

---

46. See Just, *Heaven on Earth*.
47. This will be documented and discussed in the two chapters below.
48. Dever, *Marks of the Church*.

The Medicine of Immortality

The church, as the gathered community of God, professes faith in Christ's cross by partaking of bread and wine. The focus is shifted from God's grace given to man, to man's profession of faith. Calvin's modified doctrine of the Supper corrects Zwingli's purely human-centered symbolism by emphasizing God's action through bread and wine. However, Calvin's approach still emphasizes man's ascent up toward God rather than God's descent. In Calvin's view, the miracle of the Supper is that the Spirit brings the human soul, spiritually, toward God. The direction is reversed from Luther's position, emphasizing the change that occurs within the regenerate believer rather than God's continual condescension in an incarnational manner.

Second, in the Lutheran approach, the Eucharist brings forgiveness. As Ignatius famously wrote, it is the "medicine of immortality."[49] The words of institution contain the promise that this body and blood is given to the church "for the forgiveness of sins." Not only does Christ's historical atonement bring forgiveness, but this is a continual gift in the Christian's life. Through the Eucharist, God gives the believer Christ's true body and blood, the same body and blood which was crucified and resurrected two thousand years ago, and through reception of that body and blood one receives forgiveness.[50] One's union with Christ is strengthened through the elements, wherein a special communion is experienced.[51] In the Eucharist, Christ continues to give himself to the recipient as one's righteousness. Whereas in Reformed theology, justification is described a one-time experience at the beginning of the Christian's life, in Luther's view, justification is continual. Each time one receives the bread and wine, one receives Jesus as one's righteousness and is granted forgiveness. One's justification is re-enacted and made apparent through Jesus' giving of himself. This is only possible because it is the *incarnate* God who delivers himself, both human and divine.

The Eucharist also brings about sanctification. Through participating in Christ's body and blood, the Trinity's presence within the believer's heart is strengthened. The resurrected Christ is given to the believer, causing the recipient to grow in his or her own resurrection life through participation

---

49. *Epistle to the Ephesians* 20:2.

50. "That is to say, in brief, that we go to the sacrament because there we receive a great treasure, through and in which we obtain the forgiveness of sins" (LC V.22).

51. "Therefore the Lord's Supper is given as a daily food and sustenance so that our faith may be refreshed and strengthened and that it may not succumb in the struggle but become stronger and stronger. For the new life should be one that continually develops and progresses" (LC V.23–26).

in him. It is a medicine strengthening one against death, sin, the devil, and the world.[52]

The Lutheran approach to the Eucharist is also a reflection of a broader conviction in which the incarnation is primary in one's worldview. The Lutheran church has historically emphasized the sacred nature of that which is "earthy" or "creaturely." In the Reformation, good works were brought from heaven to earth, with the focus being service to one's neighbor in ordinary vocations, rather than in abstract other-worldly practices. Because of the sacredness of the ordinary, Lutheranism was able to retain the liturgy, vestments, and art of the medieval church. The Lutheran church has sometimes been called "the church of the musicians" because of its rich musical heritage. Human innovations in the realm of the arts and architecture are to be celebrated, being used as instruments of praise and adoration. This is due to the conviction that God has made the earthly sacred by coming to his world through flesh and blood; God still comes to earth, through the elements of bread and wine, bringing himself into the realm of that which is created. The finite receives the infinite.

The Reformed approach to the Eucharist is also a sign of the broader conviction originally enunciated by Zwingli that the finite is not capable of the infinite. There is a dualist tendency in Calvinistic theology which is not present in Lutheranism. Zwingli, for example, at first rejected music altogether in worship, and the Reformed tradition later allowed for the use of Psalms without hymnody or instrumentation. Calvin rejected the use of religious art altogether, and Reformed churches are often purposefully unadorned. A common phrase about Puritan churches is that they contained "four bare walls and a sermon." This conviction of the transcendent nature of God denies that the infinite God could be contained in the finite elements. Thus, in Calvin's approach, the elements are instrumental in bringing the believer to Christ rather than bringing Christ through bread and wine.

Finally, the Lutheran approach to the sacrament is determinative for its importance in Christian piety and the church's liturgical life. The Eucharist has a central place in Lutheran worship, being guided by the principle of word *and* sacrament. The practice of weekly communion has been restored in many Lutheran churches and its central role in the Divine Service is being rediscovered.[53] The Supper is approached with reverence

---

52. LC V.23–27.

53. Wieting, *Blessings of Weekly Communion*.

and devotion. As communicants receive the bread in their hand with the message, "The body of Christ given for you," they are given a reminder that they are holding the very body of their Lord and Savior, and that God is, through this bread, granting eternal life.[54] As they drink the wine, they are reminded that this is the same blood of Christ which was shed on the cross for their sins. There is no greater comfort to be found than in the knowledge that God is present, and is present as a means of forgiveness rather than judgment.

Though Calvin attempted to uphold a high view of the Supper, the Reformed tradition has often regressed into pure Zwinglian symbolism. This has resulted in a consistent emphasis of the word *over* the sacrament, though the Supper has some importance when it is received. Though there are some laudable attempts in contemporary Reformed works to reintroduce Calvin's higher approach to the Eucharist, such a view of Holy Communion is still often missed by congregants.[55] Calvin's explanation of the Eucharist is often too convoluted to be understood by the average layman and thus is rejected. Though Calvin's attempt to improve Zwingli's doctrine is commendable, it ends up as a difficult central position to maintain, often forcing one to adopt either a Lutheran or Zwinglian perspective.

CONCLUSION

The Eucharistic debates of the sixteenth century have great relevance for today's church. Zwingli's symbolism is difficult to maintain exegetically and has resulted in a lack of Eucharistic piety in many churches. Calvin attempted to adopt a mediating approach to the Supper which accepted Zwingli's Christology along with a modified realism. However, the approach of Calvin fails to convince exegetically, and pastorally it remains confusing and unhelpful. Luther's reasons for insisting on agreement regarding the Supper were not arbitrary; without a robust Eucharistic theology, one's piety, worship, and study are greatly affected. It is only Luther's view which has thorough biblical support, theological rigor, and pastoral application.

---

54. There is a debate within Lutheranism over the time of Christ's presence. The consecrationist position (which this author maintains) holds that the bread and wine become Christ's body and blood at the time of the words of institution, whereas the receptionist position states that this union only occurs during the actual eating and drinking.

55. See Mathison, *Given for You*; Leithart, *Blessed Are the Hungry*; Nevin, *Mystical Presence*.

PART III

Salvation

7

Justification by Faith
The Doctrine upon Which the Church Stands or Falls[1]

BOTH THE LUTHERAN AND Reformed traditions have emphasized the doctrine of justification by faith. Being the primary issue dividing the Protestant and Roman Catholic churches, the doctrine of justification had a prominent place in the theology of Luther and of Calvin. Luther called the doctrine of justification the "article upon which the church stands or falls." Similarly, Calvin called it "the hinge on which all else turns."[2] Both traditions were in agreement regarding the central points of this doctrine, especially the *sola gratia* principle and the denial that works aid one's justification. However, despite the similarities, there are some nuances which differentiate Luther and Calvin on this central doctrine.

THE REFORMED DOCTRINE OF JUSTIFICATION

The Westminster Confession of Faith defines justification as follows:

> Those whom God effectually calleth, He also freely justifieth: not by infusing righteousness into them, but by pardoning their sins, and by accounting and accepting their persons as righteous; not

---

1. Large sections of this chapter are from my article Cooper, "A Lutheran Response."
2. Calvin, *Institutes* III.I.1.

Part III: Salvation

for any thing wrought in them, or done by them, but for Christ's sake alone; nor by imputing faith itself, the act of believing, or any other evangelical obedience to them, as their righteousness; but by imputing the obedience and satisfaction of Christ unto them, they receiving and resting on Him and His righteousness by faith; which faith they have not of themselves, it is the gift of God.[3]

The Confessional doctrine of justification in the Reformed tradition is linked to the highly emphasized doctrine of predestination.[4] Thus, justification is described as an effect of predestination. God's predestination establishes man's standing before God in eternity past; justification is the realization of this act in time through faith. Justification is the property of the elect alone. There is no possibility of justification apart from predestination unto life.[5] This justification is a one-time act and initiates the Christian life. One is first regenerated, receiving the gift of faith, and subsequently is justified. Justification is a purely legal event which consists of the imputing of righteousness and the non-imputation of sin.[6] The believer's sin is imputed to Christ, and Christ's righteousness is imputed to the believer. The righteousness of Christ is further divided into two distinct categories. The active obedience of Christ is Jesus' positive fulfillment of the law; his passive obedience refers to the cross whereon Christ passively takes the punishment of sin upon himself. This approach to justification is highly indebted to the Anselmian atonement tradition.

The Calvinist approach to justification is also connected with Reformed covenantal theology.[7] Covenant or federal theology is a system of theology which reads the Bible through a succession of covenants. There are two primary covenants: the covenant of works, and the covenant of grace. The covenant of works began in the garden, wherein prior to sin,

---

3. WCF XI.1.

4. See, for example, the popular work on Reformed soteriology from former Westminster Seminary professor John Murray: Murray, *Redemption Accomplished and Applied*.

5. "Not only some but all of those and only those whom God chose before time began in Christ are effectually called, justified, and glorified (Ro 8:30) . . . There is no indication in Scripture that the Spirit effectually calls (i.e. regenerates) those whom he has not chosen or that he draws into vital union with his Son whom he allows finally to perish" (Horton, *Christian Faith*, 681).

6. A good overview of the Reformed doctrine of justification can be found in the classic work Buchanan, *Doctrine of Justification*.

7. In my opinion, the best introduction to covenant theology is Horton, *God of Promise*.

Justification by Faith

man's relationship to God was determined by obedience. Continual obedience to the law would result in man's being sealed and confirmed in righteousness, thus partaking of eschatological blessedness; disobedience to the law would result in death. Having broken the covenant of works, Adam is then placed into a covenant of grace. This occurs through the *proto evangel* of Genesis 3:15. The covenant of grace then is realized through several other covenants, such as the Abrahamic, Davidic, and New Covenants. In Reformed theology, justification works within this structure. Jesus, as the second Adam, fulfills the covenant of works.[8] Adam served as a federal head to all mankind. This means that he served a representative function. Adam was the representative of all humankind, thus the actions of the representative are imputed to those whom he represents. Through Adam's sin, all of his offspring are counted as sinful because of his breaking of the covenant. Christ then comes as a second Adam, representing a specific people—namely, the elect—and fulfills the covenant of works where Adam failed. This is the grounds for the covenant of grace. One enters the covenant of grace through Christ's fulfillment of the covenant of works. As in Adam one is counted as sinful through Adam's breaking of the covenant of works, in Christ one is counted as righteous through Christ's fulfillment of the same covenant.

Because of this covenantal structure, the Reformed approach to justification is strictly tied to a legal understanding. In Reformed theology, Adamic sin is more often tied to the imputation of guilt, whereas in the Lutheran tradition Adamic corruption is central or even confessed to the neglect of any imputation of Adam's guilt.[9] In the same manner, the Reformed have tended to emphasize the active obedience of Christ, whereas the Lutheran tradition confesses the imputation of Christ's active obedience[10] but emphasizes the cross and resurrection over Christ's law-keeping.[11]

---

8. Some Reformed theologians argue that the covenant of works was republished at Sinai; the Mosaic covenant serves as both a covenant of works and of grace. It promises temporal blessings based on relative obedience, which Israel failed to perform, recapitulating Adam's exile from the garden through the Babylonian exile. This perspective is promoted by Meredith Kline and Michael Horton.

9. There were some in the late medieval Occamist tradition who denied Adamic corruption, arguing for a strictly imputational understanding of Adam's guilt. Because of this, some Lutheran reformers, including Martin Chemnitz, rejected the concept of imputed guilt.

10. FC SD III.15.

11. There are some modern Lutheran theologians, such as Gerhard Forde, who reject active obedience altogether.

Part III: Salvation

This distinction is the cause for a Reformed emphasis on legal soteriological categories, whereas the Lutheran tradition has viewed salvation in broader terms.

DEFINING JUSTIFICATION ACCORDING TO THE LUTHERAN CONFESSIONS

The first Confessional statement of the Reformation on justification comes from the Augsburg Confession:

> Our Churches teach that people cannot be justified before God by their own strength, merits, or works. People are freely justified for Christ's sake, through faith, when they believe that they are received into favor and that their sins are forgiven for Christ's sake. By His death, Christ made satisfaction for our sins. God counts this faith for righteousness in His sight. (AC IV)[12]

Justification is not defined per se in the above quotation, but several realities are affirmed: first, that justification comes through faith alone; second, that it involves an imputing of righteousness; and third, that it is a result of Christ's death.

In the Smalcald Articles, Luther gives a more straightforward definition of the term "justification":

> I cannot change at all what I have consistently taught about this until now, name, that "through faith" (as St. Peter says) we receive a different, new, clean heart and that, for the sake of Christ our mediator, God will and does regard us as completely righteous and holy. Although sin in the flesh is still not completely gone or dead, God will nevertheless not count it or consider it. (SA III.3.1)

Note that Luther's definition of justification contains two aspects: the legal and the effective. On the one hand, Luther confesses that we are imputed as entirely righteous through the alien righteousness of Jesus Christ, and on the other, he confesses that through the means of faith, we receive a new heart. Both are subsumed under the term "justification" in this article.

Not only in the Smalcald Articles, but also in Melanchthon's Apology, justification is seen as a regenerative work with effective implications. "We have shown that through faith alone we are justified, that is, unrighteous people are made righteous, or regenerated" (Apol IV.117). This is not to say,

---

12. McCain, *Concordia*.

Justification by Faith

however, that an effective change in the heart is ever the cause of imputation. Rather, imputation is the cause of sanctification and a renewed life. As Schlink states, "the 'making righteous' must be understood exclusively in the light of the 'pronouncing righteous'; the 'pronouncing righteous' is not to be understood in the light of the 'making righteous.'"[13] Justification is an act of imputation and declaration which consequently makes the Christian righteous.

The Formula of Concord affirms a more legal view of justification in contradistinction to the Apology of Melanchthon. The Solid Declaration states that "the word 'justify' here means to pronounce righteous and free from sins and to count as freed from the eternal punishment of sin because of Christ's righteousness which is 'reckoned to faith by God'" (FC SD III.17). This tension can be resolved by acknowledging that the term "justification" has two different senses in the earlier and later Confessional documents. In the definition of Melanchthon and oftentimes of Luther, the term was used as a synecdoche in reference to imputation, union, and regeneration.[14] In the proper sense, however, as used in the Formula of Concord, justification is a forensic declaration, and effective righteousness is simply its *result*. The seventeenth-century Lutheran scholastic theologians followed the Formula of Concord in defining justification as a primarily judicial term. In a typical explanation of the scholastic approach, Hoenecke writes, "Justification is a judicial act of God, since out of grace he declares sinful human beings, who have fallen into eternal punishment on account of sin, to be righteous for Christ's sake without any merit on their part."[15] Justification properly speaking is thus a legal declaration, but it is an effective declaration.

JUSTIFICATION AS GOD'S EFFECTIVE SPEECH

To gain an understanding of the relationship between imputation and renewal, one need not go directly to Paul, but to the beginning of the Bible: "And God said, 'Let there be light,' and there was light" (Gen 1:3). God is a God who speaks. Not only does he speak, but he speaks with power. He does not speak descriptively, but as a divine potentate giving a command

---

13. Schlink, *Theology of the Lutheran Confessions*, 95. Schlink states this in relation to Melancthon's Apology.

14. Jacob Preus makes this argument in *Just Words*, 15–25.

15. Hoenecke, *Evangelical Lutheran Dogmatics* 3:318. This of course is theologically correct in defining the narrow sense of the term.

which is then brought into reality. Whereas human speech either describes, questions, or gives commands, God's pronouncements enact what they proclaim. God says that it is so, and it is so.

When God justifies the sinner, he is declared righteous and consequently *is* righteous. God's word is a life-giving word and a creative word. As God declares the sinner to be justified, life is brought from death; spiritual impulses are created *ex nihilo*. This is the point Paul makes in Romans 4:

> That is why it depends on faith, in order that the promise may rest on grace and be guaranteed to all his offspring—not only to the adherent of the law but also to the one who shares the faith of Abraham, who is the father of us all, as it is written, "I have made you the father of many nations"—in the presence of the God in whom he believed, who gives life to the dead and calls into existence the things that do not exist. In hope he believed against hope, that he should become the father of many nations, as he had been told, "So shall your offspring be." He did not weaken in faith when he considered his own body, which was as good as dead (since he was about a hundred years old), or when he considered the barrenness of Sarah's womb. No unbelief made him waver concerning the promise of God, but he grew strong in his faith as he gave glory to God, fully convinced that God was able to do what he had promised. That is why his faith was "counted to him as righteousness." But the words "it was counted to him" were not written for his sake alone, but for ours also. It will be counted to us who believe in him who raised from the dead Jesus our Lord, who was delivered up for our trespasses and raised for our justification. (Rom 4:16–25)

Abraham had faith that God's promise to give an offspring would come to pass despite Sarah's barren womb. Abraham was aware of the fact that biologically, having a child with a barren woman is impossible. However, Abraham knew that God's word is powerful and brings to pass what it declares, despite what human reason might speculate. In the Pauline argument, Abraham's faith in God's creative power is analogous to the new life that Christ brings to those of faith. Those who have faith are pronounced righteous and consequently a resurrection occurs. A new spiritual life is placed in the human creature. As God's act, it occurs monergistically. One's justification, and one's rebirth, is solely the result of God's omnipotence as displayed in the act of creation.

Justification by Faith

In the text above, Paul writes, Jesus was "delivered for our trespasses and raised for our justification." This oft-ignored statement of Paul's connects justification, not with Christ's merit, nor his death, but with his resurrection. Protestant orthodoxy has typically connected justification with Christ's active obedience in fulfilling the law and his passive obedience in taking sin's penalty upon himself on the cross. The resurrection is often viewed as the proof of Christ's deity, or as a testament that the cross is efficacious. However, Paul's theological conception (as well as Luther's) is much bigger.

Paul describes the cross as the antidote to human trespasses. Man's sins were done away with on the cross, when Christ became sin for us. God's people no longer have a debt owed to God because it has been wiped out. Paul then describes the resurrection as the instrument of righteousness. Through Christ's resurrection, one's righteousness is sealed before God, and resurrection is enacted. Through the resurrection of Christ, God proclaims his people righteous, causing their resurrection. One's justification causes union with Christ's resurrection, wherein his victory is imputed to the believer, and God creates spiritual life from death. God's creative word is an eschatological word. Expounding upon Galatians 1:1, Luther writes,

> Thus at the very outset Paul explodes with the entire issue he intends to set forth in this epistle. He refers to the resurrection of Christ, who rose again for our justification (Rom 4:25). His victory is a victory over the Law, sin, our flesh, the world, the devil, death, hell, an all evils; and this victory of His He has given to us. Even though these tyrants, our enemies, accuse us and terrify us, they cannot drive us into despair or condemn us. For Christ, whom God the Father raised from the dead, is the Victor over them, and He is our righteousness. Therefore "thanks be to God, who has given us the victory through our Lord Jesus Christ" (1 Cor 15:57). Amen.[16]

One's eschatological vindication and resurrection has invaded the present age, bringing people into the kingdom of God. This, for Paul and for Luther, is connected to justification.

---

16. *LW* 26:21–22.

Part III: Salvation

OBJECTIVE JUSTIFICATION

In the nineteenth century, American Lutherans began making the distinction between objective justification and subjective justification. Objective justification refers to the *historia salutis* reality of Christ's justification at his resurrection. The resurrection is Christ's own vindication before God, and consequently becomes that of the Christian through faith. This appropriation of Christ's objective work through faith is subjective justification. Thus objective justification precedes all aspects of the order of salvation.

C. F. W. Walther explains the purpose of the resurrection of Christ, writing, "Christ is now free and declared now and forever free of all the debt and penalties taken by him, it means, in a word, that he is absolved."[17] This declaration placed upon Christ was done on behalf of all humanity. Walther notes: "Christ's life is the life of all people. Christ's proclamation of freedom, all people's proclamation of freedom, Christ's justification, all peoples' justification, Christ's absolution all peoples' absolution."[18] Objective justification flows from the reality of the incarnation. In being born as a human, Jesus takes upon himself not simply the nature of one individual man, but of all humanity. Thus all Jesus accomplishes and does with his life is accomplished for all of humankind. His vindication at his resurrection is thus the justification of all people. There is a sense, then, that through Jesus' resurrection the entire human race is justified. Robert Preus explains: "Objective justification is not a mere metaphor, a figurative way of expressing the fact that Christ died for all and paid for the sins of all. Objective justification has happened, it is the actual acquittal of the entire world of sinners for Christ's sake."[19] Objective justification is thus tied to the Lutheran contention of universal atonement but is not identical with it.

This universal justification is not alone sufficient to save without faith, however. Though sin has been taken by Christ on the cross, and the world has been vindicated before the Father, these benefits must be subjectively appropriated in faith. Faith then is not a cause of justification, but the reception of a justification which already occurred at the moment of Christ's resurrection from the dead. The Reformed church has not generally made such distinctions, especially in light of the contention that the atonement

---

17. Walther, *From Our Master's Table*, 72.
18. Ibid.
19. Preus, "Objective Justification," in *Doctrine Is Life*, 149.

is limited in scope. Thus objective justification remains a distinctively Lutheran contention in Reformation theology.

Christ's resurrection as his justification is seen in 1 Timothy 3:16, which states that Jesus was "vindicated (ἐδικαιώθη) by the Spirit." This vindication is spoken of in Romans 5, wherein Paul parallels Christ's universal act of redemption and Adam's universal act of bringing death and sin into the world. He writes, "Therefore just as one man's trespass led to condemnation for all, so one man's act of righteousness leads to justification and life for all" (Rom 5:18). There is a clear parallelism in this text, wherein Adam brings sin and death to a group of people (being all people), and Christ brings righteousness and life to this same group. If this is Paul's intent, then there is clear precedence for saying that in some sense, all are justified due to the work of Christ.

THE PLACE OF JUSTIFICATION IN THE ORDO SALUTIS

The Reformed tradition has often made a distinction between the *historia salutis* and the *ordo salutis*. The *historia salutis* is the order of God's redemption worked out in history. Thus, the fall, the giving of the law, the exile, and the incarnation all belong in the *historia salutis*. The *ordo salutis* describes the personal aspect of redemption. It describes the order in which the benefits of Christ are applied to the believer. A typical Reformed approach to the *ordo* might include election, effectual call, regeneration, illumination, union with Christ, definitive sanctification, faith, repentance, justification, adoption, progressive sanctification, perseverance, and glorification.[20] The orthodox Lutheran approach to the *ordo* often includes calling, illumination, repentance, faith, justification, mystical union, sanctification, and preservation.[21] The development of an *ordo salutis* was a generally beneficial move in scholastic theology, but the exposition of the *ordo* has sometimes led to the forensic judgment of justification being divorced from other soteric benefits, as if there is no direct connection between justification, sanctification, and union with Christ.

A fear of Osiandrian doctrine caused Lutherans in the seventeenth century to become more cautious about Luther's wording of Christ's presence in faith, causing this union with Christ to be placed solely under the

---

20. See Murray, *Redemption Accomplished and Applied*.
21. See Hoenecke, *Evangelical Lutheran Dogmatics* 4.

rubric of the mystical union, which is subsequent to justification. Andreas Osiander, a seventeenth-century Lutheran theologian, contended that justification is not a legal term caused by the objective death and resurrection of Christ in history, but describes the process whereby the Christian becomes righteous through the indwelling of divinity. The greatness and vast nature of divinity swallows up and defeats sin, causing both forgiveness and growth in righteousness. This approach is condemned by the Formula of Concord (FC III).

For Luther, Christ gives himself, both human and divine, to the one who has faith. In being united to the God-man, one receives all that is his: his righteousness, wisdom, sanctification, sonship, and immortality. In turn, Christ takes unto himself all that is wicked in the believer.[22] This union is only effective through the objective life, death, resurrection, and ascension of Christ in history. For Luther, the resurrected Christ dwells in faith. As Luther states, "For those who maintain that righteousness comes by works deny Christ's resurrection and even ridicule it."[23] Christ's resurrection is essential for God's justifying decree.

The last of the great Lutheran dogmaticians of the scholastic era, David Hollaz, describes two different manners of speaking about union with Christ, which helpfully explains the relationship between justification and union. On the one hand, mystical union is the divine indwelling of Christ wherein one is granted virtue and strengthened in faith. This is the *unio mystica* spoken of in the Formula of Concord (FC III). This union is not a cause but a result of justification. There is, however, another union spoken of by Hollaz: the *unio fidei formalis*. This formal union of faith unites one to Christ and occurs prior to subjective justification. Hollaz writes,

> Though mystical union, where God inhabits man as in a temple, according to our mode of understanding comes after justification

---

22. Mannermaa justifies this in part by the following quotation from Luther: "Christian faith is not an idle quality or an empty husk in the heart, which may exist in a state of mortal sin until love comes along to make it alive. But if it is true faith, it is a sure trust and firm acceptance in the heart. It takes hold of Christ in such a way that Christ is the object of faith, or rather not the object but, so to speak, the One who is present in the faith itself. Thus faith is a sort of knowledge or darkness that nothing can see. Yet the Christ of whom faith takes hold is sitting in this darkness as God sat in the midst of darkness on Sinai and in the temple. Therefore our 'formal righteousness' is not a love that informs faith; but it is faith itself, a cloud in our hearts, that is, trust in a thing we do not see, in Christ, who is present especially when He cannot be seen. Therefore faith justifies because it takes hold of and possesses this treasure, the present Christ" (*LW* 26:2432).

23. *LW* 2:167–68.

Justification by Faith

> according to the order of nature; however, I must confess that the formal union of faith, by which Christ is apprehended, put on, and united with us, where Christ is the mediator and conveyer of grace, and the remission of sins, is prior to justification. For as faith is prior to justification, insofar as the merit of Christ is received and is united with us to become ours. "If we take the spiritual regeneration, the rebirth wrought by God, as consisting mainly in our union with Christ, this differs from justification as an effect to a cause. For we are justified because we are from God, or because we are in Christ," see Rom. 8:1: "For there is now no condemnation for those who are in Christ Jesus." The righteousness of Christ is the chief spiritual benefit reckoned to those who believe being closely united to him, his members, who are found in him, Phil. 3:9.[24]

This manner of dividing union into two separate moments in the *ordo salutis* guards against both the danger in conflating Christ for us and in us, and that of dividing Christ's person from his work of justification.

Another unfortunate result of the Reformed *ordo salutis* is that justification is described as a pure transfer term. This perspective has been debated among the interpreters of Paul in recent years. Does justification in Paul serve as a transfer term, a term of identification, eschatological vindication, or perhaps all three? In Reformed (and sometimes Lutheran) orthodoxy, justification is an initial one-time event wherein the believer is imputed righteous and forgiven. In essence, it is a transfer term and constitutes the beginning of the Christian life. The Christian life is then an ongoing process of sanctification wherein the Christian is gradually made intrinsically righteous as he grows in holiness.

In Luther's theology, good works never become the essence of the Christian life *coram Deo*. Faith is continually the means by which man's standing before God is evaluated, secured, and renewed. As Luther confesses, "For so long as I go on living in the flesh, there is certainly sin in me. But meanwhile Christ protects me under the shadow of His wings and spreads over me the wide heaven of the forgiveness of sins, under which I live in safety."[25] God's declaration of justification is not a one-time event but is continual. As Christ gives himself as the resurrected and ascended eschatological Son of God in the Eucharist, the Christian receives this declaration of justification again. This union is strengthened, and alien righteousness

---

24. My translation, originally published as Hollaz, "Mystical Union," *Just and Sinner*.
25. *LW* 26:231–32.

is continually imputed as the means by which man's relationship to God is mediated. When a pastor proclaims absolution to the penitent sinner, this human's words become, sacramentally, God's own declarative word by which he imparts life, forgiveness, and the righteousness of Christ. God's creative act in his people and for his people is a continual act. It is not a gradual sanctification which continues after, and apart from, a one-time justification, but is a life of justification, not as a process, but of continual imputation. Every time the ruling of justification is placed on the sinner, he is again strengthened in sanctification as he participates in the eschatological life of Christ.

The continuous aspect of justification can be demonstrated from the two examples of Old Testament saints that Paul discusses in Romans 4 to defend his concept of justification apart from works. First Paul uses Abraham, citing the book of Genesis: "For what does the Scripture say? 'For Abraham believed God and it was counted to him as righteousness'" (Rom 4:3). It is worthy to note that Genesis 15 is not the beginning of Abraham's life of faith. It is in Genesis 12 that Abraham is called out of paganism, places his faith in God, and is promised to become a great nation. Surely Abraham was justified already in Genesis 12, but Paul is willing to place justification in Genesis 15. In Pauline theology, justification is not only a transfer term denoting one's transition from wrath to grace (though it certainly is that), but it encapsulates the whole life of faith. This strengthens Paul's point that "God justifies the ungodly" (Rom 4:5) because it is not only that the pagan Abraham is ungodly; rather, the Abraham of Genesis 15 who had already abandoned everything he knew solely to follow God's command is ungodly. Even after his good deeds, Paul writes that Abraham is one who "does not work" (Rom 4:5). Even after walking in faith, performing seemingly righteous actions, it is solely God's gracious imputation through faith that establishes Abraham's righteousness before God. This is a clear demonstration of *simul iustus et peccator*.

The second example given by Paul is that of David. Paul writes,

> [J]ust as David also speaks of the blessing of the one to whom God counts righteousness apart from works: "Blessed are those whose lawless deeds are forgiven, and whose sins are covered; blessed is the man against whom the Lord will not count his sin." (Rom 4:6–8)

David does not speak in Psalm 32 about his initial conversion to a life of faith. He is not discussing his circumcision, or his entrance into the national blessings given to Israel. Neither is he speaking of table fellowship and ethnocentric Judaism, as some contemporary interpreters have argued. David is describing himself in a state of confession and repentance. As David, after having ruled as a righteous king over Israel for some time, confesses his sin to God, his sins are forgiven and covered. As Paul states, God counted David righteous without regarding his works. David's justification, throughout life, rests solely on God's gracious imputation through faith. In his argument in the book of Romans, Paul significantly is pointing to two of the most venerated and righteous figures of the Old Testament. Abraham was given the promise that he would become a great nation, and David was promised that a descendant of his would continually reign on the throne; yet Paul is willing to call both of these saints "ungodly," and righteous apart from works. Paul is as patent as Luther in declaring the righteous and sinful natures of believers.

A common criticism to the Lutheran approach to justification is that the centrality of this single benefit of the *ordo salutis* neglects the rich Pauline conception of salvation. However, it has been shown that justification is not solely a soteric benefit but also encapsulates imputation, forgiveness, and God's act of spiritual resurrection, and it brings about a real union with Christ that occurs through faith. Justification is also connected with what has been an oft neglected teaching in some communities: adoption. Melanchthon, in his Apology, freely interchanges the concept of justification and adoption: "Since we receive forgiveness of sins and the Holy Spirit through faith alone, faith justifies. For those reconciled are counted as righteous and as God's children" (Apol IV II.86). Reformed theologians have often separated adoption from justification as two separate benefits. John Murray, in his classic work *Redemption Accomplished and Applied*, distinctively separates justification and adoption as different benefits of the *ordo salutis*.[26] In this view, justification is a purely forensic metaphor, whereas in the Lutheran approach it is also familial and relational. The Lutheran approach coheres with Paul's own discussions of justification wherein the soteric benefit is connected to one's place in the family of Abraham.

In line with Melanchthon's Apology, Paul freely interchanges the two concepts in his epistle to the Galatians:

> Did you suffer so many things in vain—if indeed it was in vain? Does he who supplies the Spirit to you and works miracles among you do so by works of the law, or by hearing with faith—just

26. Murray, *Redemption Accomplished and Applied*, 117–40.

> as Abraham "believed God, and it was counted to him as righteousness"? Know then that it is those of faith who are the sons of Abraham. And the Scripture, foreseeing that God would justify the Gentiles by faith, preached the gospel beforehand to Abraham, saying, "In you shall all the nations be blessed." So then, those who are of faith are blessed along with Abraham, the man of faith. (Gal 3:4–9)

For Paul, the strict theological categories which developed in certain strands of scholasticism are not to be separated. Imputation, forgiveness, regeneration, and adoption are all encapsulated in the same reality that God saves sinners by grace alone, through faith alone.

The charge that Lutherans privilege one aspect of salvation, namely, imputed righteousness, over all others, making it the sole criterion of Christian orthodoxy, is unfounded. When Luther claims that justification is the *praecipuus articulus christianae doctrinae*,[27] his precise meaning is not simply the importance of imputed righteousness, but that *Christ for us* always has precedence over *Christ in us*. God's work for sinners is at the heart of the Christian faith. This is why the common proof text used by Lutheran theologians for the centrality of justification is 1 Corinthians 2:2: "For I decided to know nothing among you except Jesus Christ and him crucified." The text doesn't state directly that Paul was preaching imputed righteousness only, but God's work for fallen humanity in the cross of Jesus Christ for salvation. This includes our imputation, forgiveness, regeneration, adoption, and redemption. This is why Chemnitz, while admitting that Augustine did not have a legal understanding of the doctrine of justification, still claims that Augustine understood the heart of the Christian message.[28]

JUSTIFICATION AND SANCTIFICATION

The issue of justification cannot be addressed properly without discussing the issue of good works in the Christian life. In Reformed theology,

---

27. The "principle doctrine of the Christian faith."

28. "Thus Augustine describes 'righteousness' as the new obedience, 'grace' as the aid of the Holy Spirit, and 'to justify' as making an unrighteous man righteous. But on the real substance of the matter he is one with us in holding that the new obedience is never perfect in this life, and that thus there is only one hope for all the godly, namely, that they have an Advocate with the Father, who is the Propitiation for their sins" (Chemnitz, *Loci Theologici* 1:31).

justification and sanctification are described as separate benefits. Though one cannot be justified and not sanctified, nor be sanctified without justification preceding, there is no causal relationship between the two aspects of Christian existence. Justification is not the result of sanctification, nor is sanctification the result of justification. They are both simultaneous benefits of the reality of covenantal union with Christ.[29] Justification is a monergistic act, wherein God imputes the sinner righteous through the merit of Christ through faith; sanctification is a work of cooperation between the regenerate man and God's renewing grace.

For Lutheran theology, sanctification and justification have an intimate connection which cannot be severed. Sanctification is the effect of justification. It is not a separate benefit of union with Christ, but is the declarative reality of righteousness (in justification) becoming an effective intrinsic reality. Sanctification is thus the "working out" of justification.[30]

Resurrection is thoroughly intertwined with the Pauline concept of sanctification, as it is with justification. In encouraging good works in the Christian life, Paul states, "If the Spirit of him who raised Jesus from the dead dwells in you, he who raised Christ Jesus from the dead will also give life to your mortal bodies through his Spirit who dwells in you" (Rom 8:11). Sanctification is a result of the resurrecting act of God through the declarative act of justification. As God's declarative word is continually given through preaching, Holy Communion, and absolution, the decree of justification is efficacious unto sanctification. The resurrection life of Christ grows in us. Paul also uses this language as a motivation to perform good works in his epistle to the Colossians:

> If then you have been raised with Christ, seek the things that are above, where Christ is, seated at the right hand of God. Set your minds on things that are above, not on things that are on earth. For you have died, and your life is hidden with Christ in God. When Christ who is your life appears, then you also will appear with him in glory. (Col 3:1–4)

---

29. See Gaffin, *By Faith*.

30. "It is also the doctrine of Scripture that, as we in faith bear the form of the perfectly righteous Christ before God by virtue of the imputation of Justification, so also the same righteous Christ is to be formed in those who are justified (Gal. 4:19)" (Hoenecke, *Evangelical Lutheran Dogmatics* 3:382). Stump, to the contrary, argues that justification "has no reference to any moral quality in man, and produces no inner change in him" (Stump, *Christian Faith*, 222).

Part III: Salvation

It is God's act of spiritual resurrection which sanctifies the Christian. His good works do not sanctify, nor does the law. God sanctifies through the means of grace. This does not mean, however, that the Christian is idle. Through God's act of sanctification, as the Christian participates in the resurrection life of Christ, he joyfully and freely performs good works. As Luther writes, "Faith cannot help doing good works constantly. It doesn't stop to ask if good works ought to be done, but before anyone asks, it already has done them and continues to do them without ceasing. Anyone who does not do good works in this manner is an unbeliever."[31] Yet these works are not to be identified *as* sanctification, but as the *result* of sanctification.

Sanctification, like justification, comes, in some sense, through the alien righteousness of Christ. Luther states this clearly: "There is a double life: my own, which is natural or animate; and an alien life, that of Christ in me. So far as my animate life is concerned, I am dead and am now living an alien life."[32] For the Lutheran Reformation, both justification and sanctification are granted through gospel rather than law.[33] "For the Gospel contains the promise of the Spirit of renewal, who writes the Law into the heart of believers, Jer. 31:33. It also teaches how the beginnings of obedience, although imperfect and contaminated in many ways, are pleasing to God in those who are righteous for the sake of Christ."[34] For Luther, and for Paul, sanctification is primarily God's act, which consists in progress in holiness resulting from justification.

Luther also formulated the distinction between justification and sanctification within his doctrine of "two kinds of righteousness," first explained in a 1519 sermon by that title.[35] The first kind of righteousness is passive righteousness, wherein the sinner is imputed righteous by simply receiving the righteousness of Christ. This is how the Christian's relationship before God (*coram Deo*) is established. Humans are in relationship not only to God, however, but also with one another. Before the world (*coram mundo*), the Christian is not simply passive, but active. This is the second kind of righteousness, or active righteousness.[36] The first kind of righteousness is

---

31. "Luther's Definition of Faith," Smith.

32. *LW* 26:170.

33. The law does play an intimate role in guiding Christian sanctification by ethical instruction. It cannot, however, grant the power to obey.

34. Chemnitz, *Loci Theologici* 2–3:826.

35. *LW* 31:297.

36. There is some debate amongst theologians between the "two kinds of

Justification by Faith

the only one that avails before God for justification; the second describes the Christian's actions within the world. The alien righteousness which is received establishes one's vertical relationship with God, and this then gives the motivation and drive for the Christian to love his or her neighbor in the horizontal plane before fellow men. This is one of the primary manners in which the relationship between justification and sanctification is explained in Luther's writing.

JUSTIFICATION'S SACRAMENTAL CONTEXT

In the Lutheran tradition, justification is placed within an ecclesial and sacramental context. It is not a single spontaneous moment of the *ordo salutis* wherein one is imputed righteous, but it is an action which occurs through concrete means that God has instituted. This is through both word and sacrament.

When one is justified, faith grasps Christ and one is counted wholly and entirely righteous for the sake of Christ even while remaining a sinner. Righteousness is imputed rather than infused. The faith that receives Christ is not that which man chooses, but is given through grace. Both justification and the faith which receives justification are gifts of God. In this sense, Reformed theology is in agreement. However, a difference arises regarding the means that bring about the gift. Whereas the Calvinistic tradition has adopted a spontaneous and free understanding of the Spirit's gifting of faith, the Lutheran tradition has confessed that the gift of faith is given through the means of word and sacrament.[37] God has so tied himself to the means of grace that forgiveness is always offered, and grace is always present when the word is proclaimed and the sacraments are administered.

The proclamation of God's word is a means of regeneration. As Peter states, "you have been born again, not of perishable seed but of imperishable, *through the living and abiding word of God*" (1 Pet 1:23).[38] The Lutheran tradition has argued that God's word is not merely descriptive of God, but

---

righteousness" paradigm in that some have argued for three kinds of righteousness. In this scheme, active righteousness can either be civil, so as to include the non-believer, or it can refer to the new obedience of the Christian. Joel Biermann argues for this model in Biermann, *Case for Character*.

37. This is not to say that the Reformed don't believe that God uses the means of word and sacrament as an instrument of regeneration, but God does not tie himself to these means in such a way that he is *always* present and acting through them.

38. Emphasis mine.

that it has power in its proclamation. The word acts toward the sinner as law and gospel. The word does not merely tell the sinner what law and gospel are and explain the distinction, but they are both functions of the word itself. Thus proclamation of the law crushes. It attacks self-righteousness and pride. As the prophet Jeremiah writes, "is not my word like fire, declares the Lord, and like a hammer that breaks the rock in pieces?" (Jer 23:29). As in prophetic literature, the word brings both destruction and redemption. Along with crushing one's pride and ego, the word also proclaims forgiveness and redemption. This is not merely a description of what salvation is or how to receive it, but the word actually *delivers* what it promises. In this way, the promise that one's sins are forgiven, the proclamation of the gospel, gives both faith and the forgiveness that it proclaimed.

Pastoral absolution, both during the service and in private, is a means by which this forgiveness is brought about. When a sinner is confronted with his or her sin and confesses that sin before the minister of the word, the pastor declares forgiveness in the Trinitarian name. This is an instance of justification. The proclamation of the pastor that one's sins are forgiven actually forgives sin and consequently grants spiritual life. Each time absolution is practiced, one is justified. Sin is forgiven, righteousness is imputed, and one's old self is drowned and the new man is raised to life. Because absolution occurs during each worship service and in times of private confession, justification serves as an act which frames the Christian life. It is enacted and proclaimed at the beginning of each worship service, implying that forgiveness is necessary and given before one approaches God in praise and adoration. Later in the service, one prays the Lord's Prayer, wherein one requests forgiveness. This prayer for forgiveness characterizes one's life throughout the week, until the next Sunday morning when absolution is declared as the answer to that prayer. Justification in this way frames the Christian life, from the prayer for forgiveness made daily, to the weekly absolution during worship.

Baptism is also an instance of justification. Through baptism one is united to Christ. One's sinful self is drowned and the new self is raised to life. Being baptized in the Triune name, the baptized receives the Trinitarian acts of redemption. The forgiveness won on the cross, the eternal life secured by the resurrection, and the indwelling of the Spirit are delivered through the water and the word proclaimed. This initial act of forgiveness and granting of new life is to be continually in view throughout the Christian life. Through this act, one has died. Sin and death no longer have any

Justification by Faith

dominion. One confesses and remembers this through the ancient practice of the sign of the cross. Through this act, Christians engage in remembrance of the fact that they are wholly righteous, forgiven children of God who live continually in light of their baptismal promise.

As with the other two sacraments, the Eucharist is also an instance of justification. The words of institution contain the phrase "for the forgiveness of sins," defining the central purpose of the Lord's Supper. It is significant that the Supper communicates Christ's true body and blood. Christ's body and blood are the same body and blood that were crucified, rose from the dead, and ascended. Through partaking of Christ through the Eucharistic elements, one receives all of the benefits that Jesus won for his people. Thus the participant in the Supper receives forgiveness and imputed righteousness. In the Supper Jesus is giving himself to his people as their righteousness and life. Thus justification is again enacted, received, and sealed as one partakes of the body and blood of Jesus.

CONCLUSION

The differences between Luther's approach to justification and that of the Reformed tradition have been made apparent. There are significant areas of agreement between the two branches of the Reformation. Both affirm that justification is by faith alone, that it is a result of the imputation of Christ's alien righteousness, and that it is a legal term. There is also agreement in the confession that salvation is monergistic. However, for Luther, justification is not limited to a bare legal declaration, as is the case in the standard Reformed approach, but it is an efficacious declaration. Reformed theologians miss the sacramental context for Lutheran doctrine. There is no justification with an absent Christ, or without one baptism for the remission of sins, or Christ's true body and blood coming to his church through the Eucharist. The Reformed tradition also divides justification from the other benefits of the *ordo salutis* in a manner incommensurate with the Book of Concord. In both the biblical and Lutheran approach to the doctrine of justification, both legal and effective dimensions are confessed, and justification is something which is continually effective and pertinent, being the basis for Christian life and worship.

8

New Life in Christ
Sanctification and Vocation

THE LUTHERAN AND REFORMED traditions have both defended a monergistic view of salvation. Election, regeneration, and justification are solely acts of God wherein man's efforts play no significant role. It is also confessed by both traditions that one's final perseverance comes through an act of grace. However, the area of sanctification is not so simplistic as to promote a strict monergism/synergism divide on the subject. That being said, there are certain trajectories within Reformed and Lutheran theology which emphasize either man's active role in sanctification or God's active role as sanctifier. Both traditions are not as internally unified on this specific topic as on others because there are various trajectories within each tradition. However, a general outline of the positions and differences can be extrapolated from various confessional documents and popular writings on the subject.[1]

---

1. One should not try to make a hard and fast distinction between the Lutheran and Reformed approaches to sanctification. Some attempts have been made in the past which have compromised the biblical and Confessional stance of the Lutheran church. Werner Elert, for example, attempted to explain the difference in terms of the third use of the law by saying the Reformed believe in a third use, whereas Lutherans do not. This contradicts the Formula of Concord. On the third use of the law, see Murray, *Law, Life, and the Living God*. Others, such as Gerhard Forde, in his article "The Lutheran View of Sanctification," have argued that there is no progressive sanctification in Lutheranism. This is also in error.

New Life in Christ

THE REFORMED TRADITION ON SANCTIFICATION

Sanctification is defined as a process which proceeds after justification in the *ordo salutis*. After justification has been received, one begins a process wherein one grows in actual holiness, being gradually conformed to the image of Christ.[2] The Reformed Confessional tradition is not always clear about the nature of sanctification and the nature of cooperation between the divine and human elements at work. The Westminster Confession of faith emphasizes the gracious nature of God's activity within sanctification:

> They who are effectually called and regenerated, having a new heart and a new spirit created in them, are further sanctified, really and personally, through the virtue of Christ's death and resurrection, by his Word and Spirit dwelling in them; the dominion of the whole body of sin is destroyed, and the several lusts thereof are more and more weakened and mortified, and they more and more quickened and strengthened, in all saving graces, to the practice of true holiness, without which no man shall see the Lord. (WCF XIII.1)

As are the other elements of soteriology, sanctification is placed within a personal *ordo salutis*. Sanctification is a link on the so-called golden chain of salvation following justification and regeneration, yet preceding glorification. It is a result of election. The Confession attributes the work of sanctifying grace primarily to the operation of the Holy Spirit, though connected to the death and resurrection of Christ. The Reformed Confessions admit that one's sanctification is always imperfect prior to glorification: "This sanctification is throughout in the whole man, yet imperfect in this life: there abideth still some remnants of corruption in every part, whence ariseth a continual and irreconcilable war, the flesh lusting against the Spirit, and the Spirit against the flesh" (WCF XIII.2). The later Wesleyan concept of "entire sanctification"[3] is expressly denied, as the Christian life involves a continual reliance on grace and is placed within the context of a war between the sinful and redeemed natures.

Though admitting that imperfection always remains in the Christian, Reformed theology lays a heavy emphasis on the progressive nature of

---

2. Frame defines sanctification as "our gradual growth in holiness and righteousness, our progress in God's way, the way of good works" (Frame, *Systematic Theology*, 987).

3. For a description and defense of the Wesleyan view, see Grider, *Entire Sanctification*.

181

sanctification. Christians are said to "grow in grace, perfecting holiness in the fear of God" (WCF XIII.3). Though there may be times of lapsing, in which growth will not be apparent, the ordinary nature of Christian life is that of growth and maturation. Holiness is an actual reality, belonging to the Christian not simply by imputation, but by the manifestation of a holy life. Sanctification is visible through action and is apparent in the Christian through the gradual cleansing of sinful motives to holy motivations for one's actions. This is displayed largely by obedience to the law according to the third use.[4]

The Puritan tradition developed a heavily emphasized concept in relation to sanctification labeled the "mortification of sin." The fullest explanation of this approach to the Christian life is contained in John Owen's book of that title.[5] Owen argues that the Christian's sanctification is a cooperative effort between God and man. God justifies, regenerates, and saves, but man is responsible for the putting off of the flesh, the killing of the old man. Owen argues that mortifying sin is necessary because it hampers one's spirituality, it harms the soul. Sin also affects the witness of the gospel that Christians are to give to those around them. This act of mortification is not complete; one will never cease sinning. However, it is real and progressive. One has a duty to kill sin in a war against the flesh. Owen provides several steps in the process to guide the killing of sin. This involves faith in Christ, reliance on the Spirit's sanctifying work, assurance of a true conversion, and an intent to obey God in all actions. Owen then gives his readers several steps by which one may become more obedient to God's law and more effective in killing one's sinful nature. This includes an intense focus on one's sinful nature, increasing sorrow over sin, and placing oneself in situations wherein this sin is hard to commit and temptation is absent.

The Puritanical approach to sanctification lays a higher emphasis on the involvement of the sinner in the sanctifying process. In the mortification-of-sin model, sanctification arises not merely through the gospel as contained in the means of grace, but through one's efforts, which include both gaining a greater trust in God's work and also actively subduing the flesh.[6] The Puritanical approach to sanctification also has an impact on

---

4. "When Scripture motivates us to pursue holiness, it often calls us to be obedient to God's commands" (Frame, *Systematic Theology*, 989).

5. This and Owen's other works on the topic are compiled in Owen, *Works* 6.

6. I am not implying that the Lutheran model ignores the importance of one's activity or subduing of the sin nature, but the emphasis is different within Puritan theology.

New Life in Christ

one's view of assurance. Since sanctification is a necessary result of regeneration, and is visible through the killing of sin in one's life, the fruit of sanctification becomes necessary for one to gain assurance. Mark Jones gives the following syllogism in relation to Christian assurance: "Major Premise: Those who keep God's commandments love Christ. Minor Premise: By the grace of God, I keep God's commandments. Conclusion: I love Christ."[7] Because Reformed theology denies the *gratia universalis* as promoted by the Lutheran reformers, one must look for evidence of salvation through the effects of the Holy Spirit in sanctification. This is prominent in the Puritan tradition, and often results not only in the contention that outward works are a necessary fruit of salvation, but also that one's motives should be examined continually in a process of testing faith's genuineness. This leads to unnecessary introspection and leads one away from the objectivity of the gospel.[8]

Though there is no strict Confessional position on the issue, there has been a tendency in Reformed theology to view both the law and the gospel as instruments of sanctification.[9] The gospel gives a motive for sanctification by reminding one of the grace given and the promise of future eschatological blessings. The law serves to demonstrate what good works are and the importance of them, and also aids one in performing them. Thus, the Christian participates in sanctification by both looking to the grace of

---

7. Jones, *Antinomianism*, Kindle location 1905.

8. This has been recognized by several Reformed theologians and pastors in recent years, due to the popularization of Puritan literature by Banner of Truth Publishing House and the Puritan Reformed Theological Seminary. This contra-Puritan movement, known as the "federal vision," seeks to promote the objectivity of the new covenant, arguing that grace and election are in some sense universal and are given through the church. Many major Reformed denominations have issued statements against this movement, fearing that a high ecclesiology will cause some to convert to Roman Catholicism rather than stay faithful to the Reformed tradition. The theologians associated with Westminster Seminary in California have also sought to depart from the popular Puritan tradition by promoting the centrality of law and gospel and the doctrine of justification. This attempt has also seen a lot of backlash in the Reformed community. See, for example, Frame, *Escondido Theology*.

9. A lot of this distinction comes from various approaches to covenant theology. In the approach of Meredith Kline, Michael Horton, and others, the Mosaic covenant is a republication of the covenant of works in the garden. This being the case, it serves to condemn Israel so that they may be led to Christ. The other approach, following John Murray, argues that the Mosaic covenant is an administration of the covenant of grace. Thus the law serves, in redemptive history, primarily as a means to demonstrate the nature of covenant life. This debate is chronicled in Koo Jeon, *Covenant Theology*.

the gospel and the commands of the law. Reformed theologian Joel Beeke writes on this issue, "To promote piety, the Spirit not only uses the gospel to work faith deep within the souls of his elect, as we have already seen, but he also uses the law."[10] Beeke points to Calvin's Genevan Catechism, in which he writes that the law "shows the mark at which we ought to aim, the goal towards which we ought to press, that each of us, according to the measure of grace bestowed upon him, may endeavor to frame his life according to the highest rectitude, and, by constant study, continually advance more and more."[11] The didactic use of the law is primary for Calvin. Though the law does serve as both the foundation for society through natural law, and the convicting of sinners, the believer's primary attitude toward the law is of trying to obey it. Though the law does continue to convict the Christian, ultimately it becomes a delight as the Christian continues the sanctifying process wherein obedience to God's law is improved. The goal of the Christian life is greater obedience to the law; this will be made perfect at the consummation of God's kingdom.

Calvin speaks of justification and sanctification as the "double grace" of salvation.[12] Sin condemns on two fronts: first in that it makes one guilty, and second that it overpowers and enslaves. Thus both a legal and a transformational solution are necessary for the problem of sin to be resolved. As the popular eighteenth-century hymn "Rock of Ages" pleads, "Be from sin the double cure. Free me from its guilt and power." Guilt is overcome through the legal declarative word of justification, and the power of sin is overcome through the Spirit's work of sanctification. In Reformed thought, it is generally taught that these two benefits of redemption are distinct. One does not flow from the other. The Reformed tradition has historically emphasized the concept of union with Christ.[13] Through the believer's union with Christ, both justification and sanctification are received as a cure from sin. There is no causal relationship, but both are separate benefits received through union with Christ.[14] This divorces the legal and transformational

---

10. Beeke, "Calvin's Piety," 45.
11. Beveridge, *Selected Works of John Calvin*, 69.
12. Calvin, *Institutes* III.XI.1.
13. See Letham, *Union with Christ*.
14. "By virtue of union with the person of the crucified and resurrected Christ, believers receive every soteric benefit, whether justification, sanctification or adoption, because the benefits of redemption cannot be separated from the person of the crucified and resurrected Christ" (Lane Tipton, "Union with Christ in Justification," in Oliphant, *Justified in Christ*, 25).

aspects of sin and salvation so that the two necessitate different detached graces.

Finally, it is worth noting that recent Reformed scholars have divided sanctification into two distinct categories.[15] Along with the traditional approach, wherein sanctification is a gradual process of becoming intrinsically righteous, there is an aspect of sanctification which occurs along with justification. The distinction is made between progressive sanctification and definitive sanctification. Progressive sanctification is the traditional approach to the term, referring to a process; definitive sanctification is one definitive event which occurs along with justification, or perhaps prior to justification, wherein one's relationship to sin is definitively breached and the Christian becomes holy.[16] Some have denied this distinction, arguing that definitive sanctification is merely another way of speaking of regeneration and is thus not a different aspect of the *ordo salutis*.[17] Whatever the state of the debate, it is important to realize that several Reformed theologians are now using the term to speak of two distinct acts of God.

SANCTIFICATION IN THE LUTHERAN TRADITION

It has been an unfortunate fact of history that the Lutheran tradition has continually been painted as antinomian, as if the centrality of justification negates any significant doctrine of sanctification.[18] This charge was leveled against Luther and Melanchthon in the sixteenth century, and unfortunately it is still prominent. Though the Lutheran Confessions do not include any article specifically on the topic of sanctification, it is often discussed within the context of good works. The Augsburg Confession answers this misrepresentation by expounding upon the nature and purpose of good works:

> Further, it is taught that good works should and must be done, not that a person relies on them to earn grace, but for God's sake

---

15. The primary proponent of this approach is John Murray, and it has had a significant impact on Westminster Seminary in Philadelphia. Murray's classic work on the *ordo salutis* is Murray, *Redemption Accomplished and Applied*.

16. Representative of this school of thought is Oliphant, *Justified in Christ*.

17. For a more traditional approach, see Fesko, *Justification*.

18. Though it is my fear that certain Lutherans almost absorb sanctification into justification, such as in Forde's chapter "The Lutheran View of Sanctification," in his book *Preached God*, 226–44.

and to God's praise. Faith alone always takes hold of grace and forgiveness of sin. Because the Holy Spirit is given through faith, the heart is aso moved to do good works. For before, because it lacks the Holy Spirit, the heart is too weak. Moreover, it is in the power of the devil who drives our poor human nature to many sins, as we observe in the philosophers who tried to live honestly and blamelessly, but then failed to do so and fell into many great, public sins. That is what happens to human beings when they are separated from true faith, are without the Holy Spirit, and govern themselves through their own human strength alone. (AC XX.27)

The focus of the Augsburg Confession's discussion of good works, along with that in the Apology, is the necessity and nature of good works. Contrary to the arguments of some Roman Catholics, the doctrine of justification by faith alone supports good works rather than negating them. Faith not only causes one to be justified in a declarative sense, but it also is an instrument of receiving the Holy Spirit. Through faith, the Holy Trinity is present and dwells within the Christian. This divine indwelling causes the believer to participate in eschatological life; the believer is regenerated and renewed.[19] Through this act of regeneration, Christians begin to do good works, not out of necessity or fear of judgment, but by free choice.[20] A favorite analogy of Luther is that of a tree and its fruit. A tree can and must bear fruit which is according to its nature. An apple tree thus grows apples rather than oranges or bananas. A peach tree can't grow grapes or plums, but only peaches. A tree does not do this through effort or a conscious continual decision to do so, but merely because of its nature. In the same manner, it is the nature of a Christian to perform good works. Thus, a Christian performs good works.

In his *Loci Theologici*,[21] Martin Chemnitz outlines several reasons why good works are necessary for the Christian. Some theologians who were opposed to Luther's teaching on justification argued that if works were not meritorious regarding justification, then good works would serve no purpose. Thus, delighting in cheap and free grace, Christians would cease

---

19. This has been described as the twofold aspect of faith. Stump writes, "The effect of faith is twofold, namely, justification and sanctification. Through faith the believer is justified before God; and through faith he also becomes increasingly sanctified in heart and life" (Stump, *Christian Faith*, 214).

20. I have written on this subject, with reference to the Eastern Orthodox teaching of theosis, in my book *Christification*.

21. *Loci Theologici* 3:1183–84.

to care about the nature of their sinful lives. This is far from the truth, as Chemnitz demonstrates through several biblical examples. These are the following reasons that Chemnitz outlines as to why Christians should perform good works:

I. Good Works as They Apply to God Himself
   1. It is the command of God
   2. It is the will of God
   3. If God is our Father, we should be obedient sons
   4. Christ redeemed us that he might purify us
   5. Good works are the fruit of the Spirit
   6. We glorify God through our works
   7. That we might become imitators of God
   8. That we might walk worthily of God

II. Causes Which Apply to the Regenerate
   1. Because they have been born again, and are new creatures
   2. Because they are sons of light
   3. That they might witness to the genuineness of faith
   4. That they may be assured that they don't have dead faith
   5. So that faith might not be lost
   6. So that we may avoid the punishments of God in this life
   7. We should have zeal for doing good

III. The Impelling and Final Causes of Good Works as Over Against Our Neighbors
   1. That our neighbor might be helped and served
   2. That others may be invited to godliness by our example
   3. That we give no one a cause for offense
   4. That by blessing we may shut the mouths of our adversaries

As is clear, the reasons why good works should be performed are numerous. Christians should perform works simply because they desire to do the will of their heavenly Father, because they have been made new creations, and so that their neighbor might be served. These motivations are in fact more laudable and less selfish then doing good works purely out of a fear of hell. Rather than causing good works, this medieval approach being attacked by Chemnitz brings about either pride, or fear and anxiety.[22]

The subject of sanctification and the Christian life is discussed throughout the Lutheran Confessions, because it continued to be a subject of debate. Some argued that good works were unnecessary or even harmful to salvation, whereas others argued that good works were necessary to obtain salvation. Both of these approaches were rejected by the Formula of Concord.[23] Good works are necessary for the Christian to perform, because faith always produces good works. To say that they are necessary for *salvation*, however, is in error because it implies some type of meritorious cause in salvation. Good works are the fruit of salvation, never its cause. The statement that good works are harmful to salvation is also in error because it implies that good works are a negative thing, whereas in Scripture they are described as something good and holy.

The Formula of Concord's treatment of the subject of free will also sheds much light on the issue of sanctification. After expounding upon the lack of freedom in the unregenerate, the Formula discusses the nature of free will in the Christian:

> When, however, people have been converted and thus have been enlightened, and the will has been renewed, then such people desire the good (insofar as they are born anew and are new creatures) and "delight in the law in the inmost self" (Rom. 7[:22]). From that point on people do good only to the extent that and as long as the Holy Spirit impels them. As Paul says, "For all who are led by the Spirit of God are children of God" [Rom. 8:14]. This leading of the Holy Spirit is not a *coactio* (or compulsion), but rather the converted person does the good spontaneously...
>
> It follows from this, as has been said, that as soon as the Holy Spirit has begun his work of rebirth and renewal in us through the Word and the holy sacraments, it is certain that on the basis of his power we can and should be cooperating with him, though still in great weakness. This occurs not on the basis of our fleshly, natural powers but on the basis of the new powers and gifts with which the Holy Spirit initiated in us in conversion, as St. Paul specifically

---

22. The Wesleyan approach, which places the necessity of good works into the discussion of perseverance, similarly fails, as does the Roman Catholic tradition, using good works as a crutch rather than free acts to be performed in joy.

23. FC SD IV.

and earnestly admonished, that "as we work together with" the Holy Spirit "we urge you not to accept the grace of God in vain" [2 Cor. 6:1]. This should be understood in no other way than that the converted do good to the extent that God rules, leads, and guides them with his Holy Spirit. (FC SD II.63–66)

There is a personal change which occurs when one converts to the Christian faith. Prior to faith, one lacks free will with regard to spiritual righteousness. Through faith, the will is transformed. After conversion, one is placed in a state where partial obedience to God is possible, though never complete.[24] The Christian is *simul iustus et peccator*, both regarding imputation and actual transformation. One is sinful insofar as one still exists in Adam, the old sinful age. One is righteous insofar as one has been changed through the Spirit and participates in the eschatological life of Christ through his resurrection. As Quenstedt notes, in sanctification, "The old man is the starting-point (terminus a quo), the new man the goal (terminus ad quem)," though the old man "cannot in this life be entirely eradicated."[25] Though the old man is gradually being destroyed, and the new gradually gaining control in the Christian's life, the battle continues until death.

The Confessions in the above statement do speak of cooperation, as is prominent in the Reformed approach. In distinction from the passivity confessed regarding justification and regeneration, the Lutheran Confessions assert that "through the power of the Holy Ghost we can and should cooperate," allowing some activity in the Christian regarding sanctification. However, the Formula is also quick to qualify this statement by stating that "This should be understood in no other way than that the converted do good to the extent that God rules, leads, and guides them with his Holy Spirit. If God would withdraw his gracious hand from such people, they could not for one moment remain in obedience to God" (FC. II.66). The Christian does perform good works and in that sense "cooperates" with the

---

24. "By regeneration the sinner has undergone a radical and fundamental change in the very center of his being. He has been brought into harmony with God; he loves God and wills what God wills. Sin has been cast out from the citadel, and faith and love have been installed in its place. But sin has not been eradicated from his nature. It remains in the believer alongside the new nature wrought by grace. Though cast out of the citadel, it lingers in the surrounding regions, ready at the first opportunity to retake the citadel and retake control . . . sin is strongly entrenched in his nature, and the gradual reduction of all the territory of our being under the new law of love entails a lifelong conflict, in which the believer makes headway, but in which he never achieves a victory so complete as to drive sin over the border" (Stump, *Christian Faith*, 279).

25. As cited in Schmid, *Doctrinal Theology*, 489.

Part III: Salvation

work of the Holy Spirit, but it is qualified that this cooperation is solely the result of the Spirit's work within the Christian's heart.[26]

This leads to the question regarding monergism and synergism in sanctification. The Reformed approach has tended toward a bold form of synergism in allowing both God's work and human cooperation through the law and the gospel as means of sanctification. The Lutheran tradition is also synergistic in the sense that it is admitted that the Christian's heart is truly changed, and one's desires are changed, so that good works are done by the Christian believer. The Christian is then called to strive in this work of renewal. The Lutheran scholastics distinguished between two uses of the term sanctification. In the broad sense, sanctification refers to the entirety of God's work of redemption, and in that meaning, is monergistic. In the narrow sense, sanctification refers to inward renewal demonstrated through good works; here the Christian cooperates with God.[27] As was shown in the previous chapter, Luther speaks, at times, of alien righteousness being an instrument of both justification and sanctification. In Luther's view, sanctification is initiated through the work of God apart from human effort. This is consistent with the Confessions' insistence that any goodness that humans perform is due to the Spirit's working and willing within the heart. The moment that the Spirit departed from someone, his good works would cease.[28] Even though the Christian can be said to cooperate with God in performing good works, this cooperation is simply a result of the Spirit's sanctifying work in the heart wherein one is transformed and given the desire and ability to perform good works.

With these qualifications, it is to be noted that the Lutheran Confessions do speak of growth in sanctification. Luther writes, "When we become Christians, the old creature daily decreases until finally destroyed" (LC IV.71). This growth demonstrates itself through good deeds and ceasing of sin: "Now, when we enter Christ's kingdom, this corruption must daily decrease so that the longer we live, the more gentle, patient, and meek we become, and the more we break away from greed, hatred, envy, and

---

26. Quenstedt writes, "The regenerate man co-operates with God in the work of sanctification, not by an equal action, but in subordination and dependence on the Holy Spirit, because he works, not *with native*, but *with granted* powers" (as cited in Schmid, *Doctrinal Theology*, 491).

27. "This is based on the twofold concept of 'holy,' insofar as it designates the imputed holiness of Christ and also the holiness of life proceeding from justification" (Hoenecke, *Evangelical Lutheran Dogmatics* 3:395).

28. FC SD II.66.

New Life in Christ

pride" (LC IV.65-67). Thus, in agreement with Reformed theology, Lutherans speak of "progressive sanctification,"[29] though the primary worker in this process is God rather than the creature. This causes the sinner to grow in righteousness and begin to fulfill the law.

In the Lutheran approach, there is not a strict justification/sanctification divide as in Reformed theology. Though they are distinct acts, they are not enacted apart from one another. Sin does include the aspects of both guilt and slavery, as is confessed in the Reformed tradition. These two ideas are not, however, divorced from one another; both are answered through the same act: justification. Justification does not involve a purely legal declaration absent of any moral effect within the Christian's life. As discussed in the previous chapter, justification is a declarative act, through which God imputes righteousness and brings forth new life. The legal is the means by which the effective is enacted. They both encompass the same reality. Thus, rather than describing justification and sanctification as redemptive benefits enacted apart from one another, sanctification arises through justification, as an effect does from a cause. The reality of imputation causes inchoate righteousness, which shows itself through works of love and service.[30]

Lutherans have tended to discuss good works within the category of vocation.[31] In the medieval church, the status of clergy promoted the concept that there was an ontological superiority of clergy over laity. Those with a radical conversion experience were, for example, expected to then join a monastic order because to remain in a secular calling was viewed as less spiritual.[32] This led to a division between two levels of spirituality: the clergy and the laity. The ethical commands of the Sermon on the Mount were often said to apply only to those of a monastic lifestyle and not "ordinary" Christians. Joining a monastic order was often labeled as a "second baptism" (a term which Luther hated).

---

29. "It is important to remember, however, that the word sanctification has acquired a definite and restricted meaning, and now refers to the progressive growth in holiness which follows in the life of the believer after his justification by faith alone" (Stump, *Christian Faith*, 276).

30. Peter Lillback argues that this is the primary flaw in the Lutheran view of justification. See Peter A. Lillback, "Calvin's Development of the Doctrine of Forensic Justification: Calvin and the Early Lutherans on the Relationship of Justification and Renewal," in Oliphant, *Justified in Christ*, 51–80.

31. The best work on the subject remains Wingren, *Luther on Vocation*. A more recent and accessible work on the subject is Veith, *God at Work*.

32. See King, *Western Monasticism*.

Part III: Salvation

This was among the primary problems Luther had with the late medieval church. In light of this two-level spirituality, Luther developed the concept of Christian vocation. In Luther's view, no vocation is superior to another.[33] The clergy do not have a higher spiritual status than the laity; Luther rejected ordination as a sacrament which places an indelible mark on the character of the one ordained. The man who is a baker and the woman who stays at home with her children are just as spiritual, through faith in Christ, as the monk, nun, priest, or theology professor. The doctrine of justification assures that one's relationship with God is settled in the same manner for everyone, namely, through faith in Christ.

Luther promoted this perspective on vocation by radically "secularizing" good works. Good works do not refer to the number of prayers one recites, or the penance performed, but they primarily refer to acts which serve the neighbor. As Luther is credited with saying, "God doesn't need your good works. Your neighbor does!"[34] A distinction is made between one's vertical relationship with God and one's horizontal relationship with humankind. Through faith, one's vertical relationship with God is settled. Faith ascends up to God, receiving Christ and his righteousness. No good work will contribute to this, but only faith. Thus good works cannot and do not have primary reference to an individual's relationship with God. It is the relationship which goes outward, the horizontal relationship with one's neighbor, which needs good works. Since one's status before God is settled through the forgiveness of sins, one has the freedom to live a life of love and service.[35] Because the Christian's heart has been changed, the believer delights in good works which take the form of service to neighbor.

Everyone has a number of vocations within life. This refers not only to careers but also to obligations with family and society. Each of these roles has distinct duties and obligations. For example, a man could be a soldier. In war he would justly be able to take life because of the purpose of this

33. "This is why all vocations are equal before God. Pastors, monks, nuns, and popes are no holier than farmers, shopkeepers, dairy maids, or latrine diggers. In the spiritual kingdom, in a divine egalitarianism (which would also come to have cultural implications) peasants are equal to kings" (Veith, *God at Work*, 39).

34. As Senkbeil observes, "God doesn't need our love, after all, but our neighbor does" (Senkbeil, *Dying to Live*, 175).

35. "In the gospel the gate of heaven is opened, and a miracle takes place. He who enters heaven immediately descends in love, in 'free bondage.' He gives himself to the care of his neighbor, concerned about his well-being . . . The freedom of faith does not dissolve vocation. On the contrary, it sustains it and gives it new life" (Wingren, *Luther on Vocation*, 66).

New Life in Christ

distinct vocation. However, this same person would not be able to take the life of a family member, or even harm a family member physically. This is because his role as soldier is distinct from his role as husband and father. Everyone serves in different vocations.[36] Within each of these vocations are different rules and manners in which one should act. In Luther's view, the duty of Christians to serve and love one another does not apply to an other-worldly sphere, wherein one must become a monastic or priest. It applies to simple, ordinary roles one has in life. Through faith in Christ, one becomes a new creation and desires to serve those around him. This is done by being faithful to one's vocation. A Christian mother serves her neighbor in being a good mother. She treats her children well and shows them mercy rather than being harsh. A Christian baker makes the best bread he can and treats his customers with kindness, not charging an unnecessarily high price for his food. The primary ways in which Christians are to do this are by showing love and mercy and working hard and well.

When the Christian responds to someone's earthly needs, this is a reflection of the grace that Christ shows to sinners through the gospel. It can even be said that the one performing the good work becomes a "mask" of God.[37] It is God himself who is acting with love toward his sinful creation; those who do these works are simply the means by which God serves his creation. In this manner, God hides himself as he works to serve the world.[38] In the same way that God hides himself under water, bread, and wine to bring spiritual grace to his church, so he hides behind the works of individuals to bring physical help and healing to the world.

---

36. "Our vocation is not one single occupation. As has been said, we have callings in different realms—the workplace, yes, but also the family, the society, and the church" (Veith, *God at Work*, 47).

37. "The casual observer looks at daily life in this world and sees only industrial policy, economic theory, cultural anthropology, and political structures. But these are masks of God. Behind this human interplay, behind these ordinary structures of society, lies the extraordinary work of God. He uses ordinary people, motivated as they often are by selfish interests, to provide for the needs and wants of His whole creation" (Senkbeil, *Dying to Live*, 171–72).

38. "Through vocation God's presence is really with man. As the God of the law, he places himself above man's self-will, and drives man to prayer, which is answered by God's love and care. In vocation works are constrained to move toward one's neighbor, toward the earth; and faith alone, trust, prayer, all without works, ascends heavenward" (Wingren, *Luther on Vocation*, 33).

While Lutherans do boldly confess the third use of the law, good works are often placed in the category of vocation.[39] Whereas in the Reformed tradition good works are primarily that which accords with God's moral law, and the goal of sanctification is greater obedience to the law, in the Lutheran tradition, good works are often defined by that which serves one's neighbor, without negating the importance of fulfilling God's law. The law does serve as a guide for good works for Lutheranism. It helps defend against creating self-made works to perform in obedience to God by pointing to that which God actually desires. However, the law still accuses even the regenerate. *Lex semper accusat* (the law always accuses) is a principle which defines the use of the law in the Christian's life (Apol IX.38). Thus, rather than hoping to obey the law perfectly, as is impossible in this life, the Christian focuses his striving on the good of the neighbor.[40]

THE SECOND AND THIRD USES OF THE LAW— CORAM DEO AND CORAM MUNDO

The Lutheran approach to the second and third uses of the law can be explained by examining the difference between one's standing *coram Deo* (before God) and one's life *coram mundo* (before the world). Before God, the law serves in its second function. God does not judge Christians based upon their new obedience, but upon the obedience of his Son, Jesus Christ. As James writes, if one breaks any of God's commandments, then one is guilty of breaking the entire law (Jas 2:10). God does not judge based on percentages regarding justification. In that realm, God wholly condemns sinners. There is no differentiation between one who has broken one commandment or hundreds of commandments. All are guilty. In this realm, the only thing which avails is the perfect righteousness of Christ that the Christian receives passively. *Coram Deo*, it can be said that one is both wholly a sinner (due to the breaking of divine law) and wholly righteous (due to the imputed and perfect righteousness of Christ). Before God, then, the law functions in its second use, and the gospel is the final word to the Christian. It is here that the *lex semper accusat* principle applies.

---

39. On the third use of the law in Lutheranism, see Engelbrecht, *Friends of the Law*; Murray, *Law, Life, and the Living God*; and Gieschen, *Law in Holy Scripture*.

40. The Christian should strive for perfection, because that is what God's law requires. However, one should not be hopeful that one will actually achieve this.

New Life in Christ

The believer does not only live *coram Deo*, however, but also *coram mundo*. The Christian who is declared perfectly and wholly righteous in Christ also lives in the world before others. Here, one is not guided by the gospel, but by the law. Thus, while the second use of the law is primarily a *coram Deo* use of the law, the third use functions primarily *coram mundo*. God's law is a delight to the perfectly justified Christian, because it serves as a guide for the believer in the world. Through the law, one is given instructions about how to live in the world, how to love one's neighbor, and how to live in holiness within the various stations in life within which one is placed. This is the realm of sanctification and good works. It is here that Christ is not only *extra nos*, but dwells within believers, guiding them in obedience and service to the world. In this realm, Christ also serves as an example of love and service. In the *coram mundo* realm, it can also be said that the Christian is *part* saint and *part* sinner. While *coram Deo* holiness cannot progress, as it is perfect, one's holiness *in the world* does grow, as one is further changed by God's Spirit, and thus further serves the neighbor in obedience to God's law.

By distinguishing between one's life *coram Deo* and *coram mundo*, the Lutheran tradition boldly confesses the third use of the law, as well as the centrality of salvation by passive righteousness alone. Justification and new obedience must both be taught, but they must always be distinguished. Each has an important role in its proper realm. This distinction helps to demonstrate some of the flaws within some Reformed explanations of sanctification. One example of such a confusion of these two categories is Mark Jones's book *Antinomianism: Reformed Theology's Unwelcome Guest?* This book is a critique of what Jones perceives to be a contemporary trend of antinomianism within the Reformed tradition. In combating antinomianism, however, Jones conflates passive and active righteousness throughout.

The problem in this work is not that Jones emphasizes the goodness of the law or the necessity of the good works in the Christian life. These contentions are correct. The problem is that Jones often places good works in the *coram Deo* category and in doing so conflates passive and active righteousness. For example, Jones states that good works are a "necessary means of our salvation."[41] He adamantly defends the proposition "good works are necessary for salvation," which is condemned in the Formula of Concord. For Jones, a rejection of such phraseology is tantamount to antinomianism. In his assertions, Jones (perhaps unknowingly) condemns the

---

41. Jones, *Antinomianism*, Kindle location 1352.

Part III: Salvation

Lutheran church as fundamentally antinomian. Jones also further argues that good works are not simply the "way *of* life" for the Christian, but are actually the "way *to* life."[42] In doing this, Jones utilizes *coram mundo* language in relation to one's *coram Deo* relationship. To be clear, Jones does confess justification by faith alone and is quick to clarify such statements in light of that. However, this confusing language still places good works in an unnecessary place in Christian soteriology, and thus confuses a clear proclamation of *sola fide*.

There are two further issues in Jones's work which demonstrate, again, why the distinction between the two kinds of righteousness is essential. One of Jones's contentions is that God's love differs depending upon the progress of one's sanctification. He writes, "God cannot help but love us more and more if we become more and more like him."[43] This is held in contradistinction to Luther's argument that "The love of God does not find, but creates, that which is pleasing to it. The love of man comes into being through that which is pleasing to it."[44] For Luther, God's love precedes all goodness in man and is not affected by man's sanctification. Rather, sanctification is a result of the preceding perfect love that God has for the human creature. Jones does not deny that God's love precedes human love either, but he distinguishes between various kinds of love, and thus argues that God's *amor complacentiae vel amicitiae* (love of delight or friendship) is dependent upon human performance.[45] This, again, is a confusion of language which bases one's *coram Deo* relationship upon one's *coram mundo* performance. This is further demonstrated by the fact that Jones contends throughout the book that assurance is to be found not in the universal means of grace, but in one's inner renewal. He argues, citing John Flavel, "The examination of our justification by our sanctification, is not only a lawful, and possible, but a very excellent and necessary work and duty."[46]

Jones thus encourages Christians to examine the state of their sanctification for assurance of their justification. One's works *coram mundo* become the basis for assurance that the *coram Deo* relationship is intact. He puts this in a syllogism, writing, "Major Premise: Those who keep God's commandments love Christ. Minor Premise: By the grace of God, I keep

42. Ibid., 1316.
43. Ibid., 1617.
44. *LW* 31:57.
45. Jones, *Antinomianism*, Kindle location 1578.
46. Ibid., 2027.

God's commandments. Conclusion: I love Christ."[47] Though good works certainly are a necessary result of saving faith, placing assurance in one's sanctification points one inward, often leading to despair due to the lack of desired fruit in the Christian life.

Ultimately, Jones has the wrong answer to a real problem. For Jones, the only way in which to battle antinomianism is to place active righteousness language within the context of passive righteousness. This leads to a rejection of the law-gospel distinction. Jones argues, "When a sharp distinction is maintained between the law and the gospel in the Christian life, the first use of the law tends to replace the third use of the law as its primary function. Despite claims to the contrary, the law takes on a decidedly negative tone in the preaching and writing of those who hold to such a sharp distinction."[48] Jones's claim here is simply mistaken. The law does not necessarily take a purely "negative tone" for those who hold to a strong law-gospel distinction. This confusion stems from Jones's failure to understand the two kinds of righteousness. One can boldly proclaim the goodness and necessity of the law while still holding firmly to the law-gospel distinction, so long as one sharply distinguishes *coram Deo* from *coram mundo* righteousness. With this distinction in mind, one can argue strongly against antinomianism, while just as strongly rejecting phrases like "good works are necessary for salvation" and "good works are a means of salvation." This distinction also ensures that one's assurance is always placed in the passive, rather than active, righteousness category.

Jones's book is not the sole piece of Reformed literature that utilizes language which confuses passive and active righteousness. It is merely one contemporary example of how such confusion is endemic in the Reformed theological system. In some ways, then, the difference between the Lutheran and Reformed approaches to justification and sanctification is that Lutherans are more careful about placing each reality within its proper sphere, whereas the Reformed, at times, conflate the two.

DEFINING THE PRIMARY DIFFERENCES

Through examining both the Reformed and Lutheran approaches to the Christian life, various differences can be observed. First, in the Reformed tradition, sanctification plays a larger role in discussion than it does in

47. Ibid., 1905.
48. Ibid., 2277.

Lutheranism. For the Reformed church, one of the primary emphases in preaching is exhortation to obey the law. In Lutheranism, sanctification is important but is always subservient to the doctrine of justification. The perfect work of God in justification has primacy over the incomplete process of sanctification. This demonstrates itself through different approaches to the law. In Calvinism, the third use of the law is primary, whereas for Lutheranism the second use is primary. Calvin viewed both law and gospel as means of sanctification, but Luther promoted the idea that it is only the gospel which sanctifies through word and sacrament. The Calvinistic approach emphasizes synergism in sanctification, focusing on the Christian's work of mortification and attempted obedience to the law, whereas the Lutheran tradition teaches a theocentric understanding of sanctification, giving primacy to divine action. The goal of the Christian life in Calvinism is greater obedience to God's law, whereas in Luther's view one's focus is on serving the neighbor through one's various vocations in life. Finally, Lutherans distinguish between the two kinds of righteousness, whereas Reformed theology sometimes confuses the two realities. Junius Remensnyder defines Lutheran sanctification in the following words:

> The Lutheran piety, then, is the brightest gem in her coronet of Christian graces. It is joyous, as well as stable; practical, while Churchly and conservative; and knows how, from the still closet of a holy mysticism, to go forth in the world and serve God with works of power. The purest orthodoxy should not be dead, but the tree that bears the best and most plentiful deeds of practical piety. Lutherans best serve their Church, and honor its faith, when "having the form of godliness they do not deny the power thereof," but when it can be said of them as of Luther that "the confessor of the righteousness of faith had what he confessed and was what he taught."[49]

DEFENDING THE LUTHERAN VIEW OF SANCTIFICATION

There are several points which merit defense and discussion regarding the Lutheran approach to sanctification and good works. It must be demonstrated that Scripture teaches the priority of justification over sanctification, the primacy of the second use of the law and the *lex semper accusat*

49. Remensnyder, *Lutheran Manual*, 138–39.

principle, an emphasis on divine priority in sanctification, and Luther's doctrine of vocation.

The primary reason why justification assumes a theological priority over sanctification is that it is a completed act. The work of justification establishes God's eschatological decree of "righteous" placed upon the sinner. As Romans 4:5 states, "And to the one who does not work but believes in him who justifies the ungodly, his faith is counted as righteousness." As was discussed in the previous chapter, this text has specific reference to Abraham. In Genesis 12 Abraham was made an heir of the covenant and given the promise of being the forefather of the future Messiah and the nation of Israel. Thus Abraham's journey of faith began earlier than the text Paul utilizes from chapter 15, wherein Abraham's faith was credited as righteousness. Paul explicitly labels Abraham as one who "does not work" and even calls him "ungodly." This does not refer merely to the beginning of Abraham's life of faith, but to the Abraham who had already left his pagan idolatry in order to serve God. Thus even after Abraham had some level of sanctification and displayed that through his good works, he is still labeled by Paul as ungodly, and is righteous apart from works. This demonstrates that justification is primary, not only in the beginning of the Christian life, but in one's continual journey in faith. Even after one is sanctified to an extent one can still be labeled as "ungodly" and "without works."

There is a prominent pastoral concern in this discussion as well. As one progresses in the Christian life, rather than seeing victory over sin, one often struggles with the fact that the sins which should be done away with keep returning. The old Adam continually reasserts himself, bringing God's children back into the sin which previously enslaved them. If I as a pastor were to emphasize the work of sanctification and progress in the Christian life to the neglect of the reality of *simul iustus et peccator*, my hearers' state of mind would likely become that of despair. The progress that we hope to find in our spiritual journeys is often not there. Rather than pointing to that work of God which is still incomplete, that work by which God would still only be able to call his people "ungodly," I as a pastor have a duty to point primarily to that work of God which *is* complete, that work by which alone one will be received into God's kingdom and participate in the resurrection unto life. Alien righteousness is full and complete and is the only thing which one can cling to in assurance that eternal life is a present possession, not the incomplete work of renewal which will only lead to the Christian's realization of personal failure to progress as far as one should.

Part III: Salvation

Paul demonstrates this principle in a pastoral manner in the first epistle to the Corinthians. Of all his letters, this is the one in which Paul deals with the broadest moral problems. The Corinthian congregation is struggling with sectarianism, sexual immorality, a lack of concern for the sins of others, and a tendency to take other Christians to court. Despite this group of people's seeming lack of the fruits of sanctification, Paul is willing to address them as "saints." Even though they are full of obvious sin that Paul addresses throughout this epistle, they are righteous and holy people. After chastising the Corinthians for their tendency to desire taking others to a law court in order to settle church disputes, Paul warns them that those who practice wickedness will not inherit the kingdom of God. But then, rather than pointing then, to the sinfulness of their own lives and the lack of fruit that they demonstrate, he reminds them of something which is a past reality. He states, "And such were some of you. But you were washed, you were sanctified, you were justified in the name of the Lord Jesus Christ and by the Spirit of our God" (1 Cor 6:11). He reminds the Corinthians that even though they demonstrate all sorts of sin and wickedness within their congregation, these sins do not define who they are in Christ. Though previously slaves to sin, the Corinthians have now been baptized into Christ, they have been set apart, they have been declared righteous, and their sins have been forgiven. Even in the midst of a situation of profound sin, Paul is willing to assure the Corinthian believers of their status before God effected by their baptisms, and their justification.[50]

---

50. Kretzmann comments, "And now the apostle, after his usual manner, reminds the Corinthian Christians of the glorious gifts of mercy which they have received, contrasting their present state with that before their conversion: And these things some of you were. Such stuff, such a set, such abominations they had been, that is, some of them; the majority of them had fortunately not been guilty of such extremes of vice. But these things are now a thing of the past, for they were washed clean in Baptism, the power of God in the Sacrament took away all their uncleanness, Titus 3, 5; Acts 22, 16; Col. 2, 11. 12; Eph. 5, 26. 27. They were sanctified; they were separated from the world and consecrated to God by that same sacred act, they were translated into fellowship with God. They were justified; they had entered into that state in which God looks upon them as just and righteous, in which He imputes to them the righteousness of Jesus Christ. And all this was done in the name of the Lord Jesus Christ, through whom all gifts of grace have been made possible, and in the Spirit of our God, through whose power regeneration is effected. The believers are the sacred and living property of Christ, because the Spirit of God lives in them. Thus the entrance of the Christians into their state of grace is brought out in all its glorious contrast to the vile condition of the unregenerate, in order that the remembrance of these privileges may always incite them to a life that agrees with their heavenly calling" (Kretzmann, *Commentary*, 1 Cor 6:1–11).

New Life in Christ

It is evident that theologically, exegetically, and pastorally, justification has a priority over sanctification. This is not to imply that sanctification is not a real work of God, or that it is not important, but it is a partial work, an incomplete work. It is justification which assures one's eschatological vindication (being that very vindication brought into the present), and which is a grounds for obedience in the Christian life. Sanctification is always a struggle, and often seems to lack progress, thus it must always be tempered by a robust understanding of justification.

The prominence of justification leads to the second point, that the law's primary use is pedagogical. Though the law is useful and necessary as a guide for good works, it is primarily used to humble, to accuse the conscience of sin so that one is continually pointed to God's grace in the cross and resurrection of Jesus. To examine the New Testament theology of the law, Paul's epistle to the Romans must be studied as to how Paul himself applies the various uses of the law.

Romans begins with a discussion of the sinfulness of humankind. In the first chapter, Paul tells his readers of the gospel, which reveals the righteousness of God.[51] He continues by explaining the revelation of the wrath of God against sin. This is demonstrated through the idolatry of pagan cultures and the acceptance of homosexual practice. Paul then indicts the Jews as well for their sin and acceptance of the sins of others. This comes to a climax in chapter three as Paul uses various quotations from the Old Testament to demonstrate the universal sinfulness of humankind.[52] It is in this context that the Pauline discussion of the law begins. Paul writes, "Now we know that whatever the law says it speaks to those who are under the law, so that every mouth may be stopped, and the whole world may be held accountable to God. For by works of the law no human being will be justified in his sight, since through the law comes knowledge of sin" (Rom 3:19–20). This explains the "second use of the law," wherein the law is used to stop the mouths of all men, Jew and Gentile alike. It is used to give the knowledge of sin. This sets up Paul's further discussion of the gospel, wherein the saving righteousness of God is revealed apart from the law. Thus the law is used to condemn, and the gospel is used to forgive sin and grant righteousness. This sets up a law-gospel contrast in Pauline theology.[53]

---

51. Rom 1:16–17.

52. Rom 3:10–18.

53. For an exegetical defense of the law-gospel distinction, see Westerholm, *Perspectives Old and New on Paul*.

Part III: Salvation

The question then is whether the law continues in that function after conversion. It may be argued that Paul approaches the law as that which condemns prior to faith and guides one after faith. At this point the condemnatory use of the law either ceases or is greatly diminished. There are a couple of responses that can be made to this point. First, as was demonstrated in the previous chapter, justification is a ruling which is received continually; it is not a simple once-for-all event within the *ordo salutis*. Since justification is God's response to the condemnatory use of the law, if justification is continually received, the condemnatory use of the law must continue as valid throughout one's Christian existence. This is especially demonstrated through the example of Abraham utilized by Paul which I expounded above. Since obedient Abraham in Genesis 15 is still considered "ungodly," the law continually reminds the faithful that they remain ungodly and that their righteousness continues to be imputed rather than inherent. This is also demonstrated in Paul's use of Psalm 32 and David's confession of sin. This arises not at the beginning of David's life of faith, but during his life when he comes to a time of confession and repentance. This is a model of the Christian life; one is condemned by the law, comes to repentance and sorrow over sin, and consequently receives God's forgiveness.

The clearest text regarding the second use of the law in the Christian life is Paul's description of his own struggle with sin in Romans 7:

> What then shall we say? That the law is sin? By no means! Yet if it had not been for the law, I would not have known sin. For I would not have known what it is to covet if the law had not said, "You shall not covet." But sin, seizing an opportunity through the commandment, produced in me all kinds of covetousness. For apart from the law, sin lies dead. I was once alive apart from the law, but when the commandment came, sin came alive and I died. The very commandment that promised life proved to be death to me. For sin, seizing an opportunity through the commandment, deceived me and through it killed me. So the law is holy, and the commandment is holy and righteous and good.

Did that which is good, then, bring death to me? By no means! It was sin, producing death in me through what is good, in order that sin might be shown to be sin, and through the commandment might become sinful beyond measure. For we know that the law is spiritual, but I am of the flesh, sold under sin. For I do not understand my own actions. For I do not do what I want, but I do the very thing I hate. Now if I do what I do not want,

New Life in Christ

I agree with the law, that it is good. So now it is no longer I who do it, but sin that dwells within me. For I know that nothing good dwells in me, that is, in my flesh. For I have the desire to do what is right, but not the ability to carry it out. For I do not do the good I want, but the evil I do not want is what I keep on doing. Now if I do what I do not want, it is no longer I who do it, but sin that dwells within me.

> So I find it to be a law that when I want to do right, evil lies close at hand. For I delight in the law of God, in my inner being, but I see in my members another law waging war against the law of my mind and making me captive to the law of sin that dwells in my members. Wretched man that I am! Who will deliver me from this body of death? Thanks be to God through Jesus Christ our Lord! So then, I myself serve the law of God with my mind, but with my flesh I serve the law of sin. (Rom 7:7–25)

This text describes the *simul iustus et peccator* expounded by Luther. Paul describes an experience wherein the law shows his own sin and inability to fulfill it. The text then goes into the present tense, describing his present Christian experience. In Paul's Christian experience, the law continues to condemn as his sinful nature refuses to obey. Thus, even though in his new nature Paul is obedient to the law, the old Adam within him doesn't allow for perfect obedience. The Christian life is thus not about continual victory over sin, but about a struggle between sin and righteousness, between law and gospel.

Many scholars have rejected Luther's interpretation of this passage, arguing that Paul is speaking only of his past experience as a Jew,[54] or embodying national Israel's own struggle with sin,[55] or personifying the experience of Adam during the fall.[56] While there isn't space in a work like this to get into this complex debate, I will give a few reasons why the traditional Lutheran interpretation is preferable.[57]

---

54. This is a common patristic interpretation, especially among the Greek fathers.

55. Douglas Moo, who utilizes primarily a traditional Lutheran approach to the epistle to the Romans, is a proponent of this view. See Moo, *New International Commentary*.

56. This has been popularized by W. G. Kumel in *Romer 7*.

57. The most extensive defense of the traditional view is from Middendorf, *"I" in the Storm*. This study, based on Middendorf's doctoral dissertation, gives an excellent overview of the various perspectives in contemporary scholarship and provides extensive refutations of the various approaches. He argues that this text references Paul's contemporary Christian experience, rather than the situation of Adam, an average Israelite under the law, or Paul's pre-conversion life. I am not convinced, however, that an Edenic

Part III: Salvation

First, it is the clear reading of the text. Paul speaks in the present tense, using a first-person pronoun. The obvious clear reading of the text is that he is indeed speaking of himself in the first-person present tense. The arguments proposed wherein other similar Pauline language is used to mean something other than that is unconvincing, and the parallels are not exact. Secondly, the hope and solution to Paul's condition is not conversion, but resurrection. Paul's hope for "deliverance from this body of death" refers to the resurrection from the dead, which Paul discusses in the following chapter as the "redemption of our bodies" (Rom 8:23). The struggle thus continues until death. David Dockery explains,

> Our entire Christian life is to be lived in the light of the tension between what we already are in Christ and what we hope to be some day. Thus, the already/not yet balance in Paul's soteriology must be maintained. This is quite different from the popular view advocated by men who view Rom 7:14–25 as the experience of the Christian who is living at a level of the Christian life which can be left behind, who is still trying to live the Christian life either under the law or in his own strength. Conversion is only the beginning; the new has not swallowed up the old. While it is true that Paul says "we died to sin" (Rom 6:2ff; Gal 2:19; Col 2:11, 20; 3:3), death is not an event past and gone in the believer's experience. Rather it is an emphasis of the "already" aspect just as the "not yet" aspect is seen in Rom 8:10; 2 Cor. 4:10; and Phil. 3:10ff. The balance in Paul's theology must be maintained. To overemphasize either aspect leads to perfectionism or gnosticism.[58]

Third, even after Paul presents the final solution to the problem of sin, his conclusion is, "So then, I myself serve the law of God with my mind, but with my flesh I serve the law of sin." Following Paul's rejoicing in the victory over sin won by Christ, Paul laments that he still exists in a struggle between the "law of God" and the "law of flesh." Had Paul intended to state that he had overcome his struggle through conversion, this statement would be an unfitting conclusion to his discussion. This statement of Paul points to the eschatological tension which Dockery finds in this text. Finally, this

---

allusion in this text is negated by adopting Luther's interpretation. In my view, Paul is placing himself in the predicament in Adam, demonstrating that since Adam failed to obey the law, God's command becomes death to all of Adam's descendants. In this way, the fall of Adam demonstrates itself in each person as the law continues this condemnatory function. Another helpful article in defense of the traditional approach is Dockery, "Romans 7:14–25."

58. Dockery, "Romans 7:14–25," 256.

interpretation of Romans 7 is consistent with what Paul teaches in his similarly themed epistle to the Galatians: "For the desires of the flesh are against the Spirit, and the desires of the Spirit are against the flesh, for these are opposed to each other, to keep you from doing the things you want to do" (Gal 5:17). In both cases, the Christian life is one of struggle between flesh and the Spirit, death and life, law and gospel.

The nature of the Christian life as described in Romans 8 through more positive language is taught in light of what Paul already described in the previous chapter. Thus, the Christian does live "according to the Spirit" (Rom 8:5), but only to an extent because of the constant struggle between flesh and Spirit in which the Christian is continually condemned by the law and set free by the gospel. The ethical commands at the end of the epistle are written in view of the struggle and in view of "the mercies of God" (Rom 12:1). There is no third use of the law devoid of the second use and an admission of one's continual reliance on grace.

The Lutheran contention that the law always accuses, and that this accusatory function of the law is primary, is thoroughly Pauline. It is the primary way in which Paul introduces and utilizes the law throughout his epistles. This condemnation applies not only to one's conversion but is ongoing throughout the Christian life, because sin is continual. This is demonstrated especially in Romans 7, where Paul describes his own struggle with sin and grace, in which the second use of the law is predominant.

Now the various texts which speak of the concept of sanctification must be examined so as to determine the nature of divine and human cooperation in the process. As Murray demonstrated for the contemporary Reformed church, the actual term "sanctification" is not always used in the Bible in the same sense it is used in systematic theology. Paul writes to the Corinthians, for example, "But you were washed, you were sanctified, you were justified in the name of the Lord Jesus Christ and by the Spirit of our God" (1 Cor 6:11). Paul describes sanctification as a past event. It is something which God causes along with justifying, and one's being "washed"—likely referring to baptism. Paul also refers to these believers as being "sanctified in Christ Jesus" (1 Cor 1:2). Being sanctified is a Christological event, wherein one is set apart as holy through Christ. As Paul writes, "And because of him you are in Christ Jesus, who became to us wisdom from God, righteousness and sanctification and redemption" (1 Cor 1:30). One of the only times in the New Testament that "sanctification" explicitly refers to a process comes from the epistle to the Hebrews: "For by a single offering he has perfected for all time those who are being sanctified" (Heb 10:14). This is the concept usually associated with the theological use of the term "sanctification." Notice that even in this text, the perfection of Christ's work lies behind the progress of the Christian. This ties together justification and sanctification and places the imputing work in a primary place, as does the Lutheran tradition.

The Bible more commonly uses other terms to refer to this process within the Christian life. For example, Paul refers to a process of "being transformed into" (2 Cor 3:18) the image of God. He states that the new self is being "renewed in knowledge after the image of its creator" (Col 3:10). In Ephesians, Paul refers to this process, encouraging the Ephesians "to be renewed in the spirit of your minds, and to put on the new self, created after the likeness of God in true righteousness and holiness" (Eph 3:23–24). Paul describes it as being "led by the Spirit of God" (Rom 8:14). Peter refers to this process as being made "partakers of the divine nature" (2 Pet 1:4). There are various means in the New Testament to speak about growth in the Christian life; the most common thread in all of them is that this process refers to something in which God is active.

The process of transformation is, in Scripture, attributed to God rather than to human effort. In Colossians, for example, Paul attributes all his toil to the fact that "he powerfully works within me" (Col 1:29). He attributes the sanctification of the church to "a growth that is from God" (Col 2:19). In the same manner, Paul assures the Philippians that "he who began a good work in you will bring it to completion at the day of Jesus Christ" (Phil 1:5), demonstrating that both the beginning and continual performance of good works are the result of God's act. He tells the Ephesians, regarding good works, that "God prepared [them] beforehand, that we should walk in them" (Eph 2:10). Thus, again, the good works of the Christian are a result of God's grace, even foreordination. At times, Paul does speak of human activity. For example, he encourages the Colossians to "Put to death therefore what is earthly in you: sexual immorality, impurity, passion, evil desire, and covetousness, which is idolatry" (Col 3:5). However, this is all grounded in the fact that the new self "is being renewed in knowledge after the image of its creator" (Col 3:10). Thus, the human is active in killing sin, but this activity is a result of "being renewed," which is a divine work. This parallels Paul's admonition to the Philippians that they should "work out your own salvation with fear and trembling, for it is God who works in you, both to will and to work for his good pleasure" (Phil 2:12–13). Again, the

Philippians are called to perform good works, and do "cooperate," but then that very cooperation is attributed to the grace of God.

In New Testament theology, as in the Lutheran tradition, sanctification as a process is cooperative, though the emphasis is always on divine initiative. Christians are called to be active in killing the flesh, slaying the old Adam; however, at the same time it is confessed that when this occurs, it is solely the result of God's grace working within his people.

Finally, it remains to be shown that the Lutheran approach to the Christian life regarding vocation is a biblical manner of speaking about the Christian life. The New Testament has numerous imperative statements regarding the nature of the Christian life. It is common that these admonitions refer to one's station in life. Peter encourages his readers, for example, by writing,

> Likewise, wives, be subject to your own husbands, so that even if some do not obey the word, they may be won without a word by the conduct of their wives, when they see your respectful and pure conduct. Do not let your adorning be external—the braiding of hair and the putting on of gold jewelry, or the clothing you wear—but let your adorning be the hidden person of the heart with the imperishable beauty of a gentle and quiet spirit, which in God's sight is very precious. For this is how the holy women who hoped in God used to adorn themselves, by submitting to their own husbands, as Sarah obeyed Abraham, calling him lord. And you are her children, if you do good and do not fear anything that is frightening.
>
> Likewise, husbands, live with your wives in an understanding way, showing honor to the woman as the weaker vessel, since they are heirs with you of the grace of life, so that your prayers may not be hindered. (1 Pet 3:1–7)

Peter describes Christian living in a rather simple manner. He encourages wives to live in their station in life as wives, but to do so well, and with respect. In the same manner, husbands are encouraged to love their wives and treat them well. Paul uses the same types of admonitions in his epistle to the Ephesians. Along with describing the conduct of husbands and wives, Paul describes that of parents, children, slaves, and slave owners.

> Children, obey your parents in the Lord, for this is right. "Honor your father and mother" (this is the first commandment with a promise), "that it may go well with you and that you may live long

in the land." Fathers, do not provoke your children to anger, but bring them up in the discipline and instruction of the Lord.

Bondservants, obey your earthly masters with fear and trembling, with a sincere heart, as you would Christ, not by the way of eye-service, as people-pleasers, but as bondservants of Christ, doing the will of God from the heart, rendering service with a good will as to the Lord and not to man, knowing that whatever good anyone does, this he will receive back from the Lord, whether he is a bondservant or is free. Masters, do the same to them, and stop your threatening, knowing that he who is both their Master and yours is in heaven, and that there is no partiality with him. (Eph 6:1–9)

In a manner commensurate with Peter's, Paul views proper Christian ethics as being lived out within the ordinary spheres of human life. Not only should husbands and wives treat one another well, showing love to each other, but so also should parents and children love one another. Mothers and fathers should show love to their children, and children should show respect to their parents. In the same manner, a slave should be obedient to his master, and a master should treat a slave well. This principle would seemingly apply to contemporary situations as well. Rather than a slave and owner, think of a situation of a worker and a boss. Bosses should treat those who work for them well, and workers should treat their boss with respect. Paul gives this principle in general terms to the Corinthians: "Only let each person lead the life that the Lord has assigned to him, and to which God has called him. This is my rule in all the churches" (1 Cor 7:17). He writes similarly to the Thessalonians, "But we urge you, brothers, to do this more and more, and to aspire to live quietly, and to mind your own affairs, and to work with your hands, as we instructed you, so that you may walk properly before outsiders and be dependent on no one" (1 Thess 4:10–12).

In all of these texts, Christian living is placed in a rather "earthy" context. Rather than urging everyone to take up those careers which are often considered "spiritual," the New Testament contains many admonitions to live in light of one's calling in life. In ordinary stations, Christians are able to serve and love those around them. This can be done through family, whether one is a husband, wife, or child. It is done through various earthly institutions, such as slavery, or one's career. Paul writes that the Christian life consists in living quietly and humbly, doing whatever labor one has been assigned.

CONCLUSION

The discussion of sanctification and the Christian life has not been as simple as many of the other discussions. The Reformed tradition varies based upon different theologians and preachers; thus there is no uniform doctrine of sanctification which is easily refuted. The differences between the two traditions are largely based on emphasis. The Reformed tradition has generally emphasized the third use of the law, human cooperation in sanctification, sanctification over justification, and God-ward good works rather than the service of one's neighbor through various vocations. These various emphases are not *always* present, but they are generally true. In contradistinction to the Reformed tradition, Lutherans have emphasized the second use of the law, God's divine work in sanctification, justification over sanctification, and the concept of vocation. It has been demonstrated exegetically that the Lutheran approach to these various issues is in accord with the New Testament witness.

Bibliography

Allen, David L. *Hebrews. New American Commentary.* Nashville: B&H, 2010.
Althaus, Paul. *The Theology of Martin Luther.* Minneapolis: Fortress, 1966.
Arminius, James and John T. Wagner (editor). *Arminius Speaks: Essential Writings on Predestination, Free Will, and the Nature of God.* Eugene, OR: Wipf & Stock, 2010.
Arminius, James. *The Works of Reverend James Arminius : Volume 2*, electronic ed., Logos Library System. Albany, OR: AGES Software, 1999.
Armstrong, Brian G. *Calvinism and the Amyraut Heresy.* Milwaukee: The University of Wisconsin Press, 1969.
Aulen, Gustaf. *Christus Victor: An Historical Study of the Three Main Types of the Idea of the Atonement.* Eugene, OR; Wipf & Stock, 2003.
Baker, Kenneth. *Fundamentals of Catholicism Volume III.* San Francisco: Ignatius, 1983.
Barker, Lane, and Michaels. *The New Testament Speaks.* San Francisco: Harper, 1969.
Barth, Karl. *Church Dogmatics, Part IV, the Doctrine of Reconciliation vol. IV. The Christian Life.* London: T&T Clark, 2008.
Bateman, Herbert. et al. *Four Views on the Warning Passages in Hebrews.* Grand Rapids: 2007, Kregel.
Bavinck, Herman. *Reformed Dogmatics.* Translated by John Vriend. Grand Rapids: Baker, 2003–2008.
Bayer, Oswald and Thomas H. Trapp (translator). *Martin Luther's Theology: A Contemporary Interpretation.* Grand Rapids: Eerdmans, 2008.
Beeke, Joel, "Calvin's Piety," *Mid-America Reformed Journal of Theology*, 15 (2004): 33–65.
Bender, Donald B. *Into the Temple Courts: The Place of the Synogogues in the Second Temple Period. (SBL Dissertation Series 169)* Atlanta: Society of Biblical Literature, 1999.
Berkhof, Louis. *Systematic Theology.* Grand Rapids: Eerdmans, 1972.
Beveridge, Henry and Jules Bonnet. *Selected Works of John Calvin: Tracts and Letters*, Grand Rapids: Baker, 1983, 2:56.
Biermann, Joel. *A Case for Character: Toward a Lutheran Virtue Ethic* Minneapolis: Fortress, 2014.
Boettner, Lorraine. The Reformed Doctrine of Predestination. Phillipsburg, NJ: P&R, 1932.
Boice, James. *A Golden Chain of Five Links.* (Monergism) <http://www.monergism.com/thethreshold/articles/onsite/goldenchain-boice.html>
Brauer, Leonard James. *Lutheran Worship: History and Practice.* Precht, Fred L. St. Louis: Concordia, 1993.

Bibliography

Brown, Peter. *The Cult of the Saints: Its Rise and Function in Latin Christianity*. Chicago: University of Chicago Press, 1982.

Brunner, Peter and M.H. Bertram (translator) *Worship in the Name of Jesus*. St. Louis: Concordia, 2011.

Bryson, George. *The Dark Side of Calvinism: The Calvinist Caste System*. Costa Mesa: Calvary Chapel, 2004.

Buchanan, James. *The Doctrine of Justification*. BiblioLife 2008.

Bushell, Michael. *Songs of Zion: A Contemporary Case for Exclusive Psalmody*. Pittsburgh: Crown & Covenant, 2011.

Calvin, John and A.N.S. Lane (Translator) *The Bondage and Liberation of the Will: A Defense of the Orthodox Doctrine of Human Choice Against Pighus*. Grand Rapids: Baker, 2002.

Calvin, John. *Institutes of the Christian Religion*. Edited by John T. McNeill. Louisville: Westminster Press, 1960.

Carry, Phillip "*Sola Fide*: Luther and Calvin," *Concordia Theological Quarterly*. 71 (2009):265–281.

Cavarnos, Constantine. *Orthodox Iconography*. Belmont, MA: Institute for Byzantine and Modern Greek Studies, 1992.

Cooper, Jordan. *A Lutheran Response to Justification: Five Views*. Blogia, 2012. <http://logia.org/blogia/wp-content/uploads/2012/07/Cooper_Justification.pdf>

Cooper, Jordan. *Christification: A Lutheran Approach to Theosis*. Eugene, OR: Wipf and Stock, 2014.

Cooper, Jordan. *The Righteousness of One: An Evaluation of Early Patristic Soteriology in Light of the New Perspective on Paul*. Eugene, OR: Wipf and Stock, 2013.

Courvoisier, Jaques. *Zwingli: A Reformed Theologian*. Richmond: John Knox, 1961.

Chemnitz, Martin and Jacob A.O. Preus (translator). *Loci Theologici Part 1 and 2*. St. Louis: Concordia, 2009.

Chemnitz. Martin. *Examination of the Council of Trent Part IV*. St. Louis: Concordia, 2007

Chemnitz, Martin. *The Two Natures of Christ*. St. Louis: Concordia, 1971.

Clark, R.Scott. *Recovering the Reformed Confession: Our Theology, Piety, and Practice*. Phillipsburg: P&R, 2008.

Clowney, Edmund. *Preaching Christ in All of Scripture*. Wheaton: Crossway, 2003.

Cyril of Alexandria. *On the Unity of Christ*. Yonkers, NY: St. Vladimir's Seminary Press, 1997.

Daniel, Curt D. *The History and Theology of Calvinism*. Springfield, IL: Scholarly Reprints, 1993.

Dever, Mark *The Marks of the Church* (Ligonier) <http://www.ligonier.org/learn/articles/marks-church/>

Dockery, David S. "Romans 7:14–25: Pauline Tension in the Christian Life" *Grace Theological Journal* 2.2 (Fall, 1981) 239–257.

Driscoll, Mark. *Religion Saves: And Nine other Misconceptions*. Wheaton: Crossway, 2009.

Duffield, Guy P. and N.M. Van Cleave. *Foundations of Pentecostal Theology*. Los Angeles: L.I.F.E, 1983.

Edwards, Jonathan. *The Works of Jonathan Edwards Volume 1: Freedom of the Will*. Peabody: Hendrickson, 2003.

Edwards, Jonathan and James Houston (editor). *Religious Affections*. Vancouver: Regent College, 2003.

Bibliography

Eire, Carlos M.N. *War Against the Idols: the Reformation of Worship from Erasmus to Calvin*. New York: Cambridge, 1989.

Engelbrecht, Edward. *Friends of the Law: Luther's Use of the Law for the Christian Life*. St. Louis: Concordia, 2011.

Engelsma, David J. *Common Grace Revisited: A Response to Richard J. Mouw's He Shines in All That's Fair*. Jenison, MI: Reformed Free Publishing, 2001.

Engelsma, David. *Hyper Calvinism and the Call of the Gospel: An Examination of the Well-Meant Offer*. Jenison, MI: Reformed Free, 2014.

Fesko, J.V. *Justification: Understanding the Classic Reformed Doctrine*. Phillipsburg, NJ: P&R, 2008.

Fisher J.D.C. *Christian Initiation: the Reformation Period*. Chicago: Liturgy Training, 2006.

Forde, Gerhard. "The Lutheran View of Sanctification" in *The Preached God: Proclamation in Word and Sacrament*. Grand Rapids: Eerdmans, 2007

Forde, Gerhard. *The Captivation of the Will: Luther vs. Erasmus on Freedom and Bondage*. Grand Rapids: Eerdmans, 2005.

Forde, Gerhard. *Theology is For Proclamation*. Minneapolis: Fortress, 1990.

Frame, John *Systematic Theology: An Introduction to Christian Belief*. Philippsburg: P&R, 2013.

Frame, John M. A Fresh Look at the Regulative Principle. (Frame-Poythress, 2011) <http://www.frame-poythress.org/a-fresh-look-at-the-regulative-principle-a-broader-view/>

Frame, John. *The Escondido Theology: A Reformed Response to Two Kingdom Theology*. Lakeland, FL: Whitefield, 2011.

Frame, John and Darryl Hart. The Regulative Principle: Scripture, Tradition, and Culture: An Email Debate Between Darryl Hart and John Frame. (Frame-Poythress, 1998) <http://www.frame-poythress.org/the-regulative-principle-scripture-tradition-and-culture/ >

Franzmann, Martin H. *The Word of the Lord Grows: An Introduction to the Origin, Purpose, and Meaning of the New Testament*. St. Louis: Concordia, 1961.

Fulgentius of Ruspe and Robert Eno (translator). *Fulgentius: Selected Works*. Washington D.C.: Catholic University of America, 1993.

Gaffin, Richard B. *By Faith, Not by Sight: Paul and the Order of Salvation* 2nd ed. Philipsburg: P&R, 2013.

Gangi, Mariano D. *Great Themes in Puritan Preaching*. Kitchener, ON: Sola Scriptura, 2007.

George, Robert. *Theology of the Reformers*. Nashville: Broadman, 1988.

Gerhard, Johann. *Theological Commonplaces VIII-XI: On Creation and Predestination*. Translated by Richard Dinda. St. Louis: Concordia, 2013.

Gerstner, John. *Jonathan Edwards: A Mini Theology*. Orlando: Soli Deo Gloria, 2003.

Gibson, David and Jonathan Gibson. *From Heaven He Came and Sought Her: Definite Atonement in Historical, Biblical, Theological, and Pastoral Perspective*. Wheaton: Crossway, 2013.

Gieschen, Charles A. *The Law in Holy Scripture*. St. Louis: Concordia, 2004.

Gore, R.J. *Covenantal Worship: Reconsidering the Puritan Regulative Principle*. Phillipsburg: P&R, 2002.

Grider, Kenneth J. *A Wesleyan-Holiness Theology*. Kansas City: Beacon Hill, 1994.

Grider, Kenneth J. *Entire Sanctification: The Distinctive Doctrine of Wesleyanism*. Kansas City: Beacon Hill, 1994.

Bibliography

Gritsch, Eric W. *A History of Lutheranism (Second Edition)*. Minneapolis: Fortress, 2010.

Grudem, Wayne. *Systematic Theology: An Introduction to Biblical Doctrine*. Grand Rapids: Zondervan, 1995.

Hendrix, Scott H. *Preaching the Reformation: the Homiletical Handbook of Urbanus Rhegius*. Milwaukee: Marquette, 2003.

Hodge, Charles. *Systematic Theology*. Peabody: Hendrickson, 2003.

Hoeksema, Herman. *Reformed Dogmatics*. Jenison, MI: Reformed Free Publishing,

Hollaz, David. "Mystical Union," *Just and Sinner*, 2014. http://justandsinner.com/a-translation-of-david-hollaz-on-mystical-union/.

Horton, Michael S. *For Calvinism* . Grand Rapids: Zondervan, 2011.

Horton, Michael S. *God of Promise: Introducing Covenant Theology*. Grand Rapids: Baker, 2006.

Horton, Michael S. *The Christian Faith: A Systematic Theology of the Christian Faith*. Grand Rapids: Zondervan, 2011.

Hunt, Dave. *What Love is This? Calvinism's Misrepresentation of God*. Bend, OR: Berean Call, 2013.

James, Bruno Scott. *The Letters of Saint Bernard of Clairvaux*. Stroud: Sutton, 1998.

John of Damascus. *On the Divine Images: Three Apologies Against those who Attack the Divine Images*. Yonkers, NY: Vladimir's Seminary, 1980.

Just, Arthur A. *Heaven on Earth: the Gifts of Christ in the Divine Service*. St. Louis: Concordia, 2008.

Just, Arthur A. *The Ongoing Feast*. Collegeville, MN: Liturgical Press, 1993.

Kearney, Ray. *Works of Saint Augustine, Adulterous Marriages, Part 1, Vol. 9* Hyde Park: New City Press, 1999.

Keller, Timothy. *What is Common Grace?* Redeemer Presbyterian, 2003. <http://timothykeller.com/images/uploads/pdf/What_Is_Common_Grace.pdf >

Kendall, R.T. *Calvin and English Calvinism to 1649*. Eugene, OR: Wipf & Stock, 2011.

Keyser, Leander. *Election and Conversion: A Frank Discussion of Dr. Pieper's Book on "Conversion and Election," with Suggestions for Lutheran Concord and Union on Another Basis*. Burlington, IA: German Literary Board, 1914.

Kharlamov, Vladimir. *Theosis: Deification in Christian Theology Volume Two*. Eugene: Pickwick, 2011.

King, Peter. *Western Monasticism: A History of the Monastic Movement in the Latin Church*. Collegeville, MN: Cistercian, 1999.

Kittleson, James M. *Luther the Reformer: The Story of the Man and His Career*. Minneapolis: Fortress, 2003.

Kline, Meredith. *Kingdom Prologue: Genesis Foundations for a Covenantal Worldview*. Eugene: Wipf & Stock, 2006.

Klug, Eugene. "Free Will, or Human Powers" in: Preus, Robert D. and Wilbert H. Rosin *A Contemporary Look at the Formula of Concord* St. Louis: Concordia, 1978.

Kolb, Robert. *Bound Choice, Election, and Wittenberg Theological Method: From Martin Luther to the Formula of Concord* Grand Rapids: Eerdmans, 2005.

Kolb, Robert and Wingert, Timothy J. *The Book of Concord: The Confessions of the Evangelical Lutheran Church*. Minneapolis: Fortress, 2000.

Krauth, Charles Porterfield. *The Conservative Reformation and its Theology*. St Louis: Concordia, 2007.

Kretzmann, Paul E. *Christian Art: It's Place and Use in Lutheran Worship*. St. Louis: Concordia, 1921.

Bibliography

Kuyper, Abraham. *Lectures on Calvinism* Grand Rapids: Eerdmans, 1931.
Lawson, Steven J. *The Expository Genius of John Calvin.* Sanford, FL: Reformation Trust, 2007.
Leithart, Peter J. *The Baptized Body.* Moscow, ID: Canon, 2007.
Leithart, Peter J. *Blessed Are the Hungry.* Moscow: Canon, 2000.
Lenski, R.C.H. *The Interpretation of St. Paul's Epistles to the Galatians, Ephesians, and Philippians.* Minneapolis: Augsburg, 1961.
Long, Gary. *Definite Atonement.* Rochester: Backus Books, 1977.
Long, Gary D. *Substitutionary Atonement: A Doctrinal Study of Three Key Problem Passages on the Extent of the Atonement.* Sterling, VA: Grace Abounding Ministries, 1977.
Lohse, Bernhard. *Martin Luther's Theology: Its Historical and Systematic Development.* Minneapolis: Fortress, 1999.
Luoma, John Kenneth Reynold. *The primitive church as a normative principle in the theology of the sixteenth century: the Anglican-Puritan debate over church polity as represented by Richard Hooker and Thomas Cartwright* (Thesis). Hartford: Hartford Seminary Foundation, 1974.
Lusk, Rich. *Paedofaith.* Monroe, LA: Athanasius, 2005.
Lutheran Church-Missouri Synod. *Lutheran Service Book.* St. Louis: Concordia, 2006.
Luther, Martin and J.I. Packer (translator). *The Bondage of the Will.* Grand Rapids: Revell, 1990.
Luther, Martin. *Luther's Small Catechism with Explanation.* St Louis: Concordia. 1986.
Luther, Martin. *Luther's Works, Volume 26: Lectures on Galatians Chapters 1–4.* St. Louis: Concordia, 1962.
Luther, Martin *Luther's Works, Volume 27: Lectures on Galatians Chapters 5–6,* St. Louis: Concordia, 1963.
MacArthur, John. *Saved Without a Doubt: Being Sure of Your Salvation.* Colorado Springs: Cook, 2001.
Marshall, Howard *Beyond the Bible: moving from scripture to theology.* Grand Rapids: Baker Book House, 2004.
Marquart, Kurt. "Confessions and Ceremonies" 260–270 in Preus, Robert D. et all. *A Contemporary Look at the Formula of Concord.* St. Louis: Concordia, 1978.
Mathison, Keith A. *Given For You: Reclaiming Calvin's Doctrine of the Lord's Supper.* Phillipsburg, NJ: P&R, 2002.
Paul T. McCain et al, eds., *Concordia: The Lutheran Confessions, a Reader's Edition of the Book of Concord.* Second Edition. St. Louis: Concordia, 2006
Molstad, John. *Predestination: Chosen in Christ.* Milwaukee: Northwestern, 2000.
Mueller, Steven P. *Called to Believe, Teach, and Confess: An Introduction to Doctrinal Theology* Eugene, OR: Wipf and Stock, 2005.
Muller, Richard A. *Christ and the Decree: Christology and Predestination in the Reformed Tradition from Calvin to Perkins.* Grand Rapids: Baker, 2008.
Muller, Richard A. *Dictionary of Latin and Greek Theological Terms: Drawn Principally from Protestant Scholastic Theology.* Grand Rapids: Baker, 2006.
Murray, Iain H. *Spurgeon V. Hyper-Calvinism: the Battle for Gospel Preaching.* Carlisle, PA: Banner of Truth, 1995.
Murray, John. *Redemption Accomplished and Applied.* Grand Rapids: Eerdmans, 1955.
Murray, Scott. *Law, Life, and the Living God: The Third Use of the Law in Modern American Lutheranism.* St. Louis: Concordia, 2001.
Nettles, Thomas J. *By His Grace and For His Glory.* Cape Coral, FL: Founders, 2006.

Bibliography

Nettles, Thomas J. et al. *Understanding Four Views of Baptism*. Grand Rapids: Zondervan, 2007.

Nevin, John. *The Mystical Presence: A Vindication of the Reformed or Calvinistic Doctrine of the Holy Eucharist*. CreateSpace, 2012.

Norris, Richard A. *The Christological Controversy*. Philadelphia: Fortress, 1980.

Olin, John C. *John Calvin and Jacopo Sadoleto: A Reformation Debate*. New York: Harper, 1966.

Oliphant, Scott K. *Justified in Christ: God's Plan for us in Justification*. Ross-shire: Mentor, 2007.

Olson, Roger E. *Against Calvinism* Grand Rapids: Zondervan, 2011.

Owen, John. *The Death of Death in the Death of Christ*. Carlisle, PA: Banner of Truth, 1959.

Owen, John and William H. Goold (editor). *The Works of John Owen Volume 6: Temptation and Sin*. Carlisle PA: Banner of Truth, 1966.

Packer, J.I. *Knowing God*. Downer's Grove, IL: IVP, 1993.

Parker, T.LH. *Calvin's Preaching*. Louisville: Westminster, 1994.

Paulson, Steven D. *Lutheran Theology*. New York: T&T Clark, 2011.

Peterson, Robert and Michael Williams. *Why I am Not an Arminian*. Westmont, IL: IVP, 2004.

Phillips, Richard. *Hebrews. Reformed Expository Commentary*. Philipsburg, NJ: P&R, 2006.

Pink, A.W. *1 John 2:2*. <http://www.pbministries.org/books/pink/Miscellaneous/1_john_2.htm>

Pieper, Francis. *Conversion and Election: A Plea for a United Lutheranism in America* St. Louis: Concordia, 1913.

Piper, John. *The Justification of God: An Exegetical and Theological Study of Romans 9:1–23*. Grand Rapids: Baker Academic, 1993.

Piper, John. *The Pleasures of God: Meditations on God's Delight in Being God*. Sisters: Multnomah, 2 ed., 2000.

Piper, John. *What is Baptism and Does it Save?* Desiring God: 2012 <http://www.desiringgod.org/resource-library/sermons/what-is-baptism-and-does-it-save >

Preus, Jacob. *Just Words: Understanding the Fullness of the Gospel*. St. Louis: Concordia, 2000.

Preus, Klemet I. *Doctrine is Life: Essays on Justification and the Lutheran Confessions*. St. Louis: Concordia, 2006.

Preus, Robert *Doctrine is Life: Essays on Justification and the Lutheran Confessions*. St. Louis: Concordia, 2006.

Remensnyder, Junius Benjamin. *The Lutheran Manual*. New York: Boschen and Wefer, 1893.

Reymond, Robert. *A New Systematic Theology of the Christian Faith*. Nashville: Thomas Nelson, 1998.

Richardson, Cyril Charles. *Zwingli and Cranmer on the Eucharist*. Evanston, IL: Seabury-Western, 1949.

Robertson, A.T. *A Grammar of Greek New Testament in Light of Historical Research*. Nashville: B&H, 1947.

Robertson, A.T. *Word Pictures in the New Testament III*. Nashville: Broadman, 1931.

Bibliography

Rosenthal, Shane. *A Defense of the Classical Reformed View & a Critique of the Traditional Lutheran Approach.* <http://homepage.mac.com/shanerosenthal/reformationink/srsupper.htm>

Rudolph, Kurt. *Gnosis: the Nature and History of Gnosticism.* New York: HarperOne, 1987.

Sasse, Herman. *This is my Body: Luther's Contention for the Real Presence in the Sacrament of the Altar.* St. Louis: Concordia, 2003.

Scaer, David P. *Law and Gospel and the Means of Grace.* St. Louis: Luther Academy, 2008.

Scott, Thomas. *The Articles of the Synod of Dort, and its Rejection of Errors: With the History of Events that Made Way for that Synod, as Published by the Authority of the States-General and the Documents Confirming its Decisions.* Ulan, 2012.

Schaff, Phillip (editor). *St. Augustine: Anti-Pelagian Writings. Nicene and Post Nicene Fathers First Series, Volume 5.* Peabody: Hendrickson, 1994.

Schlink, Edmund. *Theology of the Lutheran Confessions.* St. Louis: Concordia, 1961.

Schmid, Heinrich. *Doctrinal Theology of the Evangelical Lutheran Church.* Translated by Henry Eyster Jacobs and Charles Hay. Philadelphia: United Lutheran Publishing, 1899.

Schreiner, Thomas R. et al. *Believer's Baptism: Sign of the New Covenant in Christ.* Nashville: B&H Academic, 2007.

Senkbeil, Harold. *Dying to Live: the Power of Forgiveness.* St. Louis: Concordia, 1994.

Slick, Matthew. *Baptism and John 3:5* (CARM) <http://carm.org/baptism-and-john-35>.

Spinks, Bryan D. *Reformation and Modern Rituals and Theologies of Baptism: From Luther to Contemporary Practices.* Burlington: Ashgate, 2006.

Sproul, R.C. *Chosen By God.* Carol Stream, IL: Tyndale, 1994.

Sproul, R.C. *Essential Truths of the Christian Faith* Carol Streams, IL: Tyndale, 1998.

Sproul, R.C. *Faith Alone: The Evangelical Doctrine of Justification.* Grand Rapids: Baker, 1999

St. Augustine, Mourant, John A. (translator) and William J. Collinge (translator). *The Fathers of the Church: At. Augustine-Four Anti-Pelagian Writings.* Washington D.C: Catholic University of America, 1992.

Stout, Harry S. *The New England Soul: Preaching and Religious Culture in Colonial New England.* New York: Oxford, 1998.

Storms, Sam. *Introduction to 1 John.* Enjoying God, 2005, <http://www.enjoyinggodministries.com/article/introduction-to-first-john/>

Strawbridge, Gregg et al. *The Case for Covenantal Infant Baptism.* Phillipsburg, NJ: P&R, 2003.

Stucco, Guido. *Not Without Us: The Forgotten Catholic Doctrine of Predestination During the Semipelagian Controversy.* Tucson: Fenestra, 2006.

Suelflow, August R. *Servant of the Word: The Life and Ministry of C.F.W. Walther.* St. Louis: Concordia, 2000.

Sundberg, Walter. *Worship as Repentance: Lutheran Liturgical Tradition and Catholic Consensus.* Grand Rapids: Eerdman's, 2012.

Stjerna, Kirsi *No Greater Jewel: Thinking About Baptism With Luther.* Minneapolis: Fortress, 2009.

Thuesen, Peter J. *Predestination: The American Career of a Contentious Doctrine* New York: Oxford, 2009.

Thomas, Derek. "The Regulative Principle of Worship" *Table Talk* July 2010.

Trigg, Jonathan D. *Baptism in the Theology of Martin Luther.* Boston: Brill, 1997.

Van Biema, David "The New Calvinism" *TIME Magazine*, March 12, 2009.

Bibliography

Veith, Gene Edward. *God at Work: Your Christian Vocation in All of Life*. Wheaton: Crossway, 2002.

Vischer, Lukas et al. *Christian Worship in Reformed Churches Past and Present*. Grand Rapids: Eerdmans, 2002.

Walther, C.F.W. *Predestination in Lutheran Perspective*. White Horse Inn <http://www.whitehorseinn.org/images/CFWWalther-PredestinationInLutheranPerspective.pdf>.

Walther, C.F.W. *The Proper Distinction Between Law and Gospel*. St. Louis: Concordia, 1986.

Walther, C.F.W. *From our Master's Table*. Deerborn: Mark V, 2008.

Wandel, Lee Palmer. *Voracious Idols and Violent Hands: Iconoclasm in Reformation Zurich, Strasbourg, and Basel*. New York: Cambridge, 1999.

Warfield, Benjamin B. *The Plan of Salvation*. Avinger, TX: Simpson, 1989.

Webster, William. "The Eucharist," in *Salvation, The Bible, and Roman Catholicism, The Church of Rome at the Bar of History*. Battle Ground, WA: Christian Resources, 2001.

Weidner, Revere Franklin. *Pneumatology or the Doctrine of the Work of the Holy Spirit: Outline Notes Based on Luthardt and Krauth*. Chicago: Wartburg, 1915.

Weidner, Revere Franklin. *Theologia: The Doctrine of God*. Chicago: Wartburg, 1902.

Wengert, Timothy. *Priesthood, Pastors, and Bishops: Public Ministry for the Reformation and Today*. Minneapolis: Fortress, 2008.

Westerholm, Stephen. *Perspectives Old and New on Paul: The "Lutheran" Paul and His Critics*. Grand Rapids: Eerdmans, 2003.

White, James. *The Potter's Freedom*. Amityville, NY: Calvary Press, 2000.

White, James. "Was Anyone Saved at the Cross?" Phoenix: Alpha and Omega, 2005. <http://vintage.aomin.org/Was%20Anyone%20Saved.html >

White, James. *A Brief Rebuttal of Baptismal Regeneration*. Alpha & Omega, 2005–2006). <http://vintage.aomin.org/bapreg.html>

White, James and Dave Hunt. *Debating Calvinism*. Colorado Springs: Multnomah, 2001.

Wieting, Kennith W. *The Blessings of Weekly Communion*. St. Louis: Concordia, 2006.

Wingren, Gustaf. *Luther on Vocation translated by Carl C. Rasmussen*. Philadelphia: Muhlenberg, 1957.

Zeedon, Walter Ernst and Kevin G. Walker. *Faith and Act: the Survival of Medieval Ceremonies in the Lutheran Reformation*. St. Louis: Concordia, 2012.

Zwingli, Ulrich. "On the Lord's Supper" in Bromiley, G.W. *Zwingli and Bullinger. Library of Christian Classics*. Philadelphia: Westminster, 1953.

www.ingramcontent.com/pod-product-compliance
Lightning Source LLC
Chambersburg PA
CBHW070251230426
43664CB00014B/2495